T0294066

SILVER LININGS

SILVER LININGS
Bobby Robson's England

David Hartrick

First published by Pitch Publishing, 2021

Pitch Publishing
A2 Yeoman Gate
Yeoman Way
Worthing
Sussex
BN13 3QZ
www.pitchpublishing.co.uk
info@pitchpublishing.co.uk

A CIP catalogue record is available for this book
from the British Library.

ISBN 978 1 78531 781 1

Typesetting and origination by Pitch Publishing
Printed and bound in India by Replika Press Pvt. Ltd.

Contents

To Seb.

Maybe next time
Gazza will score.

FOREWORD

*by Daniel Storey, football writer
and broadcaster*

ITALIA 90 produced my first football memories. Perhaps that makes me incredibly fortunate. As a four-year-old who was still a year away from my first season ticket but was already consuming football VHS tapes and watching *Match of the Day* at least three times every week, I was a willing test case. Never before had I enjoyed multiple live matches every day, nor even considered that it might be a possibility. Nor had I experienced football as a global entity, a festival of sport.

The brilliant aspect of establishing a love for football – for anything – at such a young age is that you latch on to the best bits without feeling the need to focus on anything that might not fit your enthusiasm. Innocence and inexperience allowed me to consume football without context. Hindsight and the passing of time provokes a series of glorious, blurry half-memories. As a Nottingham Forest supporter I was devastated by Stuart Pearce's penalty miss and England's exit, but it didn't wrap my enjoyment in a thick smog. How could it when there were two more matches to come?

But the context of England's achievement did matter. It provides the backdrop for, and backbone of, David Hartrick's book. He places Italia 90, the book's crescendo, in the extraordinary circumstances that led to its unlikely reputation as English football's Age of Enlightenment.

The 1980s was the darkest decade for our national sport, and David provides exemplary detail and discussion of hooliganism, the circulation war that provoked visceral newspaper criticism, the damaged reputation of English football and English football supporters and the public discontentment and national anger that led to it. Our footballing landscape had become synonymous with tragedy and disorganisation, our clubs were banned from European competition and the national team's support was viewed as a cast of unsavoury, unpleasant yobs.

If Italia 90 marked a sea change in the globalisation of football, perhaps the best marker of the game entering the modern age, it was also a landmark tournament for England's national team. From the media diatribe and back-page scorn of the 1980s came hope of a new England team, one that could rise up to meet the challenges and pressures of a major tournament rather than crumple under them. The glorious summer of 1966 would never, and will never, be forgotten, but in terms of a lasting legacy and the weaving of individual storylines Italia 90 really did match up.

Bobby Robson is the protagonist of Hartrick's book, England's manager for eight years in the 1980s and a coach who constructed his own legacy at that World Cup. Robson's treatment at the hands of the tabloid media is examined in faultless detail. His struggle to establish England as a serious contender, through European Championship failure and World Cup infamy in 1986, passes comment on English football as a whole and Hartrick balances the micro and macro elements of the story expertly.

Robson's crowning glory, taking England to within two spot kicks of a second World Cup Final, is framed as a testament to the enduring optimism of the manager but also the eternal warmth, generosity and kindness of the man. There is a persuasive argument that no England manager has ever got more out of his players than Robson. From the penalty-box prowess of Gary Lineker, the natural aptitude of John Barnes and Chris Waddle, to the stereotypically English courage and passion of Pearce and Terry Butcher and the unique fragility of Paul Gascoigne, Robson proved himself capable of man-management through genuine friendship.

I have known David for a decade and am comfortable in asserting that I can think of no person better placed to document this period of English football. He is a devotee both of the England national team and the research required to detail its journey through such turbulent waters. He is unafraid to criticise – where appropriate – English football's structure, hierarchy, the behaviour of supporters and the fear that once seemed to engulf the England team when it mattered most. Hartrick does not avoid scrutiny of the mistakes and the missteps.

But this is not purely a tale of woe, even if there are times during the book where hope feels like another country's property. Without Mark Wright's winner, David Platt's volley and Lineker's penalties it surely would have been just another effigy to England failure. But Hartrick frames the stumbles, the roadblocks and the failures in the context of what we know the book's denouement will bring: glorious public salvation and that open-top bus tour of Luton during which every player was adored as a hero rather than lambasted as a statue to continued non-fulfilment of potential.

ID cards, perimeter fencing, segregation, Diego Maradona, Allan Simonsen, Ray Houghton, Margaret Thatcher –

these could so easily have been the defining actors of England in the 1980s. But as the title alludes to, *Silver Linings* offers due recognition to them all while making a persuasive and illuminating argument that it was Robson who stepped forward as the defining individual and Gascoigne as a portent for the future, for better and occasionally – and infamously – worse.

PROLOGUE

Sunday, 8 July 1990

IT WAS never supposed to end like this. There should have been apologies and furtive looks to camera. A background of grey skies was meant to meet the hunched shoulders and bowed heads walking solemnly down a set of aircraft steps. A hundred newspaper columns were written and ready, each singing a joint chorus of 'I Told You So' and 'Same Old England' in perfect harmony.

Yet, here on the pavements, streets, walls and roofs of Luton on a beautifully sunny day, the scene could not have been more different. This team – boring, poorly managed, not good enough according to the tabloids – had found a way to tear up the script and write themselves a new one. In the process they had taken a nation with them and delivered something no one had seen in English football for a long time: hope.

Hope in a time of hooligans, fences and barbed wire. Hope in a time of ID cards, the Football Spectators Act and Maggie's 'war cabinet'. English football, a landscape awash with tragedy and disarray for over a decade, suddenly looked like it may yet be able to save itself *from* itself. The masses had fallen in love again and the streets of Luton were testament. The people had false idols again.

Somewhere in the ever-churning sea of red and white an open-top bus crawled along an inch at a time. The authorities had taken measures for an expected crowd of somewhere around 100,000 believing, in truth, that doing so was more than over-preparing. In reality, most reports put the figure at well over 250,000, some as high as half a million. The police crash barriers that had lined the prepared route provided the perfect way to fashion a ladder to take you to the top of the nearest wall or bus shelter. Every surface of the town centre had been ruthlessly appropriated by a crowd desperate for a glimpse of their new heroes, the stars of England's footballing summer.

Most of that cast was either drunk or on their way to being so, with a few exceptions. They took turns to appear at the front of the bus, a rapidly repurposed London sightseeing vehicle in daily life now reduced to tip-toeing through the masses. Chris Waddle and Stuart Pearce started the journey sitting down, believing they would be heckled for missing those penalties as others were lauded. They realised just a few metres in they were not only forgiven but being demanded to wave and take the thrown scarves and hats alongside everyone else. Mass euphoria through glorious defeat.

And, of course, leading the crowd was the now beloved Paul Gascoigne. Gazza. Court jester turned national hero. His tears had typified everything the fans wanted to believe about this England, *their* England again. That the players cared as much as they did. That in Gazza they had someone on the pitch who was one of them, a lad who if he hadn't been playing would have been stood on a terrace somewhere singing at their side. The fact he was obscenely talented was merely the icing on the cake.

Not on the bus, however, was the man who had masterminded England's ascent through the 1990 World Cup

which had just ignited the nation. A man who had endured
the most venomous tabloid coverage any football figure had
ever received and for a period of years rather than some mere
passing storm. Bobby Robson, no longer England manager
and bound for PSV Eindhoven – a job he had agreed to
take before Italia 90 had begun – would have rivalled Gazza
for some of the biggest ovations from a now adoring public.
Instead, he was still in Italy to attend the World Cup Final
and appear on the BBC's coverage of the game.

In eight years, he had been celebrated, derided, Diego-ed,
and everything in between. His team missed one European
Championship, self-destructed at another, were cheated out of
a World Cup and had just come within two kicks of a final.
He had managed the good, the bad, and it had sometimes
been ugly. Through it all he continued to front up for himself,
his team and England's real fans against a level of hostility in
the media few could have weathered. 'In the Name of Allah
Go.' 'World Cup Wallies.' 'Robson Out, Clough In.' And
yet, somehow, when the news of his imminent appointment
at PSV was leaked pre-World Cup to the press who had been
demanding he leave for years, they called him a traitor. Here
was his true legacy though – children blinking into the sun,
lofted high on shoulders. He may have been absent, but he
was leaving as a gentleman and a hero.

It was the unlikeliest of turnarounds but a measure of the
man. He had gone from being hounded by the back pages to
the *Daily Mail* admitting, 'It is doubtful if any sporting figure
has endured so loathsome an inquisition.' He had survived it
all and now left on his own terms with reputation not only
intact but enhanced.

Robson's England had been inconsistent, frustrating
to the point of anger at times, but at their best few could
match them. Alf Ramsey may have won it all in 1966 but

no other England manager could boast the sheer drama of Robson's time in charge. His England was shaped by football, its place in society, a vicious circulation war, and a cast of characters that veered from the sublime to the ridiculous. This is that story.

'In the old days men had the rack. Now they have the Press.'

Oscar Wilde

Before

ENGLISH FOOTBALL had spent a lifetime preparing to win the World Cup in 1966. To some it was less a sporting endeavour and more a divine right. As Bobby Moore raised the Jules Rimet Trophy high, the home nation's island mentality had only been further enhanced. Here was tacit confirmation of what many in charge had assumed either publicly or privately; England were the best team in the world, and quite possibly always had been. Football had come home.

It would be fair to say that a good part of that mentality came from the Football Association's long-standing attitude towards the international game; chiefly one of gradual adoption due to a deep-rooted superiority complex plus viewing change by where it came from rather than the actual effect it had. England created modern football, and thus would always be the ones who mastered it, many reasoned. In truth neither side of that statement was particularly sound, but it would be fair to say the game's codification at least owed the country a grand debt.

England may have played football's first official international fixture, against Scotland in 1872, but it then watched on impassively as other nations expanded their horizons. Preferring to play home internationals, on the whole there was no immediate desire within the FA to join the Fédération Internationale de Football Association upon its formation in 1904, despite being repeatedly invited. The view was taken that this was a body who would only provide interference rather than actual ideas. They did agree to recognise it as an official body despite their reservations and promptly set up a committee to review this 'FIFA' from afar.

After several meetings and reports it was eventually decided that England should reluctantly join in 1906. Rather than some great desire to embrace a world game, this was mainly as it was felt the FA should have a say in any matter relating to football, domestic or international. In real terms this translated as a will to reject any changes to *their* game. Suitably any diktat FIFA proposed was either refused or ignored, and in particular the organisation's fanciful desire to hold a world championship of football was dismissed. After all, why would you play other nations if you assumed you would win anyway?

For their part FIFA actually embraced British involvement. FA members were promoted swiftly to prominent positions within. This led to several invites for England to tour regions and play games as pioneers, most of which were, of course, swiftly rejected. England did decide to take an official foray outside the British Isles in 1908 to play matches in Austria, Hungary and Bohemia. These games afforded England four wins by an aggregate score of 28 to two. The results did little to scale back the FA's ego, bolstered further by Great Britain's amateurs taking Olympic gold in 1908 and 1912 in far more formalised conditions than their first triumph in 1900.

The First World War fractured Europe and for a while football didn't matter. Once it ended, a relatively quick return to playing meant the FA felt the need to make a stand. They wouldn't play against any nation who had fought against the Allied Powers. Furthermore, they would also refuse to play against any other nation who didn't take the same stance. They expected this to go unchallenged when they informed the relevant people of their position.

FIFA were unwilling to officially approve such an idea as they wanted to remain neutral in the hope sport would rise above. War in Europe between nations they represented either actually or in principle put them in an impossible position. The FA's response was to leave the organisation immediately.

Talks were continual; both sides knew not having the game's self-proclaimed originators involved weakened the overall optic of FIFA. As such they were pleased to welcome the British FAs back in 1924 after compromises had been reached. It was a doomed second marriage as FIFA had moved the European game on significantly. Not only had there been rule changes, but a huge row developed over the FA's insistence upon control over amateur status for all international players, against a move to compensate footballers financially that FIFA were behind. In 1928 the home nations angrily left once again. This time there would be no olive branch offered or wanted.

Before that second divorce England had slowly come around to the idea of playing against some of the emerging European nations, if only for the chance to prove their superiority. In 1923 Belgium were invited to become the first country outside the British Isles to play against England in a home international. The match took place at Highbury and ended in a resounding 6-1 victory in front of a reported 14,000 fans.

Football reporting was relatively sparse but despite the result some were impressed by Belgium's passing as opposed to England's directness. 'It sounds absurd to suggest that we might learn anything of football from the Belgians,' wrote the *Westminster Gazette*, 'but those present at Highbury yesterday, when England met Belgium, saw, at a partially developed stage, a new type of football, which bids fair, in a few years' time, to make us think furiously.'

While not seeing it in any way as essential as the Home Championship, the FA began to extend their comfort zone. By the end of 1929 England had played away games against Luxembourg, Sweden, France and Belgium, plus a 4-3 defeat in Madrid to Spain which marked their first loss against non-British opposition. Rather than accept nearly 57 years after that first international other countries were becoming footballing talents themselves, most of the British press that did run small reports on the game moved to blame other factors.

'The spectators broke all the bounds of propriety,' ran the report in the *Derby Daily Telegraph* as Spain's fans, 45,000 of them by most reports who had queued for over an hour to get into the Estadio Metropolitano, rushed the pitch after Gaspar Rubio's late goal made it 3-3. This apparently caused 'some minutes interruption' and the incident earned almost double the coverage of the actual match. The winner by Severino Goiburu barely warranted a mention. The pitch was eventually cleared by 'Civic Guards with drawn swords' and disapproving tones were universal. A further caveat was offered in the *Sheffield Daily Independent* that England showed 'palpable signs of suffering from the heat'. If only they could have known Spain would be hot in May.

Meanwhile FIFA had been busy and in 1930 finally had their much-desired 'World Cup' in Uruguay. The hosts won and, despite wider opposition across Europe than just that of Great Britain, the tournament had broadly been a success. England were invited in spite of the rift between the two organisations, as were the other home nations. The offer was point-blank refused by all. England also watched on as the 1934 and 1938 World Cups took place, a token offer to compete in 38 rejected as desired. Both had been held in Europe, in Italy and France respectively. The competition was already FIFA's crown jewel, primary revenue generator, and suited football's growing position as the world's game. If the organisation had once been desperate to court the British it had now moved on.

In 1939 history once again overtook sport and the next World Cup would have to wait. The Second World War raged across Europe and eventually beyond. At its end things had changed irrevocably, attitudes softened by tragedy. The home nations rejoined FIFA, even playing a Great Britain v Rest of Europe game at Hampden Park in front of a huge crowd to celebrate the fact. Football was escapism and the general public needed a place to lose themselves away from their immediate memories.

Places at the 1950 World Cup to be held in Brazil were offered and accepted for the first and second-place finishers in the 1949 Home Championship. England won three out of three games and set course to take part. Scotland declined to join them despite qualifying. An epic journey to South America and a general lack of preparation cost England despite a reasonable start in Pool B with a good Chile side beaten 2-0. It left them with the routine job of beating the USA and then facing what would essentially be a knockout game against Spain.

In Belo Horizonte the unthinkable happened. Rather than sweeping aside the USA as expected they fell to a 1-0 loss in a match they wholly dominated but in which they just couldn't score. Time and time again England attacked and failed to find the net, hitting the post or bar 11 times in total. 'Schoolboys would have been spanked by their masters for missing the same simple chances,' Billy Wright wrote in

The World's My Football Pitch. Defeat to Spain in the final game sealed England's fate but the sporting world was still aghast at the result four days earlier. England, with names like Finney, Mannion and Matthews, with the game's history in their DNA, with the arrogance of surety, beaten by a team of amateurs whose coach had told the press before the tournament were there to be 'sheep ready to be slaughtered'.

The British press's reaction was scathing. England had been subject to a few barbed lines in the face of a loss before but nothing with the venom of the fiasco in Belo Horizonte, now renamed 'Lost Horizon' by the *Daily Mail* whose match report stated that England had played 'ridiculously badly!' The *Western Morning News* was actually the first to go to print and stated, 'Probably never before has an England team played so badly,' a thought echoed in *The Times* which also added, 'England had only themselves to blame for defeat!' The *Yorkshire Post and Leeds Mercury* offered that England had 'No Excuse!' in the headline and that they 'ought to have sufficient skill to offset any unnecessary vigour by the opposition'. The *Sunderland Echo* titled its report 'England's Cup Display Worst Ever!' Smaller papers were no less angry, the *Coventry Evening Telegraph* sure that 'not a single player could be proud of his showing', and north of the border the *Aberdeen Journal* wrote with disgust rather than glee, 'It was pathetic to watch English football beaten by a side most amateur 11s would beat at home, and there was no fluke about it.'

Across the country, newspapers ran similar reports all highly, and rightly in their opinion, critical of the team. The language around England reporting was historically concise, as were the match reports themselves, but the reaction to losing this game was markedly different. For contrast, when England lost away to Sweden on a short tour in 1949 the

Sports Argus only ran a 12-line story despite seeing fit to headline it 'Funeral Feast of an Epoch'. There was no mention of the score, just a quote from a Swedish publication, and that was that. A year later this 1-0 defeat to the USA marked the moment the football press truly found its teeth.

Such a loss and such a reaction required seismic analysis. Things were not working and hadn't been for some time in truth. Erosion through wilful ignorance. The newspapers' sharper reactions had been noted but the reality was English football was being left behind by those around it. A technical committee was formed with Stanley Rous at the head with the aim of improving standards. This involved two things; firstly, refining the selection of the team by looking at the committee who currently did so, and secondly a lot of arguing among themselves.

If there were still some small lingering belief that just being England was enough, it was obliterated in November 1953 in a sea change of a game against the Mighty Magyars of Hungary. Wembley Stadium witnessed magic as England lost for the first time at home to a team outside of the British Isles. Hungary's football was so far ahead of England's, so technical and so fast, it caused deep embarrassment for the FA. Hungary won 6-3, a scoreline that improbably did little justice to the actual performance. Thoroughbreds against carthorses as Tom Finney famously described it. The *Daily Mirror* went further and stated, 'We must learn how to play soccer all over again.'

Worse was to follow as six months later England returned the favour by playing Hungary in Budapest. The result was an even more chastening 7-1 defeat, which was and remains England's heaviest ever, and the difference between the two teams was now a chasm. This prompted a vicious write-up from the *Daily Mirror* which felt that its advice to start again had been ignored. The 'Disaster on the Danube' was the final straw for the newspaper. England's attacking was 'comic' and the performance one of a team who had 'learned nothing, forgotten nothing' from the previous game at Wembley. English football had been 'shattered on an anvil of speed, sporting intelligence, imagination, and sheer blinding, brilliant ball control'.

However, the ire was not just aimed at the players this time. The paper also pointed to the weaknesses in the system in its summary, 'We must sweep away those plumbers and builders and grocers who select national teams and give the responsibility to men who have played and know the game. And above all, our league set-up must make sweeping and immediate sacrifices to our international game.'

* * *

The England manager watched all this unfold, somewhat powerless. It was not, strictly speaking, his fault. Walter Winterbottom had been given the job to be England's director of coaching in 1946 on the back of an RAF career teaching PT instructors how to keep their men fit. He had been a footballer, his career cut short by injury after early promise at Manchester United. He understood the game and was known to be a keen student. Beyond that there was very little qualification for the role, in part because it had never existed.

By 1947 he was the full-time manager of the England team as well as the director of coaching; a victory for Stanley Rous who had long argued the need for a full-time employee in charge who could get the best from the players he was given. To date there had been a varied cast of individuals effectively doing the FA a favour by taking over the England team in the loosest sense. This generally consisted of a group of footballers picked and largely told what to do by committee as and when asked. Unsurprisingly those damn continentals were pioneering a single international manager looking after and selecting the team, so the FA was typically adverse. This was coupled to the organisation's belief that the position should be amateur in status with the occasional exception when it suited them.

One of those came when the great innovator Herbert Chapman took charge for an away game against Italy in 1933, keen as ever to expand his knowledge of continental football. His advice to the FA after taking the game was as prescient as you would expect, 'Bring together 20 of the most promising young players for a week under a selector, coach, and trainer, the results would be astonishing!' This was completely ignored.

Selection of the team from game to game was by committee, an imperfect system as Winterbottom had very little ultimate input. Even at the height of his powers he was still a slave to the group actually acknowledging his suggestions and often that became a matter of politics over ability. To compound matters, that committee was also made up of men who many felt were not fit for the job anyway, chiefly as they had no actual grounding in the game. Those men would sit on an ever-increasing variety of panels overseeing English football and only answering to each other. If a camel is a horse designed by committee then at times the national team was a camel with several camels around it arguing with each other about why they have a hump.

In his book *England Managers: The Toughest Job in Football*, the great Brian Glanville described them as 'greedy old men' and the situation as one of taking charge of the England team 'with one hand tied behind your back'. Winterbottom was allowed to pick the side once, a home game against Sweden in 1959 in which he chose a young team who were outplayed by the team who had finished runners-up at the World Cup a year earlier. Experiment over.

While the system afforded a layer of protection from results such as the disaster in 1950 – not a single newspaper write-up I could find, having searched through and read every one available, mentioned the England manager at all – Winterbottom was also up against resistance from within the FA to the very idea of coaching itself. This was England, what could possibly be improved? He was by no means a token appointment, but the role was ill-defined at best, nigh on impossible at worst.

Despite it all he started to have a real influence across English football, changing teachers into fledgling football coaches by passing on methods for a start, and then introducing coaching courses and eventually badges players could earn to prove to clubs they were trained and ready to move into management. In reality 1950 had just been too early for him to have an impact on a country with a historically huge turning circle. By then he was actively talking to clubs and keen to see them introduce training and fitness techniques, but some players had no desire to 'blunt themselves' for an actual game by daring to practise – a position completely backed up by the clubs that employed them.

Within the FA there was also still open scepticism and Winterbottom was routinely undermined by his own employers, but the press were yet to realise the influence a manager could have on the England team. Rous remained an ardent public supporter and his one ally throughout. That 1953 Magyar masterclass had only confirmed in his mind the need for lasting change rather than a single reactionary one.

Winterbottom led England into the 1954, 1958 and 1962 World Cups and in every single one he was tasked with taking a group of players that he hadn't selected to success.

He was, by all accounts, a highly dedicated and studious man but perhaps one whose strengths lay in long-term planning rather than short-term motivation. Rous remained by his side metaphorically even if some reports say he had one or two moments of doubt along the way, particularly in 1955 when he allegedly offered the England job to Roma's Liverpudlian manager Jesse Carver. Despite that, it would be fair to say Rous believed there was a greater good represented by *his* man throughout; however, results and specifically World Cup performances would take an inevitable toll on Winterbottom's standing.

In 1954 England had once again expected at the World Cup in Switzerland but anticipation had been tempered suitably by the brilliance of that Hungary side. Winterbottom led his team through a tough group to a quarter-final against a very decent Uruguay. England played well but lost 4-2, a result put in proper context by Uruguay's earlier 7-0 mauling of Scotland.

Four years later there was a desire to see an improvement as England really should have won one of these things by now, after all. Winterbottom was given a squad which was two players lighter than most of his opponents and shorn without good reason of Stanley Matthews and Nat Lofthouse, who Glanville wrote had been in 'imposing form'. Also, several key players were either carrying injuries or tired after a gruelling end-of-season run-in in the top two leagues. Most importantly there was a huge shadow cast over English football, and specifically this squad, by tragedy.

On 6 February, British European Airways Flight 609 crashed while trying to take off from Munich Airport. The flight was carrying the Manchester United squad back from a European Cup game and three of England's most talented players – Duncan Edwards, Tommy Taylor and Roger Byrne

– along with 17 others at the scene and a further three more in hospital lost their lives. The crash placed some perspective on the summer's World Cup in Sweden and failing to get out of a group with eventual winners Brazil and a very good Soviet Union (who beat England in a play-off to qualify from Group 4 when both teams finished level) was seen as understandable. The *Daily Herald* was sympathetic, 'They had given their spirited best … they had almost run their legs off … they had played their hearts out … but it was just not good enough. Tragically it was not good enough because that vital soccer quality just wasn't with us – luck.'

In contrast, by 1962 there was pressure on Winterbottom, largely due to his own success. The seeds sowed in coaching and training early in his reign and the work with the clubs was bearing fruit. The next English generation were truly modern footballers. While nowhere near the level of today's pristine athletes, the likes of 21-year-old defender Bobby Moore, 22-year-old striker Jimmy Greaves, and 24-year-old Munich survivor Bobby Charlton were different; faster, higher skilled and more intelligent. While nobody dared say it out loud, they were European in style.

England were also in decent form going into the World Cup, beaten only once at home since the last and having found their shooting boots. In the two years leading to the tournament in Chile Winterbottom's direct and hard-running side had averaged just shy of four goals a game; remarkable when the comfort of qualifying via the Home Championship had gone. England had to top a three-team group in competition with Luxembourg and Portugal. Luxembourg were suitably dismissed by an aggregate score of 13-1 but a Portugal side containing one of football's first truly global stars, Eusebio, were dangerous. A 1-1 draw away in Lisbon was a terrific result. England finished top and unbeaten.

Despite the form, Winterbottom knew his race was nearly run. Rous, who had become Sir Stanley since appointing him, took over as president of FIFA in late 1961. The England manager's safety net had gone. Replacing him as secretary of the FA – the role in the organisation that actually held the power – was Denis Follows, a man whose main attribute for the job was that he was open in his dislike for Rous, as was the case vice-versa. Winterbottom had also applied for the role of FA secretary and many felt his time on the frontline had earned him the higher role in overall charge. The choice of Follows was unexpected but chiefly down to Rous who had alienated most members of the FA board through his desire to run a dictatorship. Winterbottom was seen as his man and subsequently a vote for him to become secretary in effect was a vote for Rous by proxy. Rous's leadership had become so divisive that Follows won by a clear 30 votes.

England travelled to Chile with high expectations but unbeknownst to the squad they had a manager who was making other plans. Winterbottom had applied to take up the position of general secretary to the General Council of Physical Recreation (GCPR) before leaving, knowing he was a marked man from all sides. The press were building their own pressure chiefly because Winterbottom's football was seen as successful but dull compared to the cut and thrust of the continental way. With a clutch of exciting young players there needed to be another level. Even in the dominance of the last two years it was felt the direct, physical style of a Winterbottom team was not enough longer term.

So Winterbottom, hindered throughout his career by a selection committee of men nowhere near as qualified as himself to pick the squad, perennially a political tool within the organisation that employed him, and now with his good work finally coming to some sort of fruition on the pitch, knew it was time to go. He dared to dream that England might win the World Cup as a parting gift and his preparation for Chile had proved he learned lessons from his last three. England had been criticised for being too relaxed, not having the correct facilities, and even being unfit going into the last two World Cups in particular. This time there was fairly unanimous agreement that Winterbottom and the FA had got the logistics right.

Everything was set up for England to get through Group 4 and into the quarter-finals but as in 1958 they faced tough opposition. First up was Hungary who were no longer the side that had twice blown England away but were still considered a threat. So it proved as England were beaten 2-1 and the press focused on the lack of imagination from England's forwards. 'We had a guileless attack in name only,' reported the *Daily Herald*. The *Daily Mirror*, the newspaper that had been so incensed in 1954, was more resigned this time, 'Hungary are still too good for us. That, without moans or alibis, is the cruelly correct summing-up.'

England's next game was against Argentina and they produced a truly excellent performance to win 3-1, comfortably their best in a World Cup at that point. The match marked the emergence of Bobby Charlton on the international stage, unplayable as an outside-left on the day. After he finished with an assist and a goal, the newspapers were reporting that Barcelona were preparing a gargantuan £300,000 bid for him at the conclusion of the World Cup. The win set up the final group game against Bulgaria and a draw would see England through to the quarter-finals.

What followed was, in effect, the final straw in regard to Winterbottom for many. England may have got the draw they required but the turgid nature of the 0-0 was blamed on a strategy that basically revolved around playing a nine-man defence. Charlton, electric against Argentina but now asked to do a shielding job, was horrified by the approach, 'I have always believed it was the worst game in which I was ever obliged to play.'

His ire was shared by Bobby Moore, who said, 'It was one of the worst internationals of all time.' Charlton was so angered leaving the pitch that he had an argument with Johnny Haynes who celebrated qualification at the full-time whistle. 'The game was a miserable betrayal of all that I thought English football stood for,' he wrote in 2008, 'I did not play football to try to sneak a result against inferior opposition.'

The press had to acknowledge the achievement of England's progress but were horrified at Winterbottom's game plan. The *Daily Herald*'s headline summed up most reports, 'We've Done It! England, You Were Dreadful!' Its writer, Peter Lorenzo, was known to be quick to point out England and Winterbottom's flaws and he didn't hold back in his assessment, 'Dull, deadly, disappointing … Perhaps even worse than we've ever been.'

He was far from the only critic. Frank McGhee of the *Daily Mirror* described the game as 'dismal' and wrote that England had 'sagged to a new low'. *The Guardian* said the draw had been 'completely devoid of atmosphere' and gave a dog running on to the pitch shortly after half-time as much coverage as the actual second half. Even *The Times*, the newspaper least prone to hyperbole around something as trivial as football, called it an 'exasperating display' and 'a feeble, insipid match'. It went even further when going over the details, 'England seldom play well against so-called "easy" opponents, but now, in the middle of the second half, there were signs of the team's control and fibre cracking. This was deplorable against the naive Bulgarian team. Some of the play bordered on the ridiculous, with players falling over their feet and the ball.'

If Winterbottom knew it was only a matter of time thanks to Rous leaving then the press had all but confirmed it. England exited the 1962 World Cup after a 3-1 defeat to eventual champions Brazil and Winterbottom confirmed his new position shortly after the tournament. On 1 August he resigned to mock surprise from some but what constituted a fair assessment from the press; a good man who had modernised English football then hit a ceiling not necessarily all of his own creation. Winterbottom was leaving behind a role he had defined, a coaching programme for both players and managers, and a job that had become one of the highest profile in the country. He had changed English football forever.

The Observer reported that having been passed over for the FA secretary position earlier in the year he had in fact now taken up the 'most powerful position in British sport' with the GCPR. Tellingly, the newspaper too knew it was time for change but held little hope, 'Little less than a revolution can now prevent England from descending, however gracefully, into the ranks of the second-class powers.' Revolution may have been too extreme for the FA but even they had to accept that it was time to change.

* * *

4. *You will have full responsibility for the selection of England teams, excluding the Amateur XIs.*

The fourth condition on the letter confirming Alf Ramsey's appointment as England manager was by far the most important. It also marked the most significant change to

English international football since it was decided in 1946 that a full-time coach was required. Ramsey had made it clear he would only consider the job if given sole responsibility for picking the squad and then the team from it, plus he would decide upon the correct course of coaching for them while they were in his care. There would be zero negotiation on that point. Winterbottom's other role as the FA's director of coaching was given to Allen Wade and the England manager was now a unique, full-time entity. The FA had relented on both counts knowing he was the right man, but the animosity between those who had made up the now disbanded international selection committee and Ramsey who had demanded their end would last a lifetime.

He had not been first choice. Winterbottom's assistant Jimmy Adamson had been offered the role but declined as at only 33 years old he wanted to keep playing. Adamson had been Winterbottom's recommendation and represented continuity, perhaps the opposite of what was actually required. Ramsey had quickly risen to the top of nearly every list, including a poll of supporters taken by the *Daily Express* and another in the *Daily Mirror* in August 1962. He had beaten Billy Wright, Stan Cullis and Bill Nicholson in both.

Ramsey's standing in football was beyond doubt. He had an excellent playing career as a right-back who was seen as more thoughtful than most. No less a judge than Billy Wright said Ramsey was 'the most remarkable defender I have met'. After Ramsey's appointment, Tom Duckworth wrote an open letter to him in his Topics of the Week column for the *Sports Argus*, describing Ramsey the player as one who 'gave a new constructive concept to post-war full-back play'. Duckworth also added that he 'did more than anyone else to get rid of the idea that a clearance should be a long hopeful punt up field'.

Ramsey had started on the coast at Southampton but moved to Tottenham Hotspur in a swap deal for Welsh winger Ernest Jones. There he won the Second and First Division championships. Eventually he retired in 1955 due to age, injury, and a difficult relationship with several people at the club over a desire to coach and then manage at Spurs. Similar stories of Ramsey's clashes with those who did not share his opinion would follow him throughout his career. He was also a full England international with 32 caps to his name, three as captain in Billy Wright's absence, and had actually played in both the fateful defeat in Belo Horizonte in 1950 and Hungary's masterclass in 1953.

Keen to become a manager and absolutely sure of his ability to do so, he had taken over at Ipswich Town and suitably performed a minor footballing miracle. Taking them from the Third Division South to the First Division in six years with highly limited resources would have made him a *de facto* candidate to be the best manager in the country. The fact he then led Ipswich to the title in their first season in England's top division, in 1961/62, removed the conversation entirely.

Having the credentials was one thing and the desire another, but it became clear to the FA that Ramsey was keen and had a single stated goal: to win the World Cup. The letter confirming his position, complete with the non-negotiable clause four, was sent to Ramsey on 26 October 1962. He would take up sole care the following year having seen out the season with Ipswich but was expected to take an active part in all of England's games from 1 January 1963. A very different era had begun.

There was also a new competition for England to refuse to participate in. In 1954 several European football associations decided that while FIFA had the world's interests at heart it would be pertinent to set up a body to represent Europe. To do so, the Union of European Football Associations, UEFA for short, was formed. Not only did they want to introduce and formalise European club competitions but also develop their own championships internationally. This was not to rival the World Cup, but as Europe now had several of football's genuine powerhouse nations it would be fit to see them compete more than just once every four years. The English FA had willingly joined UEFA, but the thought of another competition was an idea too far.

In fairness they weren't the only ones. The first European Nations' Cup, in 1960 (renamed in 1968 to the simpler European Championship), had several sceptical international teams missing. The format was clumsy partly due to those who declined to take part, but the Soviet Union won in France and it had mostly worked. There was now pressure on UEFA's higher-profile members to take part in the second edition and this time England deigned to enter. This meant that Ramsey's first official game in charge of England was a 5-2 defeat to France in the preliminary round for the tournament to take place the following year.

The game had shown the amount of work Ramsey had to do. Having taken place on a bitterly cold February night and while still in the period of his dual employment at Ipswich, reaction was reasonably muted. Everyone wanted to believe things would change going forward; a key tenet of England reporting and fandom has always been hope after all. The team had been picked by a committee with Ramsey's blessing, as it would for every game until he took full control in May, the caveat being that Ramsey himself was on the panel and active in his choices. It had shown England's deficiencies which had been there at the World Cup in Chile but even the *Daily Mirror*, the newspaper so historically active in its criticism, tempered its report by saying, 'This England team was not nearly as bad as the margin of defeat suggests.'

After defeat to Scotland and a better performance in drawing with Brazil in early May, Ramsey left Ipswich and began his job in earnest. As a man he was obsessive to the point of belligerence, and it was now with the team under full command and selection his alone he started his minor revolution. With an injury to Jimmy Armfield Ramsey made a young Bobby Moore replacement captain for his first proper game away to Czechoslovakia, the first in a mini summer tour that would then take them to East Germany and Switzerland. Gordon Banks would continue in goal having made his debut in that defeat to Scotland, but Ramsey's key changes would be in England's approach and tactics. The physicality would remain but direct and quicker passing was preferred. The W-M was gone and England moved into a 4-2-4 formation. The result was instant.

A very good Czechoslovakia were swept aside 4-2 and England were excellent throughout. They played with a speed and adventure that a late-Winterbottom era team dare not, to take apart the home side who had been World Cup finalists the previous summer. Jimmy Greaves had been magical at times, scoring twice and revelling in the faster transition from defence to attack. Bobby Charlton added another goal and another excellent game to his England history.

The press were glowing in their admiration. 'England now were playing arrogant football and stoking the ball from man to man as though they were playing ring-a-ring-o'-roses,' ran *The Times*. 'Hail Ramsey's Red Devils!' headlined a bombastic report in the *Daily Express* by Desmond Hackett. 'England found a new courage, a head-high pride, and an unflinching spirit of battle,' he wrote, on 'a night of British football splendour.'

The tour was a success as East Germany were beaten and a poor Switzerland were put to the sword by an experimental England line-up. Ramsey was bullish, he was making a difference and the press were with him. England seemed to be finally getting the best from Greaves, a formula Winterbottom had never found, and Bobby Moore looked for all the world a star in the making. Things were good and the decision to give the England side to Ramsey already looked vindicated. The only way was up.

Fast forward to the summer of 1966 and it hadn't all been as smooth sailing. As hosts England lacked the sharpening edge of competitive football to qualify. The yearly Home Championship was still a fixture but its familiarity meant it could never serve the same function as football with real consequence. In Ramsey's opening years as manager his team was dogged with that eternal foe of any England team: inconsistency.

He had shuffled his players considerably too. Gordon Banks was now the first-choice goalkeeper barring injury or rest, Moore his permanent captain and next to him Jack Charlton, a debutant in 1965 and now the heft to Moore's guile. Either side of them Ray Wilson and George Cohen were preferred, both dependable and in truth very much in the mould of Alf Ramsey the footballer. Nobby Stiles was a fixture in midfield and provided England with boundless energy and aggression, and a tactical shift away from traditional wingers had moved Bobby Charlton into a potent central position supporting the strikers.

There were other names Ramsey had brought into the squad that supplemented his spine such as Alan Ball, John Connelly, Martin Peters, Ian Callaghan and Roger Hunt. All were talented but above all would be trusted to work relentlessly in pursuit of the team over individualism. This mindset was prized by Ramsey above all others, and, as such, a reason why he had never fully trusted Greaves despite a frankly remarkable scoring record. West Ham's Geoff Hurst had been called up to deputise and looked the long-term option in the event of a Greaves absence.

The honeymoon period was over and despite Ramsey's public insistence that England would win the World Cup the recent memory was one of near-constant underperformance. There were highlights along the way but between the experimenting to get England's first team to the point where Ramsey was happy and the constant tactical shifts – refining the 4-2-4 and then dispensing with it altogether to switch between a 4-3-3 and something close to a 4-1-3-2 – there had been too many games where the players had looked lost. This had resulted in a downbeat press who harboured a frosty but still relatively respectful relationship with the manager. Were all these changes leading somewhere was the eternal question, one usually asked in hope rather than exasperation. Ramsey, as ever, only listened to himself.

That question remained after England's first group game, a dour 0-0 draw at Wembley against Uruguay. The *Daily Express*'s Desmond Hackett chose to blame the Uruguayan defence that was 'eight or nine players deep' at all times. Others were in agreement that although England had not done enough to stretch the game the mindset of their opponents had ruined the spectacle. 'The Uruguayans promised England nothing, and gave them even less,' wrote Ken Jones for the *Daily Mirror*.

England fared better five days later in a routine 2-0 win against Mexico. Bobby Charlton's brilliant first-half goal settled the nerves and while never hitting anywhere near their best the game eased them into their own World Cup easier than the Uruguayan defensive wall had. This left them needing only a point from their final match to qualify from their group just as they had in 1962. With France to play, there would be no repeat of Winterbottom's caution.

England struggled desperately for rhythm. They did achieve the 2-0 victory they needed but the game raised some genuine concerns going forward. Firstly, Greaves failed to score, just as he had also failed in his last four games, but more worryingly he never really looked dangerous either. Ramsey's switch to a near-enough 4-3-3 didn't really fit the way Greaves played but it got the best from other players such as Charlton and, in particular, Roger Hunt who enjoyed the space afforded by defenders doubling up on Greaves centrally. In stark contrast he had scored 13 goals in his 15 England games, and then added two more in this one.

Secondly, a tackle from Stiles on Jacques Simon caused a major reaction off the pitch including calls for him to be left out of the remainder of England's World Cup campaign. The tackle itself was mistimed over outright malicious but it left Simon injured and Stiles's reputation as grounds for discussion. FIFA themselves saw fit to issue a post-game warning to Stiles and state that one more would result in a ban. Ramsey then had to go out to bat for his midfielder as the FA wanted him dropped. Not only did Ramsey defend his man on the grounds of lack of intent, but this also constituted the FA meddling in his team selection – a line Ramsey would refuse to be crossed even in these circumstances. In an interview with *The Guardian* in 2002, Stiles recalled just how far Ramsey was prepared to go over the incident, 'By all accounts the committee told him in no uncertain terms I couldn't play, that England needed to make an example of me. I was a liability, they said. Alf told them he'd resign if he couldn't pick who he wanted. He was prepared to resign in the middle of a World Cup over me. I never found that out till he'd died, Alf. What a man.'

On top of Greaves misfiring, something that would be resolved by an injury in the France game meaning Geoff Hurst got his chance, the whole England team felt out of sync. This hadn't gone unnoticed by Ramsey who had not only had enough but went public with his feelings knowing criticism was coming his way. He said the performance wasn't good enough and had been 'too casual', something that had 'swept through the whole team' after the first goal. Tellingly, and perhaps the real source of the issues for both himself and the team, he went on to comment, 'I am completely stunned by the amount of pressure we have been under.'

The 4-3-3 was not working. Desmond Hackett went so far as to call England 'tactically stupid' after the France game, the 'timid untidy match' he had been reporting on. Argentina lay ahead in the quarter-final and Ramsey tinkered England into what was just about a 4-1-3-2. Stiles, the man he fought for, was given the role of playing as a midfield two all by himself. This consisted of sitting in front of the back four and providing a shield for all four of them while also playing the ball forward to Charlton at every opportunity. This supplemented a front two of Hunt and Hurst.

It's difficult to know if Ramsey's plan worked as the game descended quickly into farce. England won 1-0, Hurst taking his chance to replace Greaves with a genuinely excellent second-half header, but that wasn't really the story.

Argentina set out to disrupt England any way they possibly could. Right from the off every other challenge was just a shade heavier than it needed to be. Words were said to both players and officials almost constantly, body language doing the heavy lifting in lieu of a common tongue. After the game several English players and FIFA's neutral observer said they were spat at. England's response was to sink to their level while pretending they hadn't as Ramsey's men managed to differ their response in one somewhat key way: subtlety.

Argentina's captain Antonio Rattin took several headlines with his sending off, subsequent refusal to leave the pitch, and then a failed attempt to get his team-mates to walk off. Ramsey was incensed by the whole game and famously described the Argentine team as acting like 'animals', a comment which caused an outcry in the foreign press and which led to the South American nations standing with Argentina and threatening to leave FIFA. He also bolted on to the pitch at the final whistle and physically stopped his players swapping shirts with their opponents.

This was an important evolution in the role of England manager. Ramsey had felt the weight of it before and talked of the pressure, but here he was acting, he felt, for all of the country. The fact his men left the field having more than played their part was irrelevant. Indeed, at the final whistle they themselves had given away 35 fouls, 14 more than they would commit in any other game in 1966, and 16 more than Argentina did on the day. Still, what Ramsey had witnessed was an affront to everything he believed his team, and his country, stood for. It was time to be seen defending not just his team but the very notion of Englishness.

This essence of Bulldog Spirit carried Ramsey and his charges into the next game and their best performance at this World Cup. After the debacle against Argentina, the semi-final against Portugal was thankfully an absolutely terrific game of football. 'What a pity this isn't the final,' commentator Kenneth Wolstenholme wistfully wondered aloud during the second half. England eased into a two-goal lead thanks to the popular man of the match Bobby Charlton, his second with 11 minutes left causing an audible cry of relief from the 90,000 fans at Wembley. The actual man of the match, Nobby Stiles, had shackled the brilliant Eusebio but could do nothing about watching him score a late penalty to bring the tension right back. It was the first goal England had conceded in the tournament but they held out. West Germany lay ahead in the final.

Everyone reading this book knows what came next. Red shirts, baggy shorts. Hurst in for Greaves. Full time 2-2. Now go out and win it again. Did it cross the line? They think it's all over. Bobby's smile for the Queen. Nobby dancing.

England were world champions. A lifetime's work was complete for the FA. For Alf Ramsey a promise was fulfilled. He was calm in victory as ever, taking a moment to praise the Germans, but privately he was filled with a mixture of joy and relief. As was his way he preferred to let the players enjoy the moment publicly. 'We were the fastest and the strongest side in the World Cup,' he would later say, perhaps giving some inclination on where that inherent English way of playing lay in his own mind.

The joy across the country lasted for weeks. Good old England. Alf's Wingless Wonders. There was, however, a problem on the horizon that no one wanted to talk about. A question with no obvious answer, particularly for those at the FA. Quite simply, having a spent a lifetime believing they should be world champions, now they were what did they do next?

* * *

From 1966 to 1982, the year our story truly begins, English international football lurched from one existential identity crisis to another. Winning the World Cup was not just the only actual pinnacle available but the manner in which it had been won left its own legacy and expectations. England had been resolute in defence, unflashy in attack, used a spoiler in midfield, heavily relied on individuals to be the difference makers, and at times still employed good old-fashioned luck. Almost overnight all of that was no longer enough. There was a desire to both have all those things that had proved successful and now felt intrinsically 'English', and also to entertain. Yes we were world champions, but how come Brazil seemed to enjoy it more?

What followed over the next 16 years was a series of sliding doors moments, missteps and misadventures, coupled with some bad decisions from players, managers, FA officials and everyone in between. The immediate challenge after 1966 was to force home English football's position as the best in the world by winning the 1968 European Championship. Ramsey was now a Sir and busily trying to evolve a team in public while staying true to his principles of hard work. English football had been questioned worldwide following the success, some even suggesting its functional and physical nature was everything that was wrong with the game.

Ramsey had carried on regardless and used his new sway to make changes to the system. He had expanded his coaching staff and could now name a squad of anything up to 22 players for even a single friendly. With a World Cup in the trophy cabinet he could flex his muscles and demand more from the league in terms of providing him players, and he duly did.

England were still dogged by the eternal enemy of inconsistency. They had qualified for the 1968 European Championship finals in Italy but lost 1-0 in the semi-final to a decent but not much more than that Yugoslavia. The match was ill-tempered throughout, England played nowhere near their best and Alan Mullery was sent off for a retaliatory kick. The Euros had been set up as a stage to prove winning in 1966 hadn't been about home advantage and hard running.

A fine play-off win over two legs against a talented Spain had been for nothing and this game became, as Geoffrey Green wrote in *The Times*, 'a desert of frustration and ruthless tackling'.

Ramsey did not take the defeat or Mullery's red card well. His relationship with the press was prickly at this stage; his unwavering belief in himself bolstered by a World Cup win did not take well to being questioned. 'It would appear that you can kick a player in front of the referee and get away with it, but if you kick in retaliation and ref does not see it you get sent off!' he stated in a post-match interview. 'We have a reputation of being a team that plays over hard, but there are many other teams using more physical forces than ourselves.' The criticism was getting to him.

England won their third-place play-off but as Sir Alf admitted, as world champions, 'Third place in Europe is not our place.' The two years after the Euros were to be filled with friendlies and Home Championship games as they qualified for the 1970 World Cup in Mexico by virtue of winning the latter. This desire for something more than function put him on a collision course with the press and increasingly the fans as yet again England struggled for lasting form, never more so than after a dull match with an emerging Netherlands side in January 1970.

The Wembley fixture finished 0-0 and England were poor against the movement of a team who would go on to great things. During the second half the fans had seen enough and jeered and booed as England time and time again struggled to hold on to the ball and made basic errors. Ramsey chose uncharacteristically to be diplomatic by saying after the match, 'I couldn't decide whether the crowd was giving us or them the bird.' If he did have a genuine doubt the newspapers the following morning will have cleared that up.

England's usual line of pressmen were at the game and ruthless in their assessment. Ken Jones called England 'painfully and totally out of touch' in the *Daily Mirror* while Geoffrey Green of *The Times* said they had played with 'a sense of drabness and despair'. Desmond Hackett in his *Daily Express* report stated, 'I cannot recall an England side that played with so little spirit, so few skills,' and *The Guardian*'s Albert Barham joined him in the condemnation by saying it had been 'quite the worst performance from an England side it has been my misfortune to witness for a long time'. Sir Alf, once untouchable, was now culpable.

England's World Cup campaign in 1970 was full of colour, drama and iconic moments, but ultimately disappointment. Pre-tournament there was the scandal of Bobby Moore's farcical arrest for theft in Colombia. The case would predictably collapse but cause a genuine concern over his ability to actually travel to Mexico at one point. Once there England got through their first game, a hard-fought 1-0 win over a Romania side there only to defend.

Next up, a brilliant Brazil and a 1-0 defeat was by no means a disaster. It was a wonderful match filled with iconic moments – Banks's impossible save, Moore's perfect tackle, Astle's miss, Pelé's casual assist for Jairzinho, *that* photo at the final whistle – and England had more than played their part. It set up the pressing need to beat Czechoslovakia to guarantee progress to the quarter-finals, and they did, 1-0, but needed an Allan Clarke penalty in another game in which they struggled to find their touch in front of goal.

This all led to a rematch against West Germany on 14 June. Peter Bonetti came in for an ill Gordon Banks but other than that England picked the team who had run Brazil as close as anyone would that summer. The match went well. Until it didn't. England eased into a 2-0 lead and looked to have the measure of the Germans once again until Beckenbauer's weak shot squirmed under Bonetti with 22 minutes to go. Ramsey looked to get bodies into midfield and did the unthinkable by substituting Bobby Charlton, still England's best attacking player by a distance. As the minutes ticked by there was an inevitability and Seeler's wonderfully improvised equaliser took it to extra time. At that point there was only one winner, England's players dead on their feet and Germany's adrenaline carrying them forward. Gerd Müller's clincher didn't just settle the game but brought down a curtain on an era for this side. England were no longer world champions.

Upon returning in disappointment from Mexico, an autopsy was demanded of Ramsey but he was in no mind to give the press one. When he was pushed about putting together a successful, modern team who could entertain as well as win he delivered the line that would ultimately become his millstone, 'We have nothing to learn from the Brazilians.'

In hindsight Sir Alf Ramsey should have left the England job after 1970 and retired still just about in the glow of 1966's victory. What followed was four years of media pressure, an England team who were struggling to evolve, and a manager who demanded absolute loyalty and obedience trying to deal with a new breed of player. Rodney Marsh was a generational talent but Ramsey just never understood him. Why wouldn't you couple that talent with militant, repetitive and unquestioning hard work?

Ramsey did try and refine his team. He was a very tactically astute and adaptable manager overall. But the 1970s were about external extravagance after all the understated cool of the previous decade. Much of the conversation was about who Ramsey didn't pick or couldn't get the best from when tried. Marsh aside, talents like Frank Worthington and

Stan Bowles were only picked under duress when Ramsey knew it was too late to save him anyway.

The 1972 European Championship was a microcosm of England's troubles. They made their way through an easy qualifying group in typically stodgy fashion. Malta were far more trouble than they should have been but were eventually beaten 1-0 away from home, and then England settled into a series of processional, unspectacular victories. This put them into the quarter-finals, and laying ahead were the team with whom they had so much recent history, West Germany.

The first leg at Wembley was another footballing lesson. Not quite at the level of the Magyars running riot in 1953, but not far off. West Germany played simple, direct, fast and physical football. It was low risk in key areas but brilliantly effective in retaining the ball – key values Ramsey wished his team embodied. On top of this their decision-making was of another world to England's, German players drifting into positions instinctively rather than following the drilled patterns Ramsey prized. They knew when to quicken the pace and possessed an instinct for blood that their opposition just didn't have. England lost 3-1 on the night but were second-best everywhere.

Ramsey had made mistakes too, picking Norman Hunter to partner Bobby Moore in the absence of Roy McFarland despite their clear incompatibility together. Both would play badly. He also stuck with a 4-3-3 that had long been worked out by any opposition manager prone to a modicum of homework. Perhaps the most unforgivable was having no specific plan for Gunter Netzer, Moore admitting he 'hadn't been told a thing about him'. Netzer was sensational on the night and ran England ragged for his 84 minutes on the pitch. In his book with Jeff Powell, *The Life and Times of a Sporting Hero*, Moore commented on Ramsey's mystifying approach to the German midfielder, 'The way we were playing gave Gunter the freedom of the park. He hated being marked tight, but in the circumstances he found at Wembley his skills and brain could take any team in the world to the cleaners. He was just allowed to carry the ball from his own half, at our defence.'

The press were predictably savage, mostly towards Ramsey and even more so because the game had been televised in full, live on a Saturday night. There was no hiding place. Ramsey's reaction was to pick a team for the return leg in Berlin who would not be beaten rather than one who would win. A 0-0 draw may have been some vindication in the manager's mind but as Geoffrey Green wrote in *The Times* it left England 'in the shadows of a serious competition', something unthinkable for World Cup winners just six years previously.

Even worse, England then failed to qualify for the 1974 World Cup after being given every chance. They were drawn in a three-team group with Wales and Poland, both sides they were expected to overcome, and anything other than four wins looked improbable. They duly started with a desperately uninspiring 1-0 victory over Wales in Cardiff. The return fixture, a 1-1 draw that made it 20 months since England had won at Wembley, proved to be the ultimate vindication for many in the press who had had enough of Ramsey long ago.

Geoffrey Green, witness to so many of Ramsey highs and lows at this point, wrote in his *Times* piece that this was 'the nadir of the English game'; Albert Barham noted, 'It is seldom that an international match has not one redeeming facet.' The tabloids joined in the dawn chorus of abuse and Ramsey was on borrowed time. By the time results had fallen so that England's home game against Poland was winner takes all in qualification terms there was a creeping sense of destiny about it all.

Having been beaten 2-0 in Poland, Ramsey knew there was work to be done and picked an attacking side for the game. The 1-1 draw that followed, England foiled time and time again by Jan Tomaszewski – the goalkeeper repeatedly called a 'clown' by Brian Clough on pundit duty – was a grim end to a crawling death knell that had rung for some time. Ramsey, belligerent until the end, told the *Daily Mail*, 'If I could plan the match again I would do the same.'

Having limped through a couple of friendlies, Ramsey was summoned by the FA, still staffed by some of the international committee he had disbanded and publicly and privately goaded. There were plenty more he had alienated much more recently too. He was dismissed with unedifying glee by some there who also ensured his pay-off was small and his future pension, in the words of Brian Glanville, was 'miserable'. Ramsey had always lived by his own rules and made sure everyone knew who was in charge. It appeared he would now pay the price of defiance. Such was the contempt he held for the noise in the press and the growing hecklers at the FA, he had refused to resign and asked the FA to no less than double his wage as recently as two months prior to his firing.

He had created the modern role of England manager and furthermore the relationship between it and the press, for better and for worse. He too had shown the FA they no longer wanted a manager who battled them over the most minor concessions. The official reasons for his removal were the loss of revenue not qualifying for a World Cup would cost the FA plus a complete breakdown in press relations, but his team had let him down too. Toothless, unimaginative, and unable to beat sides who attacked with any sort of verve, England had never been quite this bad.

* * *

Joe Mercer was the man to take over on a caretaker basis and his seven-game run in charge was just about uneventful enough that some believed he should get the job on a full-time basis. That was never going to happen as Mercer didn't really want it for a start. In any case the FA had their man. Don Revie initially approached them to talk about potentially taking the role and the search ended immediately.

Mercer's brief spell was notable for how relaxed things seemed almost overnight. Ramsey's whip hand was gone and Mercer took the opposite approach – let the players play and things should be fine. Suddenly there was a place in the team for the likes of Worthington and Bowles. Three wins, three draws, and a solitary and bizarre loss thanks to two own goals to an excellent Scotland side, and Joe was gone with reputation not only intact but enhanced.

Revie was appointed and everyone was hoping he was the man to get more from a talented but disparate group of England footballers. He was a player's manager, as Ramsey had been, but was far more softly spoken and keen to mend relationships with the press and within the FA from the off. Ramsey's devotion to his own decisions had ultimately caused his downfall. Revie was immediately keen to avoid that while also believing there needed to be changes to the way the Football League worked with the international team to help them short and long-term. The press for their part had largely called for Revie's appointment after his huge successes with Leeds United, so it began with everyone very happy about how things had turned out.

Cut to July 1977, an undignified exit, and a manager who struggled to get his methods to work in international football. On the pitch England had changed the personnel but the historical issues remained. Revie was cautious in matches he had no need to be, and only cautiously expansive in others. His Leeds at their best had been a team of wasps fighting for the ball and going forward at every opportunity; early gegenpressing pioneers you might say. His England often looked anything but. As if the bravery had been coached from them.

Creative players like Charlie George came into the squad, underperformed, fell out with Don and disappeared from England duty altogether. George was picked for a game against the Republic of Ireland in 1976, played out of position on the left wing and starved of the ball. Subbed off on 60 minutes, Revie offered him a hand. 'Go fuck yourself,' came the reply. Every step forward came with a caveat and nothing quite worked. Revie began to feel like a poor fit quite early on.

Revie's Leeds had been built on an unbreakable bond of togetherness, as Brian Clough could have told you. His squad were brothers, their time together marked by shared pursuits like bowls and a manager willing to look the other way to pretty much anything for players who were performing. The problem with international football is that situation is almost impossible to achieve but even more so with Revie in charge due to the gaps between games, a regular changing of at least 20 per cent of the personnel, his meticulously crafted but somewhat exaggerated 'dossiers' taking too long to read for most, and flair players taken from London-based teams being asked to engage in pursuits more at home in a quiet northern tap room. Alan Hudson, a creative midfielder who shone under Revie initially but then inevitably fell out with him shortly thereafter, put it succinctly when asked about Revie's England bingo nights, 'I wasn't 80 years old was I?'

Revie himself was also becoming increasingly thin-skinned, and a mixture of criticism and time between games to stew over alleged slights was a powerful combination. He believed his successes were never recognised enough and no one listened to what became his eternal press comment – patience, time, it will come, etc. He had said it would take three years to build 'his' England team but the going was proving much slower. Frustration in the press, as ever, was building.

As they had with Ramsey, it would be the Dutch who brought Revie a level of criticism he struggled to deal with. A 2-0 defeat at Wembley in January 1977 as England looked leggy, bereft in attack and criminally slow defensively was met with derision from newspaper and crowd alike. Failure to qualify for the 1976 European Championship finals had been written off comparatively lightly by virtue of a tough group and a semblance of goodwill towards Revie remaining, but he had still been criticised heavily. After a chastening night at Wembley against a Dutch team who, like Hungary and West Germany, reduced England to footballing luddites, there would be no caveats.

The headlines were bad enough – 'Bottom of the Class' ran the *Daily Mirror*, while the *Daily Express* singled out the manager from the off with 'Revie gives Cruyff freedom of Wembley'. The actual write-ups were even more withering. 'Not since the visit of the Hungarians in 1953 have England been so utterly demoralised by the skill of the opposition,' opined David Lacey in *The Guardian*, his follow-up paragraph utterly damning, 'It was as if all the lessons of the last six or seven years had been rolled into 90-minute summary so that the English could enjoy a spot of revision or check their facts if they had not been heard properly the first time. In passing, positioning and shooting, covering, intercepting and tackling, Holland were so superior that long before the end it was clear that if one country had invented the game the other had developed it into, so far as England were concerned, an unrecognisable art.'

Perhaps the most telling comment of the night came from Dutch manager Jan Zwartkruis when asked about England's lack of progress, 'The English style is kick and rush, it is difficult to change that.'

In contrast to Ramsey's pig-headedness, Revie's response was to look at an exit strategy as he had fallen out of favour both in public and private. Within the FA he had clashed with several people over his desire to introduce bonuses for his and his players' performances right from his initial appointment In particular, Football League secretary Alan Hardaker was not impressed. On not qualifying for the Euros he had pointed to Revie who had been a thorn in his side going back to their dealings while he was still at Leeds, 'If we had the same national pride as Wales instead of playing for all these bonuses, we might get somewhere.'

Things had not progressed since that qualification failure and England needed to get to the 1978 World Cup for reasons both financial – and ego led. Hardaker had never changed tack on his dislike for Revie and the way he conducted himself. On Revie's initial appointment, Hardaker had phoned then FA secretary Ted Croker and stated, 'You must be off your heads.'

Revie knew he was on borrowed time anyway but the ascension of Sir Harold Thompson to head the FA in 1976 had confirmed it. Thompson had been a key figure in the removal of Alf Ramsey, the pair continually butting heads any time they were given the opportunity, and Revie's relationship with him had followed a similar path. Thompson was a divisive man, even more so than Sir Stanley Rous had been in Winterbottom's time, and he thought nothing of publicly undermining colleagues if the mood took him. Duncan Revie, Don's son, explained to *The Guardian* in 2002 the crux of their relationship, 'They genuinely hated each other.'

Revie's eventual departure was horribly messy and totally mismanaged from both sides. Revie told the FA he had to miss a game, the first of a South American tour, and the first after a horrible defeat to Scotland that had capped a lousy Home Championship for England. Officially he was going on a 'scouting mission' to watch World Cup qualification group rivals Finland and Italy play each other. Suspicions were raised from the off. Revie was to meet the group in Argentina for the next game of the tour but questions were being asked. He did watch the game in Helsinki, but he had also used the time to negotiate a potential package to become the new head of football for the United Arab Emirates.

On returning to the group Revie immediately talked with members of the FA and pointed to a conspiracy to remove him coming from the very top of the organisation. In reality his team was still struggling and had made very little progress, the press criticism justified itself, but Revie insisted that he would only go if paid £50,000 to do so. This figure has been disputed, some sources say it was £25,000, but it amounted to asking for his contract to be paid up in full for the privilege of leaving. The FA immediately denied to him there was any such plot, even though there had been conversations about making a change and they had not been too unhappy to find out word had reached Revie, in truth.

After the tour came to an insipid end with a 0-0 draw in Uruguay, Revie made his decision. The *Daily Mail* broke the story – 'Revie Quits Over Aggro' – having paid handsomely for the privilege. This was due to Revie's close relationship with its journalist Jeff Powell who over two days not only broke the news of his departure but also of Revie's new role. Powell wrote both stories and helped Don fly to Dubai. 'Nearly everyone in the country seems to want me out,' he told the journalist in a genuine exclusive, 'so I'm giving them what they want.'

Powell saw to it that Revie's resignation letter was delivered to the FA but only once the following morning's front page had been committed to the printers. The following day, 13 July, he broke the next phase of the story under the headline 'Revie Hits The Jackpot'. It seemed another important lesson had been learned: England stories on the front pages sold newspapers. The *Daily Mail* had played an industry blinder to get both the resignation and the news Revie was signing 'the most amazing contract in the history of soccer'.

Alan Hardaker's response to the news was absolutely withering, 'Don Revie's decision doesn't surprise me in the slightest, now I can only hope he can quickly learn to call out bingo numbers in Arabic.' The FA themselves were furious, learning of their manager's departure at the same time as everyone else. Thompson immediately placed a ten-year ban on Revie working in English football, at a meeting that was less a fair hearing and more an exacting of vengeance. He was seething, taking the whole incident as a personal slight. Revie, the greatest manager Leeds had ever had and one of the finest the country had produced, was now looking at a reputation in tatters outside of West Yorkshire.

Revie was gone, not just from the role but from the country. He would come back in 1979 to successfully sue the FA for money he was never paid. He was called 'greedy' by the judge in charge of the case but cared very little about it. Thompson was ruled to have acted way beyond the actual bounds of his jurisdiction. It was Revie's last shot at him, and he hit his target.

The press spent time digging into Revie's spell at Leeds in the immediate aftermath, and allegations of bribery and the tapping up of Alan Ball (who would join Everton over

Leeds anyway) were made by the *Daily Mirror*. In the end these fell down, Billy Bremner successfully sued one paper who repeated them, but the feeling of a vendetta from the FA and the national media, barring the *Daily Mail* of course, was impossible to ignore. Powell came in for criticism too as an 'acolyte journalist who touchingly still believed in the myth of Revie's infallibility' in an absolutely scathing assessment of the departing manager's failings by the *Daily Express*'s David Miller, 'Quite the worst aspect of Don Revie's backdoor resignation is that it did not come two months earlier ... The attempt to leave the sinking ship and to be paid for desertion merely confirms the impressions of those who deplored, for example, his request and acceptance of £200 merely for speaking at a football publisher's lunch.'

The piece was followed by a listing of six areas Revie had 'failed conspicuously on'. Ex-players Revie had fallen out with were also keen to put the boot in. The press were more than happy to give them a forum. Alan Ball was suddenly offended by the lack of a phone call to say he had not been called up for a game in 1975. For a few days in July it was a frenzy and despite the mud slung at Revie the FA looked incompetent too. Out-manoeuvred by their own man and the *Daily Mail*. Indignity heaped upon anger.

As an anti-venom the FA wanted a company man. Young Ipswich manager Bobby Robson was considered and had been the source of Revie's paranoia as he was certain that was the man the FA had been lining up quietly to replace him. Robson had been asked in a press conference and admitted that 'managing England is the peak of the profession', which did little to kill the rumours. The FA did have Robson in mind but he was on an initial list alongside Brian Clough, Lawrie McMenemy, Allen Wade (then FA director of coaching) and Ron Greenwood. Greenwood was the man they had turned to immediately as caretaker as he had been helping the FA with technical committees and similar anyway. Clough was the outstanding pick and the press wanted him desperately, but it was not going to happen. The FA didn't dare risk box office when they needed stability. Plus, quite simply, Clough scared them.

Greenwood had been available, was Thompson's pick, and was delighted to accept the job initially for three games. After they had been played and interviews of the five short-listed candidates conducted, plus brief discussions with Dave Sexton and Jack Charlton who both applied for the role, he was seen as the safest pair of hands and given the job permanently. In his last game of his interim period he had masterminded a very good 2-0 win against Italy to leave England with a glimmer of hope for qualification for the 1978 World Cup. It was not to be but the fixture had reinvigorated him and the FA. The caretaker became the candidate, the candidate became the chosen.

His history was already intertwined with England's, having managed England youth and under-23 sides in friendlies. He had witnessed first-hand the Hungarian destruction of England in 1953 and in stark contrast to Ramsey and Revie he became an artisan over a champion. His major success had been in creating a West Ham team that won the FA Cup and then the European Cup Winners' Cup in 1964 and 1965 respectively. In doing so he, and they, created the fabled 'West Ham way'. That team supplied the 1966 World Cup-winning side with captain Bobby Moore and both goalscorers in the final – Martin Peters and Geoff Hurst. His football was open and often his side lost games they could have won with a bigger commitment to containment, but that wasn't his wont. Whereas it would be fair to say latterly Ramsey and then Revie from the off had chosen teams on the basis of them not losing, Greenwood's philosophy on the whole was to try for more.

Greenwood's time in charge was one of steady progress. He might not have been the panacea to all the England team's woes but he started with a low bar and raised it sufficiently to see his tenure generally as a success. Age had dimmed his attacking intentions somewhat and the England manager's job now seemed to be becoming one that forced caution upon its inhabitant. His main issue was a brilliant Liverpool side supplying him with great players who all just didn't quite work the same way for England. Eternally his England will be remembered as one who looked far better on paper than they ever truly did on the pitch.

The press were cautious with him at first. They wanted Brian Clough, they believed the public wanted him too, but everyone in the loop knew Thompson didn't. Bobby Robson was a very viable candidate and a popular one too but perhaps it was just too soon. Greenwood was seen as a safe but unspectacular choice. His role was to make some lasting changes to create what the *Daily Express* termed 'an international Soccer Sandhurst, an officer's academy that will go on producing generals to win World Cup battles for years to come'. That might have been a little bombastic but there needed to be changes to the system as well as the role as even Thompson himself acknowledged. Revie's time in charge had hurt the FA, it was time to overhaul everything.

Greenwood's first target was to qualify for Euro 80, the year in which his initial contract would also run to. He was handed a huge boon by the draw. Their qualifying group would provide the comfort of playing Northern Ireland who they had played in the Home Championship nearly every year since 1954 and lost only twice. Alongside them were the Republic of Ireland who England had a similarly strong record against and whose line-ups would provide few surprises, an average Bulgaria side, and their main rivals Denmark who would provide decent opposition but were not the side they would become in the mid-1980s.

Greenwood's team eased through the group, winning seven games and drawing the other while never quite getting into a satisfying rhythm. The highlight had been an excellent encounter in Copenhagen that had ended 4-3 to England. Kevin Keegan had starred and scored twice and despite the close nature of the score the away side had just about been in control barring a crazy five-minute spell that saw Denmark score two goals to make it 2-2.

It hadn't been a revolution, but England had been attractive in spells, inconsistent in others. Greenwood's diplomacy meant relations between the FA and its international team were good. There were bad games, as there always were with England, but attack mode was dialled down as were expectations. This was mirrored in the press who had accepted England didn't currently have the best team in the world. For the moment. There were questions asked and a nervy 1-0 win against Czechoslovakia in 1978 launched a few harsh comment pieces. Most were aimed at the team rather than directly at the manager, and for the moment that suited the FA.

The Euros in 1980 had been expanded and eight teams would play in the finals in Italy. England's good fortune in the qualifying draw was not matched by their one for the tournament. They would face a decent but limited Belgium side, hosts Italy who would win a World Cup two years later, and Spain who were as inconsistent as England. They drew, lost, and then won when it didn't matter respectively. It all felt like a let-down after some promise had been shown but conversely the ratio of difficulty meant everyone within the FA was comfortable with what had happened. Greenwood was given a contract to try to take England to the 1982 World Cup.

Qualification was achieved but as ever it hadn't been as easy as it should have been and the toll on Greenwood was huge. England would go to their first World Cup since Bobby Moore had shaken Pelé's hand but cracks were showing everywhere. One of the chief criticisms of Revie was that his sides became defensive by default as he was forever changing the personnel involved or tinkering with positions and systems in areas there was little need to. For example, he had used nearly 60 players in just three years with the national side. Perhaps by nature because of the schedule involved in international management Greenwood had been afflicted with the same illness – too much time to think. Good games were followed by bad because men who were playing well were moved or dropped altogether. England also faltered because they didn't have Nobby Stiles in midfield. A revolving cast came in but none had the bite or energy of the man who had defined the role to date.

The press had halted the relative truce and were now asking questions of the man in charge. England had been incredibly fortunate to eventually qualify thanks to Romania blowing their lines and giving them a lifeline they really hadn't deserved. The papers had remained slightly more respectful than they had with Revie but the nature of this team lurching from bad to good and back again for no obvious reason was galling and the gloves were off. Greenwood too felt the pressure and had decided to retire in the summer of 1981 only to be reluctantly talked out of it by his players.

The crux had come with an awful performance and 2-1 defeat to Norway in Oslo in September 1981. The World Cup qualifier had been pencilled in for an easy victory, especially after the home game yielded a 4-0 stroll at Wembley. Yet again England had laboured through 90 minutes and struggled, particularly in front of goal. The press response was as brutal as Greenwood had faced, *The Sun* opting for 'For God's sake, Go, Ron!' Defeat to Switzerland earlier in the year had brought with it a barrage but this defeat to Norway created a deluge; even politicians asked questions of the national team as if it had relevance to their roles.

David Miller in the *Daily Express* was typical of most. His comment piece was headlined 'Blame Ron For The Futile Flop!' and got worse from there, 'This was a shambles of a performance by predominantly average players ... England's multi-million pound flops were without balance, tactical sophistication, or a real excuse ... England are short of genuinely world-class players but the inescapable conclusion is that Ron Greenwood, ardent patriot though he may be, has made less of the material than he might have done.'

Greenwood knew, just as Winterbottom, Ramsey and Revie had all done, that he was coming to the end of his time in charge. He would decide his own destiny and announced that after the tournament he would be retiring from the game altogether. The announcement also bought him some salvation from a potential press onslaught if things did not go well. He had talked of feeling 'hurt' and a walking round with a near permanent 'feeling of shame' as England struggled. The job was weighing heavily on a man who cared but couldn't understand why things were so continually disjointed.

England's eventual performance was deemed no more than okay, but okay nevertheless. Their initial entrance to the tournament was never really bettered, including Bryan Robson's excellent early goal and performance in a 3-1 victory over France. They followed it with two unfussy and unspectacular wins in stifling heat against Czechoslovakia and Kuwait to finish top of Group 4. This then placed them into another group, with West Germany and Spain, but two 0-0 draws cost them further progress.

Greenwood's performance at the World Cup came with a huge caveat of some incredibly bad luck with injuries. He lost Robson to a groin strain in the second game after that spectacular performance against France. He also didn't have his star man, and one of those who had passionately talked him into staying in the job, Kevin Keegan. Keegan only made a substitute appearance in their final game against Spain and was questionably fit enough for that, in truth, despite his own protestations. There were other absentees too, Trevor Brooking chief among them, which meant England's team had been hampered from the off. Greenwood's time had run its course and he would be remembered as a good man who had given his best. His team, however, were a contradiction. They had both failed to get anywhere near fulfilling their potential and yet somehow also restored a tiny amount of pride.

* * *

On top of England's inconsistency under Greenwood there was another shadow over the game and one the press, and increasingly parliament, were feasting on. Unfortunately, a simple change of manager wouldn't come close to eliminating it either. Greenwood's time was perhaps most noteworthy as coinciding with a marked rise in hooliganism from England's fans. Football violence wasn't new, but it had become extremely public.

Euro 80 had been marred by a stoppage in the game against Belgium caused by freely available tickets beyond those officially allocated. The fighting on the terraces with largely Italian fans, there as supposed neutrals, was visible on TV coverage and England fans chiefly among its protagonists. The FA received a relatively small fine, causing Thompson to publicly condemn those involved as 'moronic louts and saboteurs'. The 'Battle of Turin', as it would be known, only galvanised those who followed England for everything but the football. Incidents had been on the rise for some time domestically, an undercurrent that became a tide.

The incident caused major headlines and questions from MPs and ministers. Things were getting slowly worse with each away trip and every arrest brought with it new opportunities for the newspapers to shift football in to the news section and condemn the whole sport accordingly. There was a standard apology from groups who hadn't even been involved in response, but nothing seemed to be changing. Very quickly a reputation was built that meant police forces around the world were prepared to confront 'the English disease' on their own terms. In 1981 a summer tour took England to Basle to play Switzerland and again the violence was both widespread before, during, and after the match, and extremely public.

A loss compounded things further and this was the game that matters, on and off the field, conspired to cause Greenwood to make that decision to retire. He was talked out of it by a group of players on a flight home from the next game against Hungary but he felt responsible for England, its football team and its supporters. He relented and decided to take England to Spain 82 but no further. When Alf Ramsey believed he was defending England itself after the Argentina game in 1966, little did he know that several of those who would follow him would be faced with the indefensible.

Domestic football violence came to the fore. It had always been there but that now came with the boon of selling newspapers if on the front page. Football fans, and by default football itself, became a political issue and violence would blight the rest of the decade. It also became an easy target for politicians and commenters keen to raise their profile, and eventually for a Prime Minister determined to not lose her control on any aspect of political life.

England were an average team followed by a percentage of 'supporters' who had very little interest in anything other than fighting. Greenwood was leaving an unbalanced squad, a disengaged fanbase, a sport coming under increasing fire and an FA who were struggling to stay on top of things. They had tried a taskmaster and then an advocate after Ramsey; neither had worked. The next man had a huge, unenviable job ahead of him.

1982

THIS TIME there would be no drawn-out hunt or interview process; no polls or speculation in the press. In order, England's managers had been: the first, the World Cup winner, the caretaker, the hand grenade, and finally, the lighter touch. Now it was time for a new approach and one within the FA's own hands – the succession plan.

England turned to a man they knew would take it because he had been quietly lined up for the role almost as soon as Ron Greenwood had taken the job. After the chaos of Revie's departure, the forewarning this time had been welcome. Greenwood himself had helped enormously by understanding the rubble left behind by his predecessor's explosive exit. Even as caretaker he began to repair relationships with players and managers where he could. Revie's time with England had been black and white; you were either on his side or in his path. Greenwood sought to reinstall a few grey areas. Internally he also stressed to his superiors the immediate importance of an England B team to run alongside his own.

For this he had turned to two men to help him – Ipswich Town's Bobby Robson and Arsenal's Don Howe. Both would take over coaching the B team going forward, and Robson's unwritten role would be to eventually step up to the full team if all went well. Revie's suspicions of Robson had not been misplaced in truth, but it was deemed just too early for him, as it had been in 1973 when he had been briefly considered to take over from Alf Ramsey. The FA wanted Robson's involvement longer term and a B team seemed the perfect way to do it officially. 'The International Committee won't have to make any more one-off, on-the-spot choices as it did,' said Greenwood in early 1978 free of Ramsey's belligerence or Revie's paranoia. 'It should have been done years ago.'

England B games had existed since Walter Winterbottom's time in charge. Without any youth structure, Winterbottom, ever the thinker, had realised there needed to be a pathway to the senior team or at least somewhere he and committee members could look at potential future picks. This took the form of friendlies against a lesser nation's full side or a rival's own B team.

The first B international took place in Winterbottom's first year as a manager, 1947, against Switzerland B with England officially taking the form of an 'FA XI' in shirts hastily borrowed from the RAF. A 0-0 draw followed, the England team that day fielding the likes of Billy Wright, Tom Finney and Stan Mortensen. Keen to generate a crowd, their hosts had discarded the FA XI title and billed them as 'England B', both a name that would stick and one that represented a far more notable potential scalp. Any idea the game might be played in a friendly atmosphere was put to bed immediately by a series of wild fouls from the Swiss players making a claim for their full team. Early on, goalkeeper Frank Swift had to plead with local fans to leave England players alone as they jumped on to the pitch to intimidate them. Wright described it as his first 'hard game' and said, 'Some of the tackles our players had to withstand would have made hardened rugby men wince.'

Throughout Winterbottom's time he ensured regular B games took place, some in more auspicious surroundings than others. Later in 1947 England B beat FC Schaffhausen on a school playing field. Contrast that to 1952 when over 60,000 fans packed into Amsterdam's Olympic Stadium to watch England B beat Holland's full side 1-0. The result was a shock only in the sense that *The Times* reported, 'They had expected the fitter and more skilful young English players to win by a decisive margin.' England's captain that day was young Brentford defender Ron Greenwood, perhaps an indication of why he championed the benefits in later managerial life.

Alf Ramsey and Don Revie completely ignored the need for B team football despite both winning a cap at that level. This meant a gap between the last game under Winterbottom in 1957 to the first under Greenwood's regime in 1978 of 21 years. With standardised youth international football in its infancy, the FA had been fairly easy to convince knowing the need to have a plan for the future rather than listing from one manager to another. Terry Venables, Dave Sexton and Howard Wilkinson were also brought in to run the England under-21 side between them with Sexton taking the lead. Brian Clough and Peter Taylor were asked to take England's youth team although this lasted the length of a single summer tournament before they walked away.

Robson and Howe embraced both the roles they were given and the act of working together in what was a true partnership based on an enormous amount of respect for each other. They used the B team as a trial team, an audition almost. This meant they blooded several players who would go on to win 20 or more caps for the full side. Kenny Sansom, Paul Mariner and Viv Anderson all passed through to name but three, plus the player who would remain a riddle England never quite solved, Glenn Hoddle. Hoddle scored a wonderful goal in a 4-1 defeat of New Zealand in 1979, turning two defenders inside out before casually passing the ball into the net. Having caught the eye in that B international, six weeks later he made his debut for the full England side. Proof the mechanism was working.

Don Howe would have a huge role going forward. He was drafted from being Robson's number two to Greenwood's due to Bill Taylor's tragic death in 1981. Taylor had been a popular coach and his sudden death from a brain tumour at the age of just 42 was devastating. Howe could replace his organisational skills but Taylor had been immensely popular with the players and a trusted confidant to Greenwood. As a Scot by birth he had enjoyed some lively conversations on England duty, and he was missed by all as a source of levity in the very serious world of international football.

Howe was a thoughtful, intelligent and exceptional coach. A right-back by trade as a player for West Bromwich Albion and Arsenal, he had earned 23 England caps between 1957 and 1959 including four at the 1958 World Cup. His international manager Walter Winterbottom had earmarked him and Bobby Robson to stay in football after their playing days ended. He invited them on several coaching courses and to spend time with him at the FA's training centre at Lilleshall discussing the game. Howe was a willing pupil and an even more willing talker, fascinated by the game, as was Robson. For a spell the pair were both club and international team-mates at West Brom beginning what Robson would describe in his autobiography *Farewell but not Goodbye* as 'one of my life's great friendships'.

Howe's playing career was cut short by a broken leg in 1966 while on the books at Arsenal. With his ability off the pitch recognised he was employed as a reserve and youth coach by the club but within three years he had become first-team manager Bertie Mee's assistant. Between them they coached Arsenal to a golden period, winning a UEFA Inter-Cities Fairs Cup in 1970 and then a league and FA Cup double the following year. Howe was acknowledged by many involved to have played the biggest role. 'Don was instrumental … [Don] was about the tactics and the passion and making us all believe as a team,' said goalkeeper Bob Wilson talking with the BBC in 2015. George Graham, a forward and then inside-forward in Howe's time, went further when discussing that Arsenal success, 'Don was the day-to-coach with the team, he did all the tactics, he got the team 100 per cent right … We won the double and that was all due to the organisation and the coaching on the training pitch every day with Don.'

In 1971 Howe was offered the main role of manager by the club where he had made nearly 350 appearances, West Bromwich Albion, and found it impossible to turn down. His four years there were not a success, the perfect number two struggling with the ruthless nature of being a number one. After a relegation and two years in the Second Division he left the club to take up a coaching role at Leeds United, only to be immediately tempted back into full management by Galatasaray.

Again he didn't quite fit and moved back to Leeds to become Jimmy Armfield's assistant. Armfield had replaced Howe in the England team in 1959 but the pair had a great friendship. Armfield recognised Howe as one of the finest coaches available. He went so far as to describe Howe's job in Turkey as 'a waste for English football'. The opportunity to bring him back was taken as soon as it presented itself.

Howe was pulled to Arsenal to work with Terry O'Neill as his head coach in 1977. That was still his full-time employment as Ron Greenwood then brought him into the

England set-up. There really was no other choice for Bobby Robson as his number two. He needed his 'strong right arm'. As for Robson himself, *the* hero of a great many heroes in this book? Well, he had spent a lifetime as England manager in waiting, whether he realised it or not.

* * *

There are several biographies and autobiographies that detail Bobby Robson's life to the extent that to talk about his upbringing is to lurch into cliché. The miner's son who would eventually follow his father into the Langley Park Colliery. The deep and endless love of football from the earliest age. The happiness of a loving family home.

This story is not unique to those raised in County Durham in the 1930s and 1940s, but it would be fair to say it created a man who lived every moment of his upbringing throughout his football career, publicly and privately. The tireless work ethic passed on from a father who missed one shift in 51 years. The value of a personal touch key to a close-knit community understood so deeply he knew no other way to be. The passion for football manifested in honest and heartfelt enthusiasm. And, of course, the love of Newcastle United.

Robson was always destined for sporting success. That ferocious desire to work and improve meant nearly every spare minute as a child was spent with a ball at his feet. The precious few that weren't were devoted to cricket instead. He was an excellent young footballer and had offers from clubs throughout his teenage years waiting for him to turn professional, a testament to the talent that was evident rather than just raw. Middlesbrough held his amateur forms and offered him a full contract among competition from his first love, Newcastle, but also Sunderland locally, plus

Lincoln, Southampton, Huddersfield Town, and Blackpool further afield.

As was typical of the man he chose the club who made him more than an offer. While the list above sent out terms of a contract he could sign as soon as he was eligible, Fulham offered him that and a personal touch. Their manager, Bill Dodgin, travelled personally to meet Bobby at his home and persuade him his future lay in London. Financially they made the best offer to compensate for moving to the capital, but the effort made in securing his signature was the real decision-maker. Telling him how much he was wanted meant everything.

This was something Robson would never forget throughout his career. It was also something he never had to fake. He genuinely cared about people, particularly *his* people. This became even more so as England manager with the time between games allowing him to visit players, talk with them on the phone, and encourage younger talents with trips to training grounds or after-game conversations.

As England squads came together, newcomers would be announced and welcomed in their first team meeting formally by Robson, who would then make a short speech about each's talent and lead an enthusiastic round of applause. No one ever doubted the sincerity in which he greeted a young footballer making the step into the international game. It was a throwaway gesture, hollow if attempted by some, but as Paul Gascoigne wrote in his autobiography *My Story* it was a huge moment of recognition with Robson involved, 'You go up through the ranks until you achieve your lifetime's ambition: to get into the top class, with the big lads.' Robson was good at the small things that actually meant everything.

He was also good at football, very good in fact. A darting, lithe wing-half who found a home at Fulham; in his first spell with the club, he made 152 appearances and scored 69 goals, 23 of them in a wonderful 1954/55 season in which he was far better than the mid-table Cottagers were. A year later he was signed by an ambitious West Brom outfit who paid £25,000 for his services. He eventually returned to Fulham after a happy six years that ended on an unfortunate note due to a pay dispute. West Brom took him to be a troublemaker when in reality, and absolutely typical of Bobby Robson the man, he was actually fighting for the whole team who he felt were being underpaid.

He played for Fulham for five more years, ending with a total of 370 appearances to go with his 266 for West Brom. The shirt he was proudest of wearing, however, was England's. His 20 caps between 1957 and 1962 included three at the 1958 World Cup where he fell in love, 'I was intoxicated by this great gathering of nations, this rolling festival of games … I can almost feel, on my skin, the official blazer, shirt and tie that marked you out as a player in the drama … You felt special.'

But for bad luck and injury, Robson would have won a good deal more than 20 caps and played at the 1962 World Cup. A chipped ankle bone in a training match meant his place in the side was taken by a 19-year-old by the name of Bobby Moore. England failed at that World Cup but Moore emerged as the great hope to take the team forward under new manager Alf Ramsey. Robson's time playing for England was over.

He had made quite the impression on many of the most studious observers of the game. Walter Winterbottom had him at Lilleshall whenever the opportunity arose to learn but Bobby had actually taken his first course as early as 1953 as a young Fulham player four years away from a first England cap. Journalists, as they had with Ramsey, noticed he was destined for more too. In 1962 the *Sports Argus* identified him as a 'top-class tactician'. The same year Peter Lorenzo of the *Daily Herald* praised his 'experience and subtle promptings' from wing-half in a piece where in conversation it emerged Robson had helped the England coaching staff scout upcoming opponents Brazil. He was a trusted voice with a keen eye.

At this point he was well on the path to management before he had finished playing. He had helped works teams in his spare time with training sessions before taking a role in 1965 coaching Oxford University for their varsity matches for two years. That glorious work ethic meant he would train and play for Fulham while twice a week fitting in a round trip of more than 100 miles to take the university team for the afternoon. It became clear he was never really destined for anything else.

The FA had already called on Robson to help them long before retirement as a player. In 1964 a youth training programme was run at Lilleshall to form a squad to take to a Junior World Cup the following year. Allen Wade, the FA's director of coaching, had called Robson in to help run some sessions in front of the selectors who would whittle down the players to a squad. A young West Ham winger named Harry Redknapp was impressing early on. Robson was on the path to becoming a company man.

After accepting a job to become player-manager at the newly formed Vancouver Royals in Canada in 1967, Robson, now married to his childhood sweetheart Elsie and with three young sons in tow, set off for a new life in a different country. It was not to be, as the Royals collapsed financially. He headed home after a few months of not being paid what he had been promised and the club deteriorating politically around him. Fulham offered him the chance to try and save them as they were heading for relegation. It was too big a job for an inexperienced manager and behind the scenes directors and owners were making life even more difficult. Inevitably, they went down to the Second Division.

Robson was sacked, unceremoniously, as the first he knew about it was a headline in the evening's newspaper. His long association with Fulham was over in November 1968 despite being given a three-year contract just ten months previously. He never doubted his ability but in his own words, 'My life in football was being swept away.'

By the end of January 1969, he had a job. A promising one. Ipswich Town had only had three managers in their history before employing Alf Ramsey. After he had left to join England they had run through four more in a little over four and a half years. They were a good, well-run club who had struggled to replace the best manager in England. Robson was immediately happy there.

Ramsey's success at Ipswich was to take them through the leagues to a title in their first season in the top division. Robson's eventual 13 years with the club were arguably even more remarkable. He may not have won a title but he did turn Ipswich from a club perennially linked with relegation to a consistently top six First Division side. After a tough three years building his side and a philosophy around which the whole club would run, Ipswich finished outside the top six just once, 1977/78, the year in which they won the only FA Cup in their history. In 1981 he led Ipswich to the UEFA Cup having turned them into regulars in European competition. That triumph was an incredible achievement, a literal high point in the history of the club.

Between 1980 and 1982 their season finishes were third, second and second respectively – remarkable but particularly due to the nature of how they were achieved. Robson created a club where players were produced from within, a true production line of footballers who just kept getting better. Terry Butcher was given a debut at 19 years old and within two years was a starting central defender for England. John Wark, a first-team full-back at just 17, developed into a midfielder considered good enough for a £475,000 transfer to a mid-1980s Liverpool side who were winning everything. Kevin Beattie, Mick Mills, Alan Brazil and Eric Gates all became full internationals who would play hundreds of games in Ipswich's colours, and there were more.

Remarkably, in 13 years at the club, Robson signed just 14 players for a little over a million pound combined. In the that time he had sold 45 for a profit of well north of double that invested. He had trusted in youth, mixed it with experience, and practised patience with all. It had paid off handsomely. For the second time in their history Ipswich could lay claim to having the best English manager in the country. And for the second time in their history their destiny was to lose that man to the national side. Both went with grace and understanding from the owners who also considered it to be the biggest job in the country.

If there was any doubt towards his claim, with Greenwood's retirement announced he was all but anointed in June of 1982 prior to the World Cup. With Greenwood busy preparing for the summer tournament Bobby Robson took an England side for an international against Iceland. Originally billed as an England B game, the international would be upgraded to full status at the behest of the Icelandic FA. England were playing two games in two days, Greenwood taking charge against Finland the following evening. A 32-man squad was split into two with places in the World Cup 22 up for grabs for all but a handful of certainties. After his own personal dress rehearsal finished 1-1, Robson was asked about the England job. He chose diplomacy as ever, steering the question round to praising Glenn Hoddle's display, but admitted if asked he would 'have to consider it' if offered. It seemed he was the only one with any potential doubt.

Robson's appointment came to pass on 7 July 1982. The FA had their company man in place, the succession plan, but England were still an underperforming side in need of change. He wouldn't have the day-to-day involvement he had so loved at Ipswich but Robson would be able to pick the team he felt could move England's fortunes on from an entire country's worth of players. And that's where the problems started.

* * *

If England's new management team had any doubt as to the scope of their task ahead then their very first game was a microcosm of every issue they would have. Headlines, hooligans and hostility – and all before a ball had even been kicked in Bobby Robson's charge.

As was absolutely typical the communication of his appointment from the FA was shambolic. Ipswich chairman Patrick Cobbold announced that Bobby Ferguson was to be Robson's successor at the club and wished him well with England. The problem was the FA hadn't actually named Robson as their new manager. When the England squad landed home from the World Cup they were asked how they felt about their new boss and responded honestly, unaware it still wasn't official. FA chairman Bert Millichip and secretary Ted Croker had stayed in Spain to watch the conclusion of the tournament and had no plans to announce or call a press conference until they were home the following month. A statement was rushed together and a press conference was held in a hotel in Madrid without Robson actually being there. He was confirmed on the afternoon of the same day the *Daily Mirror* had already splashed 'Congrats Bobby!' as its back-page headline.

In response, Robson made sure he said the right things at first. He wanted the only option to still feel like the best one and to keep mending some of the bridges Greenwood had tried to. 'I must try to get the ball forward more than we have been doing,' he told reporters who had been decrying England's caution for the better part of 20 years. In an interview with Jeff Powell of the *Daily Mail* he offered the lovely line that 'they call me crackers, but the job was made for me', in response to Powell asking if it had been his destiny to become England's manager. There was optimism in the opinion pieces too, most genuinely pleased Howe was being retained – 'the vital link' as *The Guardian*'s David Lacey posited.

By the time Robson had picked his first team in September he was well aware of how quickly things can change. For a vital Euro 84 qualifier against Denmark to be played in Copenhagen he picked *his* England squad for the first time. Some decisions had come easily, others were going to bring him his first taste of controversy. His chosen 19 men included goalkeepers Peter Shilton and Ray Clemence; defenders Terry Butcher, Viv Anderson, Kenny Sansom, Russell Osman, Phil Neal and Phil Thompson; midfielders Steve Coppell, Ray Wilkins, Bryan Robson, Ricky Hill, Graham Six, David Armstrong, Alan Devonshire and Tony Morley; and forwards Paul Mariner, Tony Woodcock and Trevor Francis. The men selected were all fairly uncontroversial. Luton's Ricky Hill was the only uncapped member of the squad but was in impressive form for his club and had been touted by more than one newspaper as worth a look. Southampton's David Armstrong was a left-field pick but did have a cap to his name, plus both Bobby Robson and Don Howe were long-term fans, Robson going so far as trying to buy him previously as Ipswich manager. Glenn Hoddle was injured but would have been in the manager's thinking if fit.

Two available but overlooked men created the headlines. 'Captains Dropped Overboard!' according to *The Times*. Mick Mills and Kevin Keegan had both been left out of the new manager's first squad despite being fit and in form. As recent England captains it had been assumed at least one of them would play some part to provide some continuity. Robson thought differently. The fall-out was his first taste of truly being England's manager.

Mills was relatively calm. He had been captain at the recent World Cup due to Keegan's injury and one of Robson's most trusted lieutenants at Ipswich. Before leaving for the England job it had been Robson himself who had broken the news to Mills that he was no longer required by the club and would be sold that summer. At 33 years old, Mills still had plenty to give but with a race run under Robson domestically it was fairly easy to understand the decision. There was also decent competition for the full-back positions in the England team. Phil Neal was two years younger and was the main reason Mills had been in and out of the side anyway. It was a tough decision to lose all that experience, but an understandable one. When contacted for a comment on the day the squad was announced, Mills offered only, 'As the Denmark game is a competitive one I could have expected to be in,' but remained sanguine about it.

Mills was one of Dad's Army, the tabloid moniker for England's contingent of ageing stars. The World Cup squad in Spain had an average age of 28 and no less than nine players over 30. That had to change and was first among Robson's priorities. Trevor Brooking was injured and unavailable but at 33, like Mills, he had also played his last game for England.

Most of the analysis pieces had pointed Robson towards this age profile and the need to look at younger options. Frank McGhee had written in the *Daily Mirror* that Robson 'must recognise that the heady days at the top for several of England's squad are necessarily numbered'. Keegan, however, was a different case. At 31 he had passed his absolute peak but he had been England captain and talisman for the better part of a decade. The last World Cup's coverage had been almost completely overshadowed by Keegan's race to be fit enough to play any part. England historically had not been blessed with legions of world-class players but even an older Kevin Keegan, a two-time Ballon d'Or winner, was considered to be their potential difference maker. Robson saw things differently. The player was furious.

While most of the pre-squad announcement pieces had written about the desperate need to draft younger players in, Keegan's response was tabloid gold dust. Robson had been a public figure at Keegan's recent Second Division debut for Newcastle United. After the game they had a conversation in manager Arthur Cox's office that finished with Robson telling Keegan, 'I'll see you in a few weeks.' Keegan believed he would be picked, 'I felt a connection. England-wise it felt like a match made in heaven,' he wrote in his 2018 book, *My Life in Football*.

When Keegan found out that Robson had left him out, via a coach at a Newcastle training session, he went on the offensive. He was box office on and off the pitch. He had provided plenty of headlines over the years and remained a tabloid writer's dream. 'I'm finished with England. I'll never kick a ball for my country again,' he told readers of *The Sun* in a ghost-written article, adding, 'The way I've been discarded has hurt me.'

For two days the sports pages carried Keegan reports, quotes or opinions. Not all were on his side. Keegan notably had a close relationship with several reporters, meaning those outside the circle were not as enthralled. Bobby Robson chose to stay quiet. In turn Robson's silence itself became a story. He did have allies, notably Jeff Powell in the *Daily Mail* who took Keegan to task for his perceived petulance, 'Sympathy will be diluted by his reaction. Like every other player Keegan must have understood that Robson was starting a new era when he named his squad.' David Lacey in *The Guardian* had even less patience, 'So far the only cloud to spoil the honeymoon has been Kevin Keegan's whimpering response to being dropped from the squad, a back-page bellyache in one of the tabloids which demeaned nobody but himself.'

In later years both would discuss the incident in various articles, books and autobiographies. It would be fair to say Robson, a huge fan of Keegan the player, would get his side of the story across eventually. The decision wasn't taken lightly or quickly. A combination of age, a back injury Robson had been told would linger, the relative comfort of the Second Division, various reports of how disruptive he had been in trying to be fit during the summer's World Cup, and a general sense from those he talked to that Keegan had passed his best led to the omission. Robson always expressed regret that he did not take the time to ring Keegan personally and tell him about the decision as more than anything it gave the player an easy soundbite to hit him with over the years. It was also completely out of character not to have done so, as both have acknowledged.

That lack of personal touch was not just levelled at Robson but the entire FA by Keegan. He believed he had been an important-enough player to have earned better-than-average treatment. To be fair to him, he had a history of receiving it. In 1975 when dropped by Don Revie for a game against Wales, Keegan left the England squad hotel having not received an explanation personally from the manager. After playing voluntarily against Northern Ireland a few days before when it emerged the FA had received a death threat against him, he felt he had earned his place in the match. Revie eventually got hold of him after Keegan 'drove home to Wales, took the telephone off the hook and sulked'. He explained he was saving him for a game against Scotland a few days later and Keegan was returned to the fold.

This time there would be no reunion due to Keegan's self-imposed exile from all England squads in the future. If Robson had been half-hearted over the decision at first he now had no choice but to move on. His first taste of life in the tabloid headlights as England manager and he had yet to pick an actual international team. Quite an opening.

On returning to Newcastle later in the season to watch the club he loved with Keegan still in the team, Robson was loudly jeered and spat at by fans then in the thrall of Mighty Mouse's magic. While the rift would not go on to define any aspect of his management, he was deeply hurt by those reactions more than anything that was said. Keegan and Robson did reconcile to some degree in later life, and the Newcastle fans would not only apologise to Robson but eventually love him just as much as they had Keegan. Possibly even more.

After Robson's first real soap opera died down, England travelled to Denmark for his opening game in charge and to begin a new era. Their fans, however, were still stuck in the dark ages. On the day of the game Copenhagen was awash with thrown fists and smashed windows. Before kick-off 30 England supporters had already been arrested, soon to be joined by 26 more after the final whistle, amid disgraceful scenes that went on into the night. Before the game most of the trouble had been caused by bored fans with nothing to do until kick-off but drink. After the game they were met by Danish supporters, leading to a drunken battle across Copenhagen's main square between the two factions. The Danish police were surprisingly resigned about it all in a comment that explained exactly where England fans' reputations were at the time, 'We had expected roughly this amount of trouble.'

For the game itself, Robson went with a 4-4-2 system. Denmark were good, really good in reality, but it was felt they were individualistic so an organised and compact team could weather their moments of inspiration. Bucking the trend for youth, 32-year-old Peter Shilton was chosen in goal over 34-year-old Ray Clemence. England's new-look back four had Phil Neal at right-back, Kenny Sansom at left-back, and Terry Butcher and Russell Osman in a repeat of Robson's preferred central pairing at Ipswich. In midfield Tony Morley would start on the right, Graham Rix on the left, with Bryan Robson and Ray Wilkins together in the middle as graft and guile accordingly. Wilkins had also been chosen as the new captain. Robson's first striking partnership would be Trevor Francis and Paul Mariner. It was a combative and competitive line-up for a fixture they needed to win.

The draw for qualification for Euro 84 had put England in Group 3 with the Danes, Greece, Luxembourg and Hungary. It could have been kinder to England. Hungary were seen as the greatest threat due to a mass underestimation of the Danish team. With only the winners of the group through to the finals, it was vital to get off to a good start.

The Idraetspark stadium was fizzing as the teams walked out. Denmark were on the brink of becoming the team that would capture so many hearts throughout the 1980s. Their fans had created quite an atmosphere and it was instantly apparent this would be no walkover. Both teams lined up before the game in sharp contrast to each other. England's players could feel the vibration of a crowd who wanted them to know they were to be hunted. Their response was to stand with straight backs and stiff shoulders against the hum. The Danes smiled and waved, shaking a leg out and jumping on the spot. They were relaxed. They were home.

Despite the intimidation from the stands, England took the lead after just seven minutes. The first goal of the Robson era was scored by Trevor Francis but with a heavy Ipswich influence. After a wild clearance from Osman found its way to Ipswich team-mate Paul Mariner in the box, his header forced Bryan Robson wide where he managed to spin and cross in one fluid motion quite brilliantly. Mariner leapt to head the ball but under a robust challenge from Danish defender Soren Busk he could only nudge it hopefully behind him. Rix had stolen in unmarked just outside the six-yard box and he volleyed it straight into goalkeeper Troels Rasmussen. The ball dropped perfectly for a poaching Francis to tap in from two yards.

England briefly continued on the front foot, a brilliant free-kick routine nearly coming off shortly after the goal. However, as the first half wore on, it was clear the crowd was not to be silenced and Denmark started to grow into the game. Jesper Olsen's intelligence and the wonderful feet of Preben Elkjaer began to cause problems every time they had the ball. Osman in particular struggled under the pressure of a team who realised early that they just wanted to run at him every time. Bobby Robson's enthusiasm and promise of attacking football deteriorated into anxiety as Denmark's attacking players drifted from left to right or played through the centre whenever they felt like it. England did get to half-time still a goal ahead thanks to some extremely generous refereeing when Osman clattered into Elkjaer in the box.

They trudged off a goal to the good but now acutely aware there would be a massive task ahead to win this game.

The second half was all about the clearly great Danes. England were set up in straight lines against a team who were happy to play in circles. Olsen was starting to find angles that seemed to take an entire defence out of the game. Lars Bastrup flashed a shot wide as he was the only man on the pitch to read a reverse pass plucked from the pages of Pythagoras's notebook. Elkjaer again should have had a penalty as a lightning counter from an England corner saw him taken out by both a desperate Kenny Sansom and Peter Shilton racing off his goal line. The nerves were causing England to snatch at simple passes whereas Denmark seemed to have all the time in the world to settle over the sights.

An equaliser was inevitable and came after Osman, who surely just wanted the game to end at this point, stretched out a leg in the area knowing he was going to be so late his tackle would be in good time for England's warm down. The trip on Jesper Olsen was such that even this referee, Dutchman Charles Corver, had to give it. Earlier in the year Corver had been the official who saw nothing wrong in the infamous Schumacher/Battiston challenge at the World Cup. Third time lucky as a penalty was finally given for Allan Hansen to duly tuck away from the spot. It looked like there would only be one winner.

England were barely clinging on under incessant pressure and were grateful that Shilton was having a good night. Remarkably they went back into the lead. Francis again was perfectly placed to tap in when a Ray Wilkins corner found its way to his feet three yards out via a Terry Butcher flick. A very English goal. It was completely undeserved, highway robbery in fact, but no one in a white shirt cared. It was inevitably and deservedly a false dawn.

In the final minute, Jesper Olsen picked the ball up with the whole defence and a couple of midfielders in front of him. After dropping his shoulder and drifting past an ethereal challenge from Osman, a touch of pace took him past a despairing lunge from Butcher. From there he simply rolled the ball by a diving Shilton and was celebrating before it had crossed the line. A brilliant goal that he, Denmark and the game itself warranted. There would be no time left to get a winner. England had been outplayed and lucky to come away with a point. Denmark had been sensational throughout the second half.

Bobby Robson had to concede that he had not expected the Danish team to be as good as they were. 'It would have been a travesty had we won … I knew they were a good team but they have shown us they are brilliant,' he told the waiting press pack. Bold talk before the game reduced to unreserved humility. His era began with controversy but also, now, a priceless away point regardless of how it had been won. There was no longer any doubt about the level of work to do ahead.

* * *

England would next face West Germany in a home friendly that allowed Robson to experiment with his squad in less pressured circumstances. The Denmark game had crystallised a few things in his mind. He and Don Howe now knew the size of the task ahead and the single biggest issue facing them: English football. Both openly talked about how to begin an overhaul of the traditional British style to something more continental.

'If we continue to play the English way, as our players are used to with four defenders in a line across the back, we'll get murdered by teams as quick and imaginative as Denmark,' Robson told Jeff Powell. Howe too was quick to voice the problems of finding the right personnel to make the sea change required to become a force again. 'We need people who can play anywhere and meet the challenge of doing a different, unusual job if asked,' he said before returning to his job with Arsenal post-Denmark game. England needed a new system, more progressive football across the First Division, and better players immediately.

After the bombast of Keegan's omission from his first squad, Robson's second was a headline-grabbing challenge to a section of England's so-called 'fans'. He needed better, more intelligent footballers who offered more than running and playing in straight lines. Robson selected Mark Chamberlain, John Barnes, Luther Blissett, Ricky Hill, Cyrille Regis and Viv Anderson. Six black footballers in an England squad for the first time.

To get a sense of how challenging this was for a moronic section of England supporters, you only had to go back a month. The under-21s had played Denmark the night before the European Championship qualifier. Cyrille Regis became the first black footballer to captain England at any level and their win was not only resounding (a 4-1 rout) but it was also a wonderful performance of how to attack creatively, instinctively and, most importantly, quickly. Barnes had been particularly impressive, a watching Robson calling him 'a diamond' to anyone who would listen. However, England's four black players on the night – Regis, Chris Whyte, Paul Davis and John Barnes – were not only racially abused by their own fans continually, but a cheer was heard every time a white player touched the ball. From monkey noises to worse, it was a pathetic display of intolerance throughout.

Robson and Howe's squad decisions were made on no other basis than footballing ability. Six black players? As Robson himself said, 'If the 11 best players in the country were black, that would be my England team.' Anderson, Laurie Cunningham and Regis were all given debuts by Ron Greenwood but only two black players at any one time had featured together in an England squad, and only twice at that.

Anderson had been England's first senior black international, in a game against Czechoslovakia in 1978. He had become a regular in the squad and added nine further caps before being selected here. Seven months after Anderson's debut, the immensely talented Cunningham appeared for England but never quite transferred the form to international football that brought him a transfer to Real Madrid from West Bromwich Albion. Regis was a brilliant young striker who had been called into Greenwood's squad for an international against Northern Ireland earlier in 1982. As he prepared for meeting up with the squad he received a bullet through the post with a letter warning him he would 'get one of these through the knees' if he played. He kept the bullet until his tragically early death at the age of just 59 in 2018 'as a reminder of the force of anger and evil some people had inside them'. Speaking with the *Daily Mail* in 2010 about the racist abuse he received, he said, 'For the rest of my playing days, it was also a motivation, a reminder that these people were not going to stop me.'

Robson was widely praised in the newspapers for his decision to bring in these six black players to a squad in desperate need of more talent, albeit via some incredibly clumsy language around the individuals involved. Importantly, for the first time in a little under a decade the average age was 25. Denmark had mattered and Robson had got it wrong; too little respect for his opposition, too much faith in his squad. With the pressure off it was already time to look at some options.

England's youth system, enhanced by Greenwood's embracing of it when he took control, was now profiting. The night before the full international the youngsters completed a two-legged win over West Germany to seal the European Under-21 Championship for the first time. Robson knew he had to look further afield. Thankfully there were places he could.

England had played the Germans at the recent World Cup in a drab 0-0 draw. This time there would be a winner, the away side, but England emerged with a great deal of credit. Wembley welcomed the new management team for the first time and despite the 2-1 defeat on the night there was satisfaction that there had been an improvement. Robson handed a first cap to Spurs' versatile Gary Mabbutt and Blissett came off the bench for his debut too. Between six players in the starting line-up there was a meagre nine caps so the experimental side had very little baggage to bring with them, and it showed.

West Germany mixed their side up from the one that had recently lost the World Cup Final but they still just had too much for this English 11 over 90 minutes. However, there was a sharpness and desire about England's play not evident in Copenhagen. The main difference on the night was the clinical nature of the opposition's finishing, Karl-Heinz Rummenigge's two goals proving enough. Tony Woodcock's late consolation was deserved but overall the result was a fair reflection of where the two nations were.

To round out the year, England faced two vital qualifiers. In November they travelled to Greece and then in December they hosted Luxembourg at home. After the draw in Denmark had shown them the Danes were more than likely to win both these games the pressure was on for England to match that.

Greece represented the greater challenge of the two. There was a need to build on the performance against West Germany and get Robson and Howe their first win in the dugout together. After the fireworks of the last two squad announcements this one was a lot calmer. Robson called in three debutants – under-21 captain Sammy Lee, West Ham striker Paul Goddard and full-back Danny Thomas from Coventry. Thomas was now the seventh black player Robson had called upon in three squads. Regis was dropped, along with David Armstrong, and least surprisingly Russell Osman after his Copenhagen nightmare.

By the time the manager was passing his chosen 11 to the match officials on the day of the game, his squad had been decimated by injuries. Two rounds of First Division fixtures had taken place between the squad announcement and travelling to Greece. From his original 20-man list Robson had eight players struggling with injuries. He had drafted in Manchester City's Tommy Caton as cover, plus Chris Whyte was told to be ready if anyone else pulled up. Steve Coppell, Terry Butcher, Graham Rix and Alan Devonshire had all been declared unfit and sent home by the day of the game.

Of those left to play, Shilton kept his place in goal, Kenny Sansom would start on the left but was carrying a hamstring strain, and Phil Neal was on the right with a swollen calf. Phil Thompson played in the middle of the defence with Alvin Martin who was recovering from a groin strain. In midfield Tony Morley would start on the right, Gary Mabbutt was drafted to play out of position centrally, Ray Wilkins had been unavailable for selection due to injury so Bryan Robson would captain in the middle, and debutant Sammy Lee would line up on the left. Up front Paul Mariner would play with Tony Woodcock who not only needed injections for an injury to his big toe just to train but was also wearing physio

Norman Medhurst's football boots having lost two pairs since joining the squad.

They limped on to the pitch at the Kaftanzoglio Stadium to a sea of whistles and an incredibly hostile atmosphere. England fans had behaved in predictable fashion but were met with greater resistance. The Greeks had their own element. Training in the stadium the day before the game, the England players had to concentrate and ignore the continuous efforts of the Greek police to keep mobs of home supporters from entering throughout. Denied entry, they screamed and hurled insults in near perfect English instead as the team ran through a few drills. As the coach left to return the team to the hotel it was ambushed and showered with beer cans, coins and stones. Windows were smashed and the players were shaken. The Greek authorities responded by using over a thousand riot police to control the game a day later. After the final whistle it had been arranged that England would leave and head straight to the airport via a police escort and an already cleared route. Half a team in a gladiatorial atmosphere – it didn't look like it would be England's night.

One way or another though it would eventually be just that. England understandably lacked rhythm with such a cobbled-together side but didn't want for effort from anyone. Morley, Robson, Mabbutt and man of the match Lee worked tirelessly in midfield to cover their patched-up defence. It was no-nonsense stuff throughout, and gone were the neat interchanges of the West Germany game, but so too were the anxieties from Denmark.

An early goal helped enormously. Despite the circumstances Tony Woodcock had his best game in an England shirt. Just two minutes in, instinctively he latched on to a flick from Paul Mariner to touch the ball past the keeper. In an uncompromising mood, England held firm until half-time. It wasn't pretty – tackle, pass, clearance – but it was working.

The second half was a continuation of the first. Robson's men were dogged at the back and ruthless in front of goal. Woodcock read Alvin Martin's clearance and clipped the ball over the goalkeeper from the edge of the area for his second of the game just after an hour. Four minutes later, Lee's deflected free kick made it 3-0 and England could spend the rest of the game in containment mode. At the final whistle the stadium was no longer a cauldron but instead was half-empty. Robson had a result he dare not have dreamed about. Such was the nature of the performance – the balance, the control, the work ethic – not a single substitute had been used despite the walking wounded everywhere.

Robson was bullish after the result and in the build-up to the next game. He had previously stated that the Football League and the FA needed to work with him to improve the international side. What this meant specifically was that he wanted matches postponed before the bigger fixtures and Don Howe to be taken on full-time rather than splitting the job with his Arsenal duties. The nature of the disastrous preparation and ruinous effect on the squad but still having a manager who got his team over the line meant the FA were at least now willing to look at the proposals. A 3-0 away win had exacted a measure of goodwill.

Luxembourg came to Wembley for the final international of the year to face a side buoyed by a point in Denmark, a performance against West Germany, and that impressive win in Greece. The visitors were summarily dismissed 9-0 by a rampant English attack on the night. The standard of opposition was as weak as they had faced in years but England were absolutely ruthless, and if anything they were disappointed to have not been a touch more clinical and scored double figures.

Blissett got England's fourth goal on the night, the first by a black England senior international. He then added England's fifth and seventh for a hat-trick, the sixth a header from Mark Chamberlain. Progress for Robson and for England on several levels. The new manager was starting to enjoy himself.

1983

IT LOOKED like 1983 would be a busy year ahead for England with 11 games in total to play. However, just five of those would actually define success or failure. England's remaining qualifiers for the following year's European Championship were to be the real yardstick for their current position under the new management team. Bobby Robson had learnt a decent amount from his first four games. Each represented a step forward – an away point, a performance, a victory, a rout. The next 12 months would bring his first Home Championship, a summer tour to Australia and their remaining games in UEFA Qualifying Group 3.

At this point Robson was also beginning to understand that despite his perceived position as a company man, the FA were not the easiest body to work for, or indeed with. The upcoming trip to Australia had been a perfect case in point. The FA had originally organised a tour to South America with England likely to be playing Uruguay, Brazil and possibly one other local side. Robson had talked of his delight at being able to face off against the Brazilian team that had just captured everyone's hearts at the World Cup.

The difficulty in organising the games and a dispute over money – England potentially having to pay to play at least one match in a venue they would also bear the cost of among other things – meant that by the end of the year the idea of the entire tour had all but collapsed.

The hastily arranged replacement involved what was essentially a three-match series with England playing their hosts in three separate Australian cities. It had been touted originally as an England B tour to run at the same time as Robson took his men to South America. Australia's international team, many players within who were still only semi-professional, did not represent the challenge anyone in the senior England management team wanted. With a commitment in place, reluctantly it was agreed that the tour would be promoted to full international status.

Where Robson had been looking to test his England side against Brazil as a minimum – comfortably one of the best sides in the world and the most storied in World Cup history – he was now looking at a trio of games against a team who had failed to qualify for Spain 82 from a group containing New Zealand, Fiji, Indonesia and Chinese Tapai.

Coupled to this, and indeed another reason for the South American jaunt's eventual cancellation, he had also been told he would not be allowed to take his chosen squad anyway. The FA cited a 'gentleman's agreement' made in 1970 that clubs could arrange their own tours the summer after a World Cup year and all players would be expected to attend. It became apparent that England were going to be struggling to put together a squad, never mind two, to send to different parts of the world.

For the now-unwanted games in Sydney, Brisbane and Melbourne, Robson was expected to be without players from Manchester United, Tottenham Hotspur and Arsenal as a minimum. Furthermore, anyone he selected from Liverpool and Watford would only join up with the squad once their own tours of the Far East were completed, and they were to take priority in terms of travel arrangements and preparation. As the year began he was basically to be held ransom by the whims of any other First Division team who managed to arrange a money-spinning foreign jaunt before the end of the season. Not an ideal situation for a manager who had spoken frequently of the desperate need for more time with his squad.

He had also now been foiled in an ambitious plan to lead an England-heavy Great Britain side to the 1984 Olympic Games. Rule changes had opened the tournament up for a potential entry as professionals were allowed as long as they had not competed at a World Cup or earned a sportswear endorsement contract. Italy, West Germany, Holland, Brazil and others were taking the chance to compete in another world football tournament with teams of young professionals. Robson thought it would be the ideal situation to look at some of his developing players in competition circumstances.

The FA felt differently, chairman Bert Millichip stating publicly that in declining to take part they were 'sticking to the Olympic oath, even though other people are not'. Privately they simply didn't know how to sort the logistics of organising a Great Britain team even though they had nearly 18 months to organise one. The two most pressing questions were how to best cover their costs (as ever), and what mandate would they have to lay down in terms of picking the squad by national representation. A golden opportunity to spend time with young English players in a tournament scenario was gone. Robson was fast realising whereabouts on the food chain his requests actually were and specifically how easy it was for them to be dismissed.

His demands for change within the wider game were also being ignored. The notion of postponing all First Division fixtures the weekend before an important England match may have been wishful thinking longer term but some very practical ideas around coaching were being treated the same. He wanted simple reform in youth football, chiefly around the way games were played. 'No one should play 11-a-side football until they are 13,' he explained in a speech to the Northern Football Writers' Association. 'At present we have a situation where 11-year-olds are playing 11-a-side whilst professionals have five-a-side as our daily routine – it doesn't make sense.' He also wanted a limit of the amount of games youth sides could play in a season as some were playing over 100 in a little over eight months. Again, his requests were pushed to the bottom of the pile.

Back within the world of things he could influence, 1983 would start with a match against Wales in the Home Championship. Over the years the tournament's popularity had waned to an all-time low. It had also become a lightning rod for hooliganism. Once seen as the prestige cup in England's calendar, it had become an inconvenience to play three so-called competitive games a year that you actually learned very little from. To top off the relative lack of excitement about this specifically rearranged game, the Milk Cup semi-final was to be played the day before, robbing both teams of the chance to include anyone from the clubs involved – Manchester United and Arsenal.

Suitably, the attendance on a freezing February evening was a miserable record low for a full England international at Wembley. Just 23,600 fans came to a stadium that could have held nearly four times more than that. An icy pitch, a disinterested audience and a competition that no longer raised the pulse contributed to a stale game. England won, another sign of progress as it had been nearly ten years since Wales had lost at Wembley. They had also come from behind for the first time under Robson. Trailing down to a typically instinctive Ian Rush goal, they had to grind their way slowly back into the game against an impressively energetic Wales side. Shortly before half-time Terry Butcher wandered into the penalty area completely unmarked as England pushed forward. Alan Devonshire's wayward shot landed at his feet and he tapped in his first international goal.

The most notable performances came from two debutants, Aston Villa's Gordon Cowans and West Bromwich Albion's Derek Statham. Cowans won the penalty that eventually gave England the win and had been eye-catching throughout. Phil Neal scored, and a 2-1 victory was a credible result from a match no one would remember anyway.

Of far more importance was Greece's visit to Wembley in March. With England starting to find their feet under their new manager it was expected to be a relatively easy home win. Perhaps even a chance to up that goal difference further after the nine goals against Luxembourg.

They were restarting qualification football in a commanding position but wary of greater tasks ahead. As David Lacey wrote in *The Guardian*, to assert themselves at the top of the group 'they will need to beat Greece this evening by a margin at least equal to their 3-0 victory in Salonika'. The fixture schedules and rearrangements meant England sat top of the group having already played three fixtures. Denmark were in second with that draw in Copenhagen and a predictable win over Luxembourg to their name. The team everyone was supposed to fear, Hungary, had only begun their qualification journey three days before the night England would play Greece at Wembley. Predictably they too had beaten Luxembourg in comprehensive fashion.

Robson had not far off a full complement of players to choose from this time. Cowans deservedly kept his place, and Manchester United's young right-back Mick Duxbury was called into the squad for the first time after impressing

in the under-21s. A fit-again Ray Wilkins was left out despite
a niggling injury to his United team-mate Bryan Robson
meaning he would also be missing. Rather than an outright
snub, it was felt that Wilkins was still playing his way in
whereas Cowans, Gary Mabbutt and Sammy Lee had all
been impressive in recent internationals and deserved to keep
their places. The only other player who could have been in
contention was Glenn Hoddle but like Wilkins he was only
just back from injury so not risked.

Robson named his team the day before the game and
it looked as strong as any he had picked so far: Shilton,
Neal, Martin, Butcher, Sansom, Lee, Mabbutt, Devonshire,
Coppell, Francis, Woodcock. Two strikers, Coppell as an out
and out winger tasked with supplying and supplementing
the front two, Devonshire to stretch the midfield with his
pace. It all looked set fair for a comfortable night under the
Wembley lights.

It would prove to be anything but as Robson's team had
their first really bad night. Greece came for pride having
been whistled off by the few remaining in the stadium
the last time they played England. This meant that out of
possession they retreated to make sure at least eight players
were behind the ball, presenting their opponents with two
walls of four to bypass. In response England offered very
little. They were slow, predictable and passed sideways.
Midway through the second half they had been reduced to
hopeful clearances and very little else. Greece were happy to
stay tight and afford no space anywhere in their own half.
The plan worked as Woodcock had to be replaced by Blissett
having offered nothing more than middle-distance running.
Devonshire was also subbed off having had a poor night
after some early heavy tackling destroyed his enthusiasm
for the game.

The Wembley crowd had grown tired of a team bereft of a creative spark without Ray Wilkins, Bryan Robson or Glenn Hoddle as options. This was not necessarily a reflection on Robson at this stage but rather this was *the* England issue. Winterbottom, Ramsey, Revie and Greenwood had all struggled to find ways to get their team to break down defensive sides. An hour in, the jeers and whistles were audible on the TV coverage; 'unfortunate but understandable' as commentator John Motson noted. A universal chant of 'what a load of rubbish!' echoed around the stadium and continued on and off for the rest of the game.

By the final whistle England had barely troubled goalkeeper Nikos Sarganis who might have expected a busy night. The 0-0 draw was cause for great celebration among the Greek players who had all they had come for. England trudged back to the dressing rooms, Robson and Howe off the bench and down the tunnel well aware of the atmosphere around them. Ramsey, Revie and Greenwood had all received the bird at various points of their career and here was Robson's introduction to such a reception. If it was an England manager's worst rite of passage then perhaps there was an argument to get it over with early.

A shuffle through the newspapers over breakfast will have brought the management team some discomfort. Most chose to avoid any outright attack on Robson and preferred instead to split the blame three ways between the lack of Greek ambition, the same old issue with breaking sides down and a lenient referee. Harry Miller's write-up for the *Daily Mirror* may have been headlined 'Greek Farce' on the back page but his and Frank McGhee's verdicts preferred to focus on their belief that Greece were not there to play any actual football and got away with murder. McGhee, however, did write, 'Condemning the Greeks for playing with daggers in their stockings cannot and must not obscure the inadequacy of England's all-round performance.'

A reaction was required 28 days later when Hungary came to Wembley fresh from consecutive 6-2 victories over Luxembourg. This game had now taken on huge significance with Denmark bettering England's result by beating Greece at home. If the home side lost then qualification would have looked difficult. Another draw would not help that much, in truth, with the ominous sight of Denmark at Wembley on the horizon in September. England were favourites for that game still, just about, but the Danes had already given them one chastening evening. They simply had to win; nothing else would be good enough.

Fortunately, Hungary were every bit as bad on the night as Robson's men were good. After trying to scale a Greek wall they instead faced a team who took risks they were not good enough to capitalise on, conveniently leaving England some space. Stung by the draw last time out England started on the front foot and stayed that way. They got their rewards with a comprehensive 2-0 victory that but for Luther Blissett's finishing could, and probably should, have been double that or more.

The first goal had come from a routine Trevor Francis run across the near post and header. The second followed a terrific passage of play and came after good work in midfield from Sammy Lee again as he beat his man and chipped a lovely pass towards Aston Villa striker Peter Withe. Withe was a good player who had struggled in an England shirt. This was his seventh cap but now he finally had a goal to his name as he chested down the pass and struck an unstoppable shot on the half-volley across Hungarian goalkeeper Béla Katzirz. Job done, England could start looking towards the Denmark game and plotting the victory they needed.

Before that lay the remaining games in the year's Home Championship. First up was a stupefying 0-0 draw with Northern Ireland, notable only for John Barnes's debut from the bench in the 70th minute. Barnes nearly marked it with a goal, forcing the only save even approaching discomfort from goalkeeper Pat Jennings. Much of the pre-game press had focused on Glenn Hoddle's apparent inability to take his club form into international football. He had spent 90 minutes passing well enough in his first start under Robson but the game had descended into nothing around him early on.

Four days later, on 1 June, they played Scotland for the 101st time. The winner would take the title as both teams had drawn against Northern Ireland and beaten Wales. Wembley was closer to a full house than it had been since a vital World Cup qualifier against Hungary in 1981. The 83,000-strong crowd were rewarded with an early England goal as Bryan Robson made a late run to volley in Terry Butcher's flick from two yards. The lead settled English nerves and they looked comfortable from that moment on. As ever there was an edge to the game that made it scrappy but that suited this England team on the night who were happy to compete in midfield and clear anything that made its way past.

Bryan Robson had returned to the team after an injury but was lost again to a groin strain he had tweaked not long before his goal. Despite trying to play on, he was forced off as it worsened and Gary Mabbutt took his place. The reshuffle meant Gordan Cowans could drift inside a bit more as Mabbutt's defensive instinct afforded him cover. The Villa man doubled England's lead ten minutes into the second half. They played out the rest of the game trying to avoid any more injuries as it descended into a last half an hour neither side really wanted to play at full tilt after a long season. Chances came and went but the game had effectively been over after Robson's goal. Eventually it finished 2-0, Scotland had been disappointing, and England had won the Home Championship outright for a 34th time.

The whole tournament had been a hinderance in 1983 and discussions were to be held about its future. Matches had been moved around to make way for other things and the Scotland game was switched to midweek to try and avoid widespread trouble. Bobby Robson was keen to use the precious time he got with his squad in more constructive ways and with bigger tests. It felt a doomed event in the longer term but for now it was Robson's first actual achievement as England manager. Denmark still lay ahead but first there was the summer tour.

* * *

England would play Australia three times in eight days and remarkably manage to disappoint each time. The rearranged tour and cobbled-together squad, plus the timing to play at the end of a long season, all meant the perfect recipe for three flaccid, lifeless performances from the away side. Helping the overall feeling of lethargy was the fact the sports world was currently consumed with the Cricket World Cup being hosted in England and Wales. There was a feeling no one wanted these games and, to add insult to injury, no one was watching them either.

First up in Sydney was a 0-0 draw after which both teams were booed back into the dressing rooms. England gave debuts to five players during the game – Paul Walsh, Mark Barham, Steve Williams, John Gregory and man-of-a-very-poor-match Danny Thomas. Australia wanted a result from the game and dug in. England played like a side who didn't want to get out of first gear if they could avoid it. By the time it became apparent they might have to it was too late.

The tour moved to Brisbane and England were better. They upped the tempo and went at their opposition from the off but proved wasteful in front of goal. It took until the 57th minute to break through, Walsh with a tap in after Gregory hooked the ball back to him in the six-yard box. The goal was controversial as it looked very much like the ball had gone out of play before Gregory got to it. Furious yellow shirts briefly surrounded the referee but no one in white was complaining. *Shoot!* magazine cleared this up in its 15 June issue by running a sequence of photos to prove the ball hadn't fully crossed the line when Gregory pulled it back. This would have been fine if the final photo hadn't shown Gregory's foot a long way over the line and daylight between it and the ball.

Australia's Terry Greedy, a full professional goalkeeper for a little over a year at this point, had a fine game but was grateful for the opposition's profligacy as the encounter wore on. At the final whistle the score remained 1-0 and in theory England had restored a measure of pride with the win. However, the moral victory was still Australia's for keeping the score down.

Finally everyone moved on to Melbourne with a feeling of relief that this was nearly over. The last game of the tour ended in another draw but Australia getting on the scoresheet this time represented a big win for them. England had gone ahead 20 minutes in after a good spell had seen the Aussies resort to kicking anyone they could get close enough to in lieu of an actual functioning defence. Trevor Francis spun and crashed in a great shot for the lead, a high point for the away side's entire tour. A few minutes later Phil Neal had a horrible moment and it was 1-1. Joe Watson's looping cross found its way to the back post where, caught in two minds, Neal chose neither option and instead mis-controlled the ball off his thigh into his own net. The own goal stiffened Australian resolve and the tackling remained as fierce.

England pushed but Australia, aided by referee Jack Johnston who you could charitably call 'a homer', bullied them back. As they were repeatedly kicked, finally Francis had a long overdue moment of anger and picked up the first booking of the game for a late lunge. England did then get a penalty, not for Australia's captain John Kosmina tipping John Barnes's shot on to the bar with his hand, but a few minutes later for his push on Terry Butcher that even this referee couldn't pretend not to have seen. Francis scored only for Johnston to say he had not been ready and there would have to be a retake. Clearly annoyed as he had been targeted all game, Francis lashed wildly at the second one and hit it high and wide to a great cheer. The game petered out as Australia got closer to another draw and at the final whistle celebrated as if they had won.

The whole thing had proved as unsatisfactory as it had initially promised to be. Australia were delighted to have only been beaten by an aggregate score of 2-1 over the three games. Bobby Robson was less than thrilled by it all. The press reaction was one of total apathy as they were too wrapped up in the cricket and now Wimbledon previews too. The players were tired, they had travelled too far for games of no consequence, and few people actually cared. Even Jimmy Greaves was annoyed with it all in his *Shoot!* column, writing, 'The tour was a complete failure.'

No one other than the England regulars who had made the trip actually put together much of a case for inclusion in the next squad. In his *World Cup Diary* published in 1986 Bobby Robson described the tour as 'having limited value and, on reflection, scant preparation for the European Championships'. A few of the players had at least enjoyed themselves. Barnes said it had been a 'great trip' as it had coincided with Australia's centenary celebrations. This was very much shorthand for the fact they had been allowed to go out and enjoy a drink between games.

So all roads now led to Wednesday, 21 September and the showdown with Denmark. Not quite mathematically winner takes all but a Danish victory meant qualification was no longer in England's own hands. The Danes had beaten Greece at home and found yet another generational attacking star at their disposal. Nineteen-year-old Michael Laudrup had become one of the most sought-after young talents in European football and Lazio had moved swiftly to take him from Brondby in the summer.

Robson had underestimated Denmark in 1982 but he wasn't about to make the same mistake again. The problem was he was about to go too far the other way. There is a fine line between instilling respect for your opponents and implanting a fear of them instead. The build-up to the game saw a pensive Robson in press conferences, every question treated as a hindrance.

He had taken to naming his team early as was the tradition for England managers, usually the day before the game where it would then be dissected by the columnists. Now there was no early announcement, a mark of both wanting to keep his opposition guessing and a desire to leave room to refine until the last moment. His squad had been shorn of Tony Woodcock, Gordon Cowans, Alvin Martin and Bryan Robson – all lost to injury and all would have started if fit. He was incredibly wary of the physical threat of the Danes – so quick, so strong on the ball, so confident in everything they did – that he knew the midfield balance would be key. The England management team had prided themselves on trying to pick teams that would ask all the questions but here was a game where the opposition were expected to know most of the answers.

As ever, creativity was going to be the problem. That midfield was finally selected and two men were included with the responsibility of playing through the Danish press – Ray Wilkins centrally from deep and John Barnes on the left who was to stay much higher. To complement them Sammy Lee's impressive England form and high energy would be rewarded with another cap, while John Gregory would play after proving on the Australia tour that he was more than happy to get involved if the game turned into a battle at any point. Barnes and Wilkins were tasked with looking forward, Lee and Gregory were to be more defensive and track runners to try not to give the Danes the clear run at England's back four they enjoyed in the first game. Ahead of them a front two of Francis's good form and Paul Mariner's selfless work rate were to try and profit from any sight of goal they were afforded.

Defensively there was a surprise. Peter Shilton kept his place in goal as ever, Phil Neal and Kenny Sansom either side and the un-droppable Terry Butcher in the middle. Next to him was a recall, and an unexpected one. Russell Osman, the defender so overrun in Copenhagen, would play at Wembley. The injury to Martin left Robson with few options he trusted so he turned to one of his old Ipswich lieutenants for help. The decision was aided by the news Preben Elkjaer was not fit enough to start after a training-ground injury. Osman had been run ragged by Elkjaer in Copenhagen but went, partly out of necessity, to Australia and featured in all three games. Recency bias meant in Martin's absence he was now the next man in line. Even he was shocked to be in the running, 'If I am in, I'm a bit lucky to be back after that game in Denmark.'

Robson had his team but his pre-match nerves had bled into the camp. In later life he did actually recognise that mentally he had hindered his squad, 'My mistake was in exaggerating their ability in my own mind and putting it across to the England players.' Walking out, his team were nervous, straight-faced to a man with the odd stolen glance at the opposition. Wembley was noisy, expectant. England dare not lose.

In contrast their opposition were doing their upmost to appear relaxed. They were more than aware of the significance of this game but also supremely confident of their ability to overcome everything England could throw at them. Wembley's history alone was meant to be enough to cow most opposition into meek obedience. Denmark, however, took the full allocation of tickets available to them and 15,000 of their fans had taken the trip to London. Each and every one did a fine job of making themselves heard, as they would do all evening. The players, one of football's greatest-ever cult teams in the making, were inwardly nervous but had been told to give as little sign of that as possible. In the book *Danish Dynamite*, defender Morten Olsen admitted that the Oscar-worthy acting from the squad was deliberate and designed to unsettle a team they knew were on edge. 'You can bluff,' he told the authors, 'but you must also have the class to bluff.'

England's nerves meant they played in straight lines again, risk-averse football that was susceptible to anyone willing to play on the edge. As early as the first minute they were completely undone. Allan Simonsen picked up the ball after a loose piece of control from Barnes ceded possession to the Danes and immediately hit the pass into the space behind England's back four Michael Laudrup was likely to be running into. Controlling it without breaking stride, Laudrup was clean through and rounded Shilton with a mere shuffle of the hips. His shot, snatched due to coming so early in the game, hit the side netting and England had already had a huge let-off precisely 52 seconds into their night's work.

Robson shifted uneasily on the bench. It was going to be a long night. Early on, England's main source of creativity was Terry Butcher repeatedly moving out of defence and hitting a long, hopeful ball forward. In contrast the Danes were being patient, picking moments rather than building pressure. The game was less a game of chess and more a case of seeing who made the first mistake. With a sense of inevitability, the home side slipped first.

England had provided the odd spark here and there, Barnes's run and cross for Mariner's wayward header had lifted a few from their seat, but in the 37th minute their job became considerably harder. Denmark kept the ball, Laudrup popping up on the right wing as that Total Football-like fluidity of the Danish attack tied the back four in knots. His cross was aimed at an area rather than a man but with Butcher pulled out of position and beaten twice by Laudrup on the right Neal made a horrible mess of trying to head the danger clear. Simonsen's mis-control actually ricocheted the ball back into an off-balance Neal who handballed eight yards away from the referee. The penalty was given, it was scored by Simonsen, and England had a mountain to climb.

The rest of the game settled into a familiar pattern. England huffed and puffed but struggled to create anything clear-cut, while Denmark looked dangerous every time they ventured forward. The home side were sluggish again, Wembley's grass beginning to feel like quicksand as it had against Greece. Hoddle hadn't made the bench despite being in the squad and that now looked like a glaring error as England laboured. The home crowd were getting restless, but you could barely hear them over the growing Danish celebrations.

The game's biggest moment came in stoppage time. Sansom was afforded the opportunity to drop a long throw into a crowded penalty area. The Danish defence, resolute but untroubled, slipped for the first time in the match and the ball ended near substitute Luther Blissett. His turn and shot from eight yards was destined for the bottom corner before an excellent, instinctive save from goalkeeper Ole Kjaer. Kjaer had been the one player Robson had not talked up; quite the opposite as both him and Howe felt he was nowhere near the standard of the outfield players. England had been unable to test him until seconds before the final whistle, and he had passed admirably. Blissett's mixture of bad luck and bad finishing was starting to become an issue for England as he had yet to add to the hat-trick against Luxembourg.

At the final whistle, which came shortly after Kjaer's flying save, the Danes dropped all sense of calm or cool to erupt in celebration. Despite the talent at their disposal Wembley was still an incredibly iconic, and difficult, place to play football. An away win under the twin towers was something only eight nations outside of the British Isles had achieved. Of those nations Denmark were by far the smallest. This had been a different performance to the 2-2 draw in Copenhagen, more measured, but an even better result. Their qualification lay in their own hands. The home support's repeated chant of 'what a load of rubbish' was one of the first to make it over Denmark's noisy offering.

For Bobby Robson there was only despair and an early inquisition into whether he was the right man to take England forward. Qualification for the Euros, absolutely vital in everybody's minds after getting to the last World Cup, looked to be gone. In multiple books and articles written later in his life he referenced the defeat as his 'blackest day' in football. Certainly if the draw against Greece had bought an uncomfortable few days in the newspapers this would be Robson's first taste of outright contempt. He struggled to cope with the defeat and faced a cacophony of cheap shots from the red tops.

The Sun's editorial was brutal; 'Send For Cloughie!' screamed the headline. 'We were not just beaten by tiny Denmark, we were MURDERED', ran one of the less hyperbolic lines within. The newspaper had been Brian Clough's biggest advocate both when Don Revie resigned and then in vain when Greenwood's departure was announced. The *Daily Mirror* headlined Frank McGhee's verdict with the no less vitriolic 'Rubbish, Robson!' McGhee's report was a masterpiece of seething criticism, 'England can have no other complaint. Denmark were streets ahead in every department. A search for one solitary individual success for England ends in failure… It was infuriating and humbling to see men come and go, Mark Chamberlain for Barnes, Luther Blissett for Lee, and realise that nothing was going to make any difference.'

It was no better in the broadsheets in truth, England's failings laid bare once again. The simple fact was that Denmark were much the better side than England. There had been mistakes made though. The doubt sowed. The optic of not naming your team early creating the sense of running scared. A team with so little creative talent. A simplistic tactical approach against a team who could play a symphony together. Robson was depressed and blamed himself. So much so he offered his resignation to Bert Millichip knowing the words 'Brian' and 'Clough' were now in nearly every conversation involving the England team. It was immediately refused to the FA's credit.

* * *

England's remaining fixtures for the year – away to Hungary and Luxembourg – were played in a slightly sombre atmosphere. Robson, and many in the team, were glad to be away from the glare of Wembley as Denmark did as expected and qualified. Needing two wins from their last three games they could afford the hiccup of a defeat in Hungary as they eased past Luxembourg and Greece.

All England could do was win those matches, which they did in quite impressive but utterly futile fashion. In Hungary they put the game to bed by half-time with three first-half goals in a totally dominant showing. As ever with England anything good must be heavily caveated and for these 45 minutes it was very much a case of look at what you could have had. Glenn Hoddle not only scored the first with a wonderful free kick, but he was magnificent throughout. His corner was headed clear for Lee to add a second from distance with a firecracker of a shot, and then he provided the run and cross for Mariner to tap in a third.

Hoddle glided through the game, a metronomic presence of high quality in England's midfield. With pace ahead of him and Bryan Robson's return meaning some bite around him, he spent 90 minutes making a mockery of his absence against Denmark. He carried this form into Luxembourg and produced another man-of-the match performance in a 4-0 win. Against opposition considerably below his level he looked like a maestro performing in a tap room. His corner provided Bryan Robson and England's first goal, then a brilliant Hoddle cross led to John Barnes nodding the ball down for Terry Butcher to score easily. Sandwiched in between was an own goal charitably credited to Paul Mariner. England's fourth and final goal came after Hoddle picked the ball up and eased into space before flicking it through to a charging Bryan Robson, who finished for the best goal of the night. In two games in which England had got seven goals in total, Hoddle had scored one, directly assisted three and indirectly assisted two more.

The game in Luxembourg was yet another low for England's fans who ran riot in a country ill-equipped to deal with them and completely undeserving of such treatment. Before the match had even kicked off there had been violent clashes involving a section of the 1,500 England fans who had little interest in the game. Thirty-four had been arrested by the time the away coach was pulling into the stadium. After the game they went on the rampage again, turning cars over with and without people inside and smashing shop windows as they raged through the streets. Sixty arrests in total were reported. There had been far more in truth that had been dealt with without the need for paperwork by simply locking them up until they were sober. Yet again the manager and the FA were forced to apologise for the conduct of their fans.

There was a gloom over England and especially over coverage of the national team. Bobby Robson was already becoming a tabloid lightning rod for negativity and the front pages were full of hooligan stories. There were still those who believed England were on an upwards curve, a lot more in the media than those who didn't in truth but missing out on Euro 84 was a failure. Furthermore, there were aspects of that failure that undeniably lay at Robson's door. Happily, with the England job tabloid redemption was never far away. Usually, a single decent win would do it. Robson looked to next year with hope and expectation things could only get better.

1984

ONE OF football's great unspoken acts is to elevate some goals to a moment in time rather than a mere sporting accomplishment. Significance comes in all forms but usually it's either brilliance or notoriety that earns them a higher status. Their marker is that generally they require only a few words to describe. Van Basten's volley. The hand of God. Carlos Alberto charging in. These are the goals that stand the longest and mean the most. Reading this, you will immediately be able to recall some of your own club's greatest hits. None will need more than a five-word descriptor.

England have a few entries in this particular pantheon. They think it's all over. Beckham, last minute. The dentist's chair celebration. And there is another that those of a certain vintage will never forget: Barnes against Brazil.

In the first three of those goals there is an element of Englishness. Geoff Hurst tiredly collecting a long, straight clearance and hitting it as hard as he can feels about right. To a footballing country raised on *Roy of the Rovers*, David Beckham scoring a free kick in the last minute appeals to our engrained saviour complex. And Gazza's 1996 moment of inspiration was something we had all waited six years for as tacit proof we were right about his talent all along.

Barnes against Brazil, however, doesn't fit the mould. England players don't take one, two, three, four defenders on. England players don't roll their foot casually over the ball to glide past a goalkeeper. England players don't score goals that the home fans in one of football's most storied stadiums allow a standing ovation. England players don't score exhilarating solo goals. To this day it still feels like it might not go in every time you watch it, that somehow it should not have been scored. A truly otherworldly moment from an obscenely talented player, John Barnes, who admitted in a television interview 18 years later it was 'like having an out of body experience'.

The interview was part of a segment to celebrate Barnes's goal against Brazil being voted 75th in a list show, *100 Greatest Sporting Moments*, broadcast on Channel 4 in 2002. The list had been voted for by the general public long before the days of social media skewing poll results towards the most well-supported teams. It finished higher than Shane Warne's ball of the century, Martina Navratilova's ninth Wimbledon title and Ben Johnson's drug-assisted 100m gold at the 1988 Olympics. Barnes against Brazil. A moment in time.

'That's a good ball there for Barnes.'
Commentator Brian Moore has no idea what's about to happen. Mark Hateley wins a header, controls the ball on the bounce and then chips a pass out to the left wing. Barnes is waiting. He's had a good first half, and an earlier run brought a warm round of applause from the home fans. He chests it down and into space in one fluid motion. England look unfamiliar, wearing white shirts, white shorts and red socks instead of the usual variations of white and blue. Around them Brazil are in the most recognisable kit in world football.

'Now can he take Leandro?'

Barnes's first two touches take him between two defenders who can't fathom the opening for a tackle. Leandro is his direct marker, a right-back who in typical Brazilian style plays far higher than he should. Barnes has caught him square and by moving inside has opened up a pocket of space for himself. His next four touches are all taken at speed as a change of pace sees him into the penalty area. Four defenders are around him all filled with the dread of knowing they can't get anywhere near.

'John Barnes now. He might go all the way for England!'

Moore's voice rises with each touch. 'For England' – as if Barnes is doing this for all of us watching. A reactive piece of television direction sees us move from a near pitch-side angle to one higher up. It is the perfect showcase for what's about to happen. The space Barnes is working in looks so small but for the defenders it might as well be an ocean. Yellow shirts everywhere but all are now just like us – mere spectators. Only the goalkeeper waits ahead of England's left-winger.

'Barnes!'

Rather than pass it either side of him he does the unthinkable and takes a touch more. A roll of the foot, instinctive but incredibly pleasing on the eye, and he's left the goalkeeper completely stranded. Then it's time. One more touch to put it in as a last desperate tackle comes in. Goal. Barnes against Brazil. Moore waits a full four seconds, a lifetime in television terms, before speaking again. It is a moment of both disbelief and a desire to let the goal stand without comment as we all rise from our seats. It is the perfect response from a master commentator who himself can't quite believe it yet.

'He's scored! And England, amazingly, are into the lead!'
A few more words are spoken as two replays are shown. Moore exclaims on a second viewing that Barnes 'has performed a miracle there'. By the time of the third he's talking directly to us rather than commentating by asking us to 'just look at it again'. The player is hugged by a few and then disappears into a joyful mob. Something has happened. It will be remembered.

* * *

If not qualifying for the Euros was to be counted as a failure on Bobby Robson's behalf, then it had to be the *before* and a successful 1984 the *after* for everyone to keep believing in this management team. As disappointing as the campaign had been, there were caveats. Denmark turned out to be an outstanding side, the England squad was heavily in transition, and both Glenn Hoddle and Bryan Robson had been unavailable through injury for significant games.

England's slow evolution needed to continue with recognisable progress. Drawing that *before* line would be helped by a new kit creating a different visible identity. England's contract with Admiral had run its course and they switched back to Umbro. Umbro had made every England kit from 1954 until 1974, none of which carried a logo other than the England badge. By 1974 kit design was in the very early stages of what would be a revolution – shirts were no longer merely blocks of colour.

Don Revie had encouraged the FA to look at the Umbro deal on a couple of different levels. He had changed Leeds's kit believing it helped with a feeling of belonging and a sense of status. He had made it an advantage rather than just a necessity. England's plain white shirt was easy and instantly recognisable, but at odds with the advances being made elsewhere. Revie had, of course, also been aware of the rights involved in having the deal to make a high-profile team's clubwear and how profitable they could be. With his encouragement the FA sought out a new deal and went with Admiral who offered a payment immediately and a yearly royalty on the number of shirts sold. By 1984 and with the current kit design both four years old and with only notable failures to mark it, the time had come for a new look. Umbro kept it simple – a blue V-neck with red and white tipping and matching trim on the sleeves – but it felt significantly like the start of a different chapter. The FA also received a £1m payment for the five-year contract, their biggest endorsement deal to date by quite a margin.

England now knew their schedule. The South America tour would finally take place in the summer with a full squad of Robson's choosing. They would play Brazil, Uruguay and Chile. Before that they would play France and the USSR in friendlies, plus fit in the year's Home Championship games. After would come a friendly against East Germany and then, crucially, it was time to get into the qualifiers for the 1986 World Cup.

The draw had taken place in December 1983 and nobody wanted to play England. That had very little to do with the footballers, and everything to do with the fans. As it turned out Bobby Robson couldn't have asked for much more. For a start England were drawn into Group 3, one of the five-team groups, and this was hugely significant. It meant the top two would both qualify for the World Cup allowing for an element of safety from England's point of view. The high stakes of Euro 84 qualification only being possible by winning their group had proved a bridge too far. The crash mat of two places was surely too big to miss.

Then there was the draw itself. Ahead of them were home and away games against Northern Ireland, Romania, Turkey and Finland. Not only would England be heavy favourites for all eight fixtures regardless of setting, but the other four teams in the group were likely to take points off each other as qualification progressed. This meant there was every opportunity for England to have a hiccup along the way and still get to the World Cup. They could not afford to fail but they were being given a helping hand they ill-deserved.

They would also have more room in the schedule the following year as 1984's Home Championship would be the last. The Welsh FA in particular were keen for the competition to continue as it was their main revenue generator but it had run its course. When it had been abandoned in 1981 after England and Wales refused to travel to Belfast for fixtures there, a death knell for the tournament's future had stared to sound. During the previous two years, it had been a threnody in the international calendar and hooliganism was rising. The English FA announced that they were withdrawing after the year's games had been played and the Scottish FA immediately followed suit.

First up was February's away friendly in Paris. France were warming up to host the 1984 European Championship in the summer and were not aware that not only would they go on to win it, but they would become regarded alongside the greatest-ever European sides. With that in mind it was perhaps no surprise that England lost. However, the nature of the defeat was disheartening.

England were outplayed by a far better side to a degree that was worrying. If Denmark had been all energy in Copenhagen and then given them a death by a thousand cuts at Wembley, here France cruised to a 2-0 win by barely breaking a sweat. Michel Platini grew into the game after a promising opening few minutes from England and eventually became its focal point. With that went any chance of Glenn

Hoddle and Bryan Robson having some freedom. Somehow it got to half-time goalless. Patrick Battiston had missed a great chance having rounded the goalkeeper, Platini had mis-controlled when clean through, and Peter Shilton had made good saves from José Touré and Bruno Bellone. In response, England had offered only a feeble shot from Southampton's Steve Williams.

The dam could not hold for much longer as time and time again England were forced into a desperate tackle or a pressured clearance. Touré's beautiful nutmeg left Graham Roberts wondering what on earth had just happened but Shilton came to the rescue again. Platini missing an open goal on the follow up was surprising to say the least. Eventually Platini, involved in everything at this point, made the breakthrough. His header over a stranded Shilton was scant reward for just how on top France had really been.

With the lead France eased off slightly and Hoddle was allowed to curl one just wide. Bryan Robson tried to get the tempo of England's midfield up but only succeeded in creating space behind him. He was grateful to Shilton for another save as Touré again couldn't work the finish. Unfortunately the goalkeeper handled outside the area in trying to clean up the attack and Platini curled his second of the night in from the free kick.

England had been well beaten. Hoddle, who it had been hoped was going to take his form from the last two internationals into this one, had been given a masterclass by Platini. Bobby Robson had selected Brian Stein for his debut, the first African-born player to represent the full England side, just as he had been for the under-21s. It had not been his night as those around him had created next to nothing. England had played an excellent side destined for great things again and had shown just how far off the pace at the top of international football they were. David Lacey of *The Guardian* eloquently summed up France's attacking performance as 'rather like d'Artagnan fighting the Cardinal's men – the thrust of the rapier meeting unimaginative side swipes from untutored swords'.

Yet again the actual match only produced half of the column inches as violence erupted across Paris before, during and afterwards. The ease of travel afforded large groups of England fans access to the away encounter. Those who had no interest in the football came along too. During the day, trouble had flared up between England fans along club lines before they had even reached the capital. The interior of one of the Dunkirk-to-Paris trains had been damaged as Chelsea and West Ham fans fought with each other, smashing windows and using anything breakable as a weapon. Before boarding, several cars had been damaged at a British Leyland depot in Dunkirk as tensions that had started on ferries over, where four people had already been injured by fighting, carried on into France.

Once in Paris, English hooligans had fought with groups of their French counterparts, damaged cars and taxis, smashed shop windows, and fought the local police who were in no mood to let their city be destroyed by louts. Fifteen England fans ended up in hospital with injuries sustained from police batons. During the game England's fans had decided to try to 'take' the stadium, charging into French supporters and using ripped-up seats as projectiles. Some of those made their way on to the pitch along with several coins and bottles. Small groups of France fans tried to stand their ground but were met with punches, kicks and broken glass by a barrage of louts singing 'God Save the Queen'.

The police again moved to meet force with force and England fans were thrown out of the stadium, some quite literally by simply pushing them over a large concrete wall. The response was that the violence and random destruction carried on well into the night. Eventually, with the help of the English police force, the vast number of fans were kettled into returning home under escort on planes and mostly by ferry. It had been a disgraceful day and yet again both the FA and the England manager were forced to publicly apologise for the violent and vocal minority.

It had been an extremely disappointing couple of days on every level. Robson was drained by it all – the so-called fans had only succeeded in 'distracting and detracting' from his team again. Bert Millichip had 'been able to watch only half the game' as he had been called away to discuss the immediate response to the violence. The weekend before the match, boxer Tony Sibson had fought Louis Acaries at the Palais Omnisports on the outskirts of Paris and won. After the bout, English boxing fans had stayed in the arena as long as they could, eventually damaging seats and climbing into the ring, only leaving when tear-gas canisters were fired into the crowd. England's stock had never been lower among its sporting peers. Unbelievably it would eventually get much worse.

* * *

England entered the final Home International Championship as holders and in need of some sort of boost. They didn't receive it as they played their three games between April and May and fell short in each to varying degrees. There were three notable debuts – Terry Fenwick, Mark Wright and Gary Lineker – but it would be another in a growing series of disappointments from Robson's side.

Northern Ireland were first and another dismal crowd at Wembley witnessed a 1-0 win for England. Both the Northern Irish and Welsh FAs were equally angry that the Home

Championship was ending and both teams were determined not to let England walk to victory. Tony Woodcock's goal came about after an error from goalkeeper Jim Platt who pushed a Viv Anderson shot straight into his path. Chances were missed at both ends but an overall sense of boredom descended yet again on an England home game. By the final whistle the few fans that had come had already left in droves. As Mike Payne wrote in the peerless *England: The Complete Post War-Record*, the final Home Championship game at Wembley would 'only be remembered for the fact it was the last'.

England then travelled to Wales at the start of May to play at the Racecourse Ground at Wrexham. Robson's squad had been decimated by nine of his regular picks and three maybes all dropping out through injury. The fact that many of those missing played their next club fixture was no coincidence. The scheduling put the game right at the sharp end of the season with most clubs only having three or four fixtures left to determine their respective fates. Robson was sympathetic to a degree but his full international side had a distinctly England B feel for the first time since the trip to Australia.

Wales played very well, England very badly. The fact it only ended 1-0 to the home side could be classed as a positive as the English midfield and attack offered next to nothing in the game. Shilton, in a rich vein of international form, played well enough to stop Wales adding to Mark Hughes's first-half header. QPR central defender Terry Fenwick made his debut from the bench with ten minutes to go. He would go on to get 19 more caps after this game. More significantly Southampton's Mark Wright played the full 90 minutes for his first of 45 England caps. Wright was a tall imposing centre-half who Bobby Robson liked a great deal.

He would feature a lot in the immediate future but this was an inauspicious debut.

One newspaper had decided it was already enough. *The Sun* printed 'Robson Out, Clough In' badges and was represented in Wales to give them to England fans personally before the game. It also arranged a phone poll to show that its readers were demanding a change of manager. There was no denying that Robson was struggling as injuries and circumstances were conspiring against him, and bad results were stacking up. The Wales performance had been a dismal affair, particularly off the back of the drudgery of the Northern Ireland game and being given the runaround by France.

The *Daily Mail* was absolutely scathing in its assessment of England's performance. Jeff Powell, once a Robson booster, laid into the manager in his match report, 'Bobby Robson should go down on his knees and give thanks that last night's monstrosity did not take place at Wembley. The time-honoured chorus of "what a load of rubbish" would not have done justice to a performance of such embarrassing ineptitude that it is impossible to discern in which direction Robson's England are heading. We can only hope that this is the worst, the pits, the bottom of the barrel. Because if England sink any lower then Robson will drown in his own humiliation before he can complete his term of office.'

The manager needed a reaction from his team, and he got one of sorts in the final British Home Championship international, against Scotland at Hampden Park. England were better, not particularly good, but a few rungs above their previous games that year. They started at a decent tempo. Robson picked a genuine winger each side in Mark Chamberlain and John Barnes. He had largely played a four in midfield with one winger and the player on the other side tucking in to create a three. Change was needed and instantly England were able to force Scotland back more than Wales or Northern Ireland allowed.

They fell behind as an inexperienced defence watched Mark McGhee jog between them all for a free header. Tony Woodcock then scored an excellent equaliser and the game continued to ebb and flow until the final whistle. Gary Lineker came on for his debut with 17 minutes to go and showed glimpses of what was to come but wouldn't feature again until next year. With the whistle, and the 1-1 draw, the last Home Championship came to a close. Somewhat fittingly, each team had played three games, with identical records of one win, one draw and one defeat. Northern Ireland took the trophy on goal difference and it was all over. The tournament's place in British football history cannot be overstated even though it had run its course.

Despite Scotland rallying, England had shown enough to at least quieten some of the noise from the last game. There had been a collective pushback, particularly from some TV pundits who felt that *The Sun* and others had gone too far. What England really needed was a performance and a win. They would get the chance exactly a week later when the USSR came to Wembley for a friendly.

Yet again they fluffed their lines. With 19 players injured or unavailable, Bobby Robson pulled together a side he had been forced into rather than picked. He went with his two wingers again – Chamberlain and Barnes – and Trevor Francis returned up front from his injury just as Woodcock left with one. This meant Luther Blissett was tried again with a feeling that, with Portsmouth's young striker Mark Hateley on the bench for the first time, this might be the AC Milan man's last chance to add to those goals against Luxembourg.

The issue was the defence – Mick Duxbury and Kenny Sansom either side of Graham Roberts and Terry Fenwick. Sansom was rightly trusted to the point that no one expected to see him out of the starting 11 for the foreseeable future barring injury. On the other side Duxbury was inexperienced, an under-21 star who had been unable to carry that form into the full team to date. Duxbury was not a bad player by any means, but it would be fair to say he felt the weight of an England shirt.

Centrally both Fenwick and Roberts were in a similar position. With the benefit of hindsight and knowing some of the excellent central defenders and partnerships to come it's easy to say they weren't quite at the standard required. In reality they were both competent players with no real relationship with each other, facing a USSR side who were organised, extremely fit and feared neither. Ahead of them Ray Wilkins and Bryan Robson were labouring having had a long campaign in which they had played a combined 103 games between them plus a whirlwind end-of-season trip to Hong Kong. The lack of cover and trust in each other meant 90 minutes of gradually increasing pressure and an inevitably wobbly defence.

Wembley was a little under half-full. As early pressure fizzled out into the usual straight passing and creative struggle, the crowd grew restless early. An unusually hot day added to England's lethargy as they toiled having not got the early goal their first ten minutes might have deserved. Both wingers found themselves matched for energy by their respective full-backs and were forced back into midfield by their adventure. Chamberlain missed an early chance and the USSR responded by doubling up on him any time he came inside. Blissett struggled to make an impact and only registered a shot from too far out and too much of an angle to ever trouble the goalkeeper. By the end of a goalless first half the rumblings from the crowd were loud enough to hear on the television coverage. A sarcastic chant of 'Come On You Reds' took off. After only Shilton had kept it 0-0 with three excellent saves, England walked off to light but still evident booing.

In the second half things got much worse just seven minutes in. A long ball over England's midfield was dropping comfortably into Duxbury's path but he got everything wrong. A poor first touch saw him stand on the ball and then fall over, leaving Sergey Gotsmanov one-on-one with a stranded Shilton. He finished well and England never looked like getting back into the match. Ten minutes later Oleh Blokhin hit the post and the home fans were now applauding the away side in between the usual bouts of 'what a load of rubbish'.

Hateley came on for Francis and in his 20 minutes was comfortably England's best player. It was enough to make this Blissett's last England cap. A second goal felt like it could come any moment but it took until the final minute to arrive. It was incredibly soft once more. A long ball was nodded on to Blokhin who had simply jogged past three defenders and into space. Shilton saved his shot but the rebound fell to Oleh Protasov who had run through without a marker. He tapped it in under very little pressure. Wembley was not happy.

The final whistle blew and there was a cacophony of booing. England had been hounded off by their own fans before but not quite with this level of hostility. The boos gave way to loud 'Robson out!' chants. As he walked to the tunnel, beer was thrown towards the coaching team and Robson himself was spat at. Most of the players jogged past worried they were going to get their turn too. A poor performance, another depressing afternoon.

As expected the papers had their say the following morning. The *News of the World* and the *Sunday Mirror* both laid the blame at the manager's door, the *Mirror* choosing to headline its write-up simply with the word 'Bad!' *The Observer* was more reserved, actually praising Robson for going for attack, in principle at least, with two wingers. Writer Ronald Atkin was fearful for the future however, offering that the tour to South America looked like 'a disaster before it even leaves the ground'.

If Denmark had been a low-enough point for Robson to offer his resignation, his resolve here was actually strengthened by this negative response. If he could turn the tide, if he could get things going the right way, he would be a hero. So determined was he in spite of the venom directed towards him from all quarters that he turned down a contract to go and manage Barcelona after the Wales game. They had offered four times his salary paid tax-free into a Swiss bank account and a way out. He had never wavered. This was one of the hardest jobs in world football with an average team, below average fans and a wealth of other problems besides. He still wouldn't have changed it for a thing.

* * *

John Barnes, and England's performance against Brazil, brought new hope from the jaws of despair. A second goal, the first of Hateley's England career, came with a sense of absolute superiority as they had bossed one of the widely considered best teams in the world in their own back yard. In truth, Brazil were in a transitional phase, as their opponents were perpetually. There was no denying that England had gone there, stuck with two wingers, and produced the result and attacking performance they needed out of nowhere, however. There had been nothing in any game of 1984 to date, and in particular the awful afternoon eight days earlier against the USSR, to suggest it was coming.

The *Daily Mirror*, one of the newspapers so vociferous in going after everyone connected with the England team, immediately dubbed it 'The Miracle of The Maracanã' as England became only the fourth team to beat Brazil in the national stadium's history. Frank McGhee was impressed but lacked an element of self-awareness, 'What mattered most to their manager was the vindication of a policy that had been heavily criticised. Insulted and abused only a week ago after losing 2-0 to Russia at Wembley, it was Robson's stubborn persistence in a policy he believed in that produced a night to remember.'

What a difference a win makes. Instant breathing room. England then lost to Uruguay in the following game and drew against Chile in the last match of the tour, bringing a sense of reality back. The euphoria of Barnes, Brazil and the miracle just about remained to allow each result a far softer landing than they would have had.

Uruguay had resorted to a few dark arts to get their win – a fairly obvious dive being given as a penalty for the first goal and then a clear tactic at half-time meaning England came out but were left waiting on a warm evening for over five minutes for their opponents to appear. Clive Allen had been wasteful in only his second cap too, missing glorious chances twice in the first half to go ahead and another in the second half to equalise. But it had not been a bad performance compared to recent losses, far from, and the reviews reflected that.

The final game against Chile disappointed but again England created enough for their biggest critics to stay relatively quiet. They came up against a goalkeeper in Roberto Rojas who had one of the best nights of his career. Time and time again they created chances, Allen once more out of luck, but the keeper pulled off a series of unbelievable saves to deny them. A goalless draw to end the much-desired South American tour. Robson had learned a fair bit about his players and reinforced his philosophy that they needed to get on the front foot more.

The trip had been blighted once again by England's following, although they had not been able to travel in the numbers that saw them wreaking havoc in France. Instead it was a highly personal incident that left John Barnes feeling numb when he should have felt on top of the world. The touring party boarded their commercial plane to Chile for the final leg. A small group of National Front supporters were on the same flight as the England party.

They sat at the back. The touring squad took the front of the plane. Mark Chamberlain, Viv Anderson and John Barnes were then subjected to vile abuse throughout the flight. Even worse, the racist group went virtually unchallenged throughout, revelling in the chance as Barnes stated in a 2013 interview with *The Independent*, 'The white players in the squad signed autographs for the NF activists but they wouldn't be friendly because they knew it was offensive.'

Despite the offenders loudly shouting that England had only beaten Brazil 1-0 'because a n****r's goal doesn't count', and several proud unfurlings of National Front flags, the journalists on the same plane did not commit one word to print on the incident. Even FA secretary Ted Croker was heckled for preferring 'Sambos' but did nothing. In the fight against racism anywhere silence is never helpful. Not a word was said.

England broke up after the tour until a September friendly against East Germany that only served to fill a gap in the schedule. Wembley's record low crowd against Wales in 1983 was matched as there was little appetite for the game from anyone involved. East Germany did what teams knew they had to do to make England struggle and retreated to their own half. Bryan Robson scored an incredible acrobatic volley with eight minutes left to earn a 1-0 win. The goal was far better than the match deserved, and everyone moved on quickly.

What they then moved to were the final two games of the year and both had consequence attached. England's first two qualifiers for the 1986 World Cup would be against Finland and Turkey. The draw had been a boon from the off but suspicions were being confirmed as Finland had already beaten Northern Ireland, who themselves had then beaten Romania. With the other four teams in the group likely to keep taking points from each other, it really was England's golden chance to make life easy for themselves for a change.

It needed a good start and Finland were first up at Wembley in October. A small crowd for a qualifier, just over 47,000, at least provided some atmosphere. A floodlight failure meant the warm-ups were largely done in the dark much to the amusement of most involved or watching. The issue was rectified and England knew they would face their old enemy in the game ahead – a congested midfield and then a packed defence.

Bobby Robson went with Tony Woodcock and Mark Hateley up front knowing he needed his strikers to perform or it could quite quickly become a difficult night. Thankfully Hateley was in the mood. Early pressure came to nothing but for once England didn't panic or retreat. It was clear that Finland weren't going to offer much of a threat and all they really had in defence was bodies. Chances were actually coming along fairly frequently rather than the cross, clearance, shot blocked, cross, clearance, ad infinitum of other games. The opening goal to settle the nerves actually came this time too, Hateley quite brilliantly finishing a difficult chance after Barnes's shot had hit the bar.

From one came two as ten minutes later Woodcock followed his own shot in and profited from a complete meltdown between goalkeeper and defender on the line. At 2-0 England came out for the second half relaxed for a change. They ran in three more goals in a completely dominant display, much to the delight of those who had made the trip. Hateley scored his second shortly after half-time, showing a great change of pace to run through a static defence having picked the ball up 45 yards from goal. He then confirmed the man of the match award with an assist for Bryan Robson. By the time Kenny Sansom scored his first England goal with five minutes left to play, a few were making an early start home satisfied rather than disgruntled for a change.

The 5-0 win was the perfect start and marked a couple of significant changes. The experiment with Mick Duxbury ended as Gary Stevens made his debut from the bench. Duxbury had struggled to convince in an England shirt and it was time to look elsewhere. Robson also had Terry Butcher back after injury and paired him with Mark Wright, as he had against East Germany. The result was a duo who complemented rather than worked against each other.

It would also be the last cap for Mark Chamberlain. He had played six times for England in 1984 and despite occasionally sparkling he had suffered most from any manager willing to scout an England game. He often found himself the subject of a full-back instructed to man-mark him in a way Barnes hadn't been yet despite *that* goal. Bobby Robson also knew he needed another way to play in games where a bit more discipline was required and Barnes would likely be his one winger.

So England travelled to Turkey confident they were on an upwards curve. It was shallow still, but there. The USSR game had been a nadir, everything after an improvement to a greater or lesser degree. Turkey were a relative unknown and this was to be the first match between the two teams. It proved to be entirely one-sided as the away side scored eight including a Bryan Robson hat-trick.

Turkey were far poorer opposition than had been expected but England, for once, were utterly dominant. Robson's goals were joined by two from Barnes, two from Woodcock, and a final flourish from a full-back just as there had been against Finland with Viv Anderson's header. Remarkably England had scored eight but also been a touch wasteful, a sentiment echoed by the manager's immediate post-match comments to Brian Moore that he never thought he would 'win an international game 8-0 and feel like we let them off the hook'. Played two, won two, scored 13, conceded none. Quite some start to qualifying.

England's now permanent captain was the man of the match against Turkey and also by far their best player overall since the trip to South America. Bryan Robson had taken over from Ray Wilkins due to injury and never actually given the armband back. He was an inspirational figure and had become a bellwether – when he played well, England played well. Nearly all the recent disappointments had come in his absence due to injury or when he had a rare bad game. The man his team-mates knew as Robbo, the press as Captain Marvel, had become the heartbeat of the side and his form in the last three games had been incredible. Five goals, two assists, two man of the match awards.

England's Robsons, Bobby and Bryan, shared several things in common despite there being no relation. Both were born in County Durham – Bryan in Chester-le-Street, Bobby in Sacriston – to working-class families who nurtured a desire to see their sons play football professionally. The area had provided a rich vein of inspiration by the time Bryan began to show real talent. Like Bobby, his childhood was spent solely with a ball by his side. Both were spirited away to the south to begin their professional careers and went to the club who made them feel most wanted. For Bryan this was West Bromwich Albion, meaning another point of shared history.

Bryan started there as an apprentice and made his way into the first team in 1975. Two years later he was playing regularly but was also on his second fracture, the right ankle this time following the left leg a few months previously. The treatment room was the one thing that would hold him back throughout his career. Manchester United came calling in 1981 and broke the British transfer record for him. Robson had started as utility player but was by now the most dynamic midfielder in the country. By the end of 1984 he was up alongside anyone in European football in the role.

Bryan Robson was almost a cliché of himself at his best. It's impossible to talk about him without using words like all-action and marauding. He was a midfield two all by himself, a genuine goal threat, and the epitome of a captain. The fact that England finished the year so strongly was no coincidence with him in such form. There was every reason to feel incredibly confident going into 1985 for both Bobby and Bryan Robson. Unfortunately, neither knew it would be one of the darkest years in English football history.

1985

ENGLISH FOOTBALL was at war with itself. Violence was commonplace at nearly every major match in the country and the authorities were struggling to deal with it effectively. In truth often they only succeeded in enflaming already volatile situations rather than policing them. It wasn't just stadiums either – town centres, pubs, trains and service stations were becoming battlegrounds as groups affiliated to clubs began planning to meet up, sometimes regardless of whether they were actually playing each other. The 1970s had seen football violence go from isolated scuffles to a mainstream news topic. Now it was organised battalions of men ready to do battle with like-minded souls or those who wished to stop them.

Violence around football was not new. As long as there has been a form of men kicking a ball across an agreed area there have been those who have used it as an excuse to misbehave. By 1985, however, it had become more important to many involved than the actual sport from which they took their original identity. I've had several conversations with ex-hooligans from Brighton & Hove Albion, Manchester United, Leeds United and more besides. All can remember the odd game, a notable achievement or trophy. Ask them about specific instances of violence and they will tell you in minute detail about away trips that ended in pitched battles across a city, or the time they took a ground by charging through the home fans.

Fighting side by side with people in a decade of austerity and economic fear was more than just an outward identity. The sense of belonging to something that went beyond the very real worries of real life and sense of being powerless about everything was palpable. Away from the headlines and brutality of miners' strikes, cuts and a further level of demonisation of the working class there was a place to put the aggression. One of the most basic tribal urges would be satisfied.

Then there was the role of the press, tabloid and broadsheet, who realised very quickly that stories of these battles sold newspapers. Thus began the construction of an ouroboros – every young, vocal football supporter was labelled as a hooligan and so many started to act like one. Desmond Morris, in perhaps the best book ever written about football as a whole, *The Soccer Tribe*, described the process as the media making the hooligan 'the "folk devil" of modern society' – those who had not adopted the persona were branded one anyway so leant into and eventually embraced it. Misplaced aspiration crafted on an anvil of stereotype and adversity.

In 1985 hooliganism at international games afforded mainstream recognition for those involved rather than shame. A normal level of violence at a domestic match barely made a ripple anymore. Lurid stories of foreign cities under invasion from gangs came with a degree of dark excitement. There was exaggeration in certain quarters from the press, even provocation in truth – stories exist to this day of journalists and photographers allegedly paying groups to misbehave on cue. None of that excuses the behaviour of those domestically or internationally who did commit senseless crimes of violence and vandalism, regardless of any attempt to explain their behaviour.

The England manager's job came with a degree of apology attached which Robson knew and understood upon taking it. The nature of every trip abroad causing some flashpoint was wearing and a big distraction, however. The FA were also tired by 1985 and the year began with talk about everything from a ban on alcohol in football grounds and the immediate surrounding area, to ID cards possibly being introduced. Actual football was being pushed further and further down the agenda.

Because of the near-constant talk of violence, revenue was down. Attendances across all four professional leagues had slumped from a little over 24.5m combined across the 1979/80 season to 18,368,631 in 1983/84. Families and the elderly had turned away from football and away followings were dwindling down to only the hardcore who would follow their team regardless and those who were there to cause trouble. Football's image problem had come home to a financial roost.

By the time of England's first game of the year at the end of February there had already been several domestic flashpoints despite an incredibly harsh winter causing matches to be called off in all but a handful of weekends. An FA Cup replay between Darlington and Middlesbrough had made the front pages. Fans had clashed before the game and jointly with the police. With ten minutes to go and with Darlington leading 2-0, Boro's fans overwhelmed the police line at the bottom of their stand and made their way on to the pitch. The game was held up for ten minutes with both teams whisked back into the dressing rooms for protection. Darlington's element were only just kept from entering the pitch themselves to meet the trespassers head on.

With the temperature high off the pitch despite artic conditions across the country, England's first game of 1985, a trip to Belfast for a World Cup qualifier against Northern Ireland, needed to go well. Bryan Robson was missing because of a dislocated shoulder, Everton's Trevor Steven would make his debut, and Alvin Martin returned to the defence in place of Mark Wright. Gary Stevens kept his place and Mark Hateley's excellent form saw him starting next to Tony Woodcock.

The game was important anyway but of real note for Irish goalkeeper Pat Jennings as it would mark him equalling the British record for international caps, at that point held by Bobby Moore with 108. Jennings was excellent too, holding England at bay until the 76th minute when he was beaten by an excellent Hateley finish from outside the area.

England got the 1-0 win that they wanted and played just about fine. A game against any British side was always going to be a tight, tense affair and three points away from home were to be cherished. They survived a few scares at their own end but caused enough trouble in the other half of the pitch to be just about worth their win. It was very much a case of job done when looking at the Group 3 table as England were top with six points from three games, Northern Ireland and Finland just behind with four but also having played one game more, and then Romania and Turkey were yet to earn a point. It was too early to be booking flights to Mexico, but certainly difficult to see a way England could not qualify from there.

Off the pitch things were relatively quiet due to how highly policed the game had been. There was what *The Guardian* described as 'a spate of bomb threats' on the day but everyone was at pains to say it 'probably' had nothing to do with the match. It had still been an unedifying enough spectacle regardless. John Barnes and Viv Anderson were booed and whistled by fans every time they touched the ball, with several National Front flags clearly visible among club ones in the crowd.

Five days later it was domestic football in the headlines as a Milk Cup semi-final between Chelsea and Sunderland turned into a riot. Play was held up twice as fighting raged in the stands at Stamford Bridge and then out on to the pitch, mounted police forcing Chelsea fans away from the Sunderland end. Seats were ripped up, darts and glass were thrown, and Sunderland's Clive Walker (once of Chelsea) had to be protected as he was targeted by fans for the crime of scoring twice. Chelsea chairman Ken Bates had defended his club's fans against charges of hooliganism before, describing them as 'boisterous' rather than violent. Here there was no defence with over 100 arrests made and Bates forced to admit that there is 'scum at every club'. He would shortly start making ill-fated plans about how to stop them entering the field of the play.

The talk about football's problems was starting to turn serious and questions were constantly raised in parliament again, this time about the nature of sentencing that could be given to football arrests. They were so commonplace at games that most weren't even being reported by local press, and often resulted in minimal convictions and then small sentences.

After the battle at Stamford Bridge, March would provide another low point, as Millwall were drawn to play Luton in an FA Cup quarter-final. Both sides had vocal and notorious hooligan elements and the tie was always likely to be volatile, but no one expected it to be quite so inflammatory.

Millwall fans caused trouble around Luton before the game and then carried on during. At one point the match was halted and the police themselves had to seek refuge as they were bombarded with an array of projectiles including seating from the ground. With the players back in the dressing rooms the police were forced to fight truncheon battles on the pitch, finally forcing the Millwall 'fans' back into the stands. The referee brought the teams back out after a 24-minute delay having himself appealed over the PA system to let the game finish. Millwall manager George Graham had also begged the fans to stop on the touchline.

The players completed the game but were clearly nervous. On the available footage you can see them looking to the stands to make sure another wave of invaders wasn't about to appear every time they got the chance to. It ended with lines of police with Alsatian dogs around the pitch to prevent further ingress. It didn't work, the final whistle prompting another surge from the away end. Battles with a still-outnumbered police force on the pitch were shown on TV coverage as the players, officials and benches ran for the dressing rooms. Those Millwall hooligans then took to the streets after the game and attacked cars and shops, plus another £45,000 of damage to their train home. On another night of shame for English football, 47 people were hospitalised, 33 of them police officers, and only 31 arrests were made.

The trouble was on the front page of every newspaper. Crisis point was nearing and, a day later, Prime Minister Margaret Thatcher was taking 'direct control of tackling soccer violence' according to the *Daily Mail*. She would meet with the FA and everything would be on the table – ID cards, banning the sale of alcohol, penalties for clubs who had the worst persistent offenders, games kicking off in the morning, and more besides. The host nation for the 1988 European Championship was to be decided the morning after the FA Cup tie. Having been heavy favourites at one point, England's bid received no votes. The FA blamed the rise of violence over the last year, with the Luton riot just the culmination of a trend.

By the end of March, Mrs Thatcher had assembled her 'Soccer War Cabinet' and England had played their second match of the year. The Republic of Ireland came to Wembley for the first time in five years. For the Northern Ireland game Bobby Robson had resorted to going long knowing how tight it would be, and he got his reward. Here was a night to experiment and get back to attacking a different way. It was also time to look at some options with this just being a friendly.

Manchester United's Gary Bailey would make his debut in goal ahead of Peter Shilton as a search for a reliable understudy continued. Mark Wright returned next to Terry Butcher in defence, with Sansom and Anderson either side of them. Bryan Robson, fit again, partnered Wilkins in midfield, Trevor Steven had done enough to keep his place on the right. On the left there was a debut for a player everyone was excited about, Newcastle United's Chris Waddle. Up front Mark Hateley, now of AC Milan, kept his place after his excellent goal and performance in Belfast. He was partnered with a player for whom Bobby Robson had a great deal of hope, an old-fashioned striker with a genuine eye for knowing how to be in the right place at the right time. After a brief sub appearance the previous year it was time to finally give 90 minutes to Gary Lineker.

* * *

Things could have been very different for Lineker, a prodigious talent at an early age. He always seemed destined to become a sportsman but most outside the Lineker family felt that, although he was talented at football, cricket would be where he would excel longer term. Representing county teams while at school, he was scouted several times for both sports. He would choose football and never forget he was lucky enough to have the choice, signing apprentice forms with Leicester City.

He was slight in build so aware he needed to be quicker on his feet and in his head than most defenders he would play against. He broke into the first team at Leicester in early 1979 and was immediately played out of position on the right wing where he struggled. When you're born with a striker's instinct not every skill is transferable. He struggled at first, grateful for manager Jock Wallace's patience and belief. Leicester were promoted to the First Division with Lineker in and out of the side, and then he barely featured as they were relegated immediately back down. In his first three seasons in professional football, he had scored only seven times.

Leicester would be promoted back to the First Division two years later in 1983 and in that time Lineker had grasped his moment. Played and trusted as a striker he had finished as the club's top scorer in both seasons in the second tier. They had learned that Lineker was a willing runner but only into the areas he knew he could score from, therefore the game plan evolved to getting the ball to him in those key areas. He was a finisher, best played with someone alongside him who could win the ball and feed him. They had paired him with Alan Young's guile and experience. It paid off as Lineker learnt to turn instinct into end product with someone to help him take defenders away from where he wanted to run. The second season Young moved on and in came Alan Smith from non-league football. While two years younger than Lineker he was 6ft 3in and would compete for the balls his 5ft 9in partner couldn't.

Nineteen goals in 47 games in 1981/82 had seen Lineker grow up and toughen up. In the promotion season he was their difference maker and recorded his first 20-goal year, finishing with 26. Smith chipped in with 14 of his own in his debut season in professional football. The step up to the First Division for 1983/84 was taken with ease and Lineker scored 22 at slightly over a goal every other game. It was at this point that bigger clubs had begun to circle. Bobby Robson had also been forced to take notice and eventually pick him for the Scotland game. By the time of the Republic of Ireland friendly in 1985, Lineker was still with Leicester and on his way to finishing as the Golden Boot winner. In the summer he would move to Everton, having finished his fourth season in a row as Leicester's top scorer, for £800,000. An absolute bargain for a player who it was now proved guaranteed goals.

Lineker would become one of Bobby Robson's go-to men right up until the manager left in 1990. The affection was returned, the pair never less than glowing about each other. Lineker delivered a wonderful eulogy at Robson's funeral in 2009 in which he described his England manager as having 'seen something in my game I wasn't even aware of myself'. In 2001 Lineker travelled to Newcastle to record a piece with Robson for the BBC's *Football Focus*. The friendship is evident throughout as the pair chat about Newcastle United, Barcelona, and more. When it comes to their time together with England, one comment from Robson brings knowing smiles and a twinkle to the eye of both men, 'Good side in the end weren't we, Gary.' Lineker takes his hands out of his pocket to agree, 'We were a really good side.'

Robson knew that getting the best from Lineker was about pairing him with the right people and by the end of 1985 he was shaping his attack around him. Against the Republic of Ireland, Hateley dovetailed with the new man effortlessly until an injury forced him off for another debutant, Peter Davenport. Lineker provided the game's best moment with his first goal for England, a wonderfully instinctively striker's finish to lift it beyond a stranded Pat Bonner. Clinical to the point of ruthlessness, it put England 2-0 ahead. The first had come from Trevor Steven and had been deserved as the home side had played well, not 'fine' or 'just enough', but actually looked good until a late goal and rally from the Republic.

The game had been a rough one with Bryan Robson and Hateley forced off after fouls had left them both in a heap, and Ireland's Chris Hughton leaving with an injury after Spurs team-mate Glenn Hoddle had a nasty, and somewhat out-of-character, two-footed lunge at him. Bobby Robson and the press had been impressed by his new additions and by the way England had played. Waddle had looked promising, Lineker was exactly what any successful team needed up front, and they had proved they could all play together from the off.

The only blot in the copybook had been Ireland's goal, Liam Brady's shot squirming under Gary Bailey. Bailey had not had much to do but then failed when called upon for his big moment. He might not have been the long-term solution to cover Shilton, but a lot more had been learned about everyone involved.

An overall good feeling around the England side took them to Romania in April and the first dropped points of the qualification campaign. A goalless draw was seen as a good result as this away trip to Bucharest was by far the hardest they would face in the group. The atmosphere was also the most intimidating by some way, England whistled and harassed by a rampant home crowd throughout. They started well, Bryan Robson hitting the bar with a header, but slowly Romania pushed their way into the game and began to bully England in midfield.

By the time an hour had passed it had become a game for warriors. England had to dig in and really fight for the point as Romania attacked in waves led by a ravenous crowd and a referee who realised quickly he wanted to leave the stadium without an escort. The young Gheorghe Hagi was a magician, capable of anything. He continued to find space but Shilton's form and some desperate defending finally took England through to the final whistle. It could have been better; Paul Mariner missed a very presentable chance to win the game but a point was absolutely fine in the grand scheme of things. Lineker's emergence and that lack of a clinical finish contributed to this being the last of Mariner's 35 caps.

With the biggest hurdle now behind them, England really could start looking towards Mexico. Nothing could be taken for granted but they were three points and a goal difference swing of 18 from dropping out of the qualification places. With only two points awarded for a win, that already looked like enough of a cushion with three games to come at home.

Whereas things were starting to look up for the national team, the rest of English football was still a desperate, disparate mess. Ken Bates's solution to stop fans from getting on to the Stamford Bridge pitch was an electric fence, which had been fitted but permission to turn it on was denied. He was disconsolate at not being able to use his electrified wire, dismayed that things had turned, and said, 'There is all this concern that a few soccer hooligans might get their fingers burnt trying to scale the fences at Stamford Bridge.'

May 1985 would be one of English football's darkest months. On the first Bank Holiday Monday, an extremely hot day, another game was halted by fans spilling out on to the pitch and fighting with police officers as Manchester City's away following rioted at Notts County. Police horses had to push them back into the stands as the second half was delayed by15 minutes. The following Saturday, even worse was to come.

Leeds fans travelled to Birmingham for a Second Division match. The violence started on the way down, trains were vandalised and reports came in of fighting at service stations by those travelling by coach and car. It continued before and then during the game which was delayed as Leeds fans threw anything they could get to, including advertising hoardings. Riot and mounted police pushed fans back after they entered the pitch at half-time, Birmingham's own 'Zulu Warriors' trying to get at the Leeds 'Service Crew'. Fights were breaking out wherever fans could get to each other and at the final whistle there was an inevitable charge as both sets rioted. Several police officers were dragged into the crowd and beaten; several police horses were targeted and hurt. Tragically, in one of many crushes a 12-foot wall collapsed and 15-year-old Ian Hambridge was killed. Ambulances attending the many injured were attacked and the fighting continued into the town centre. At its end over 500 had been injured, over 100 of them police officers, a teenager had lost his life and the violence of the entire day had been obscene.

On the same afternoon another one of English football's biggest issues came to an awful head. Several stadiums around the country were old, barely fit for purpose, and almost perfect for fans to fight in as there was minimal segregation. While most complaints focused on stopping fans getting to each other or on to the pitch via fences – the FA were looking into potentially using Perspex as had been used at a squash tournament recently at the Wembley Arena – the actual state of many stands and stadiums was being ignored.

At Bradford City's Valley Parade a stray cigarette falling below the main stand had tragic consequences as a fire started and within four minutes it engulfed the 76-year-old structure. The nature of its design, from the pitched roof showering ash, timber and debris down on to the fans plus funnelling the smoke back into them, to the wind-tunnel effect created by its position, made it a hell on earth in a little over 240 seconds. Exits and turnstiles had been locked and some padlocked to prevent people coming in after kick-off, meaning a stampede towards a trap. Some escaped on to the pitch, others forced doors open, but 56 spectators died in the inferno. The fire was captured on TV and featured on the evening's news. The desperation of those trying to escape on to the pitch clear and unforgettable. If Bradford had installed some of the fences being discussed to stop fans entering the pitch the death toll would have been in the hundreds or worse.

The tragedy led to an inquiry led by Sir Oliver Popplewell that found major deficiencies at nearly every football ground in the country. It also concluded there needed to be huge changes to the way they were policed and stewarded. The inquiry was extended to look at the wider issues of hooliganism beyond the Bradford tragedy. One of Popplewell's recommendations was that 'the police be given additional powers of search and arrest; and that consideration be given to the creation of a specific offence of chanting obscene or racialist abuse at a sports ground'. Unbelievably this was the first time this had even been discussed as an issue.

The weekend after the tragedy at Valley Parade and the death of Ian Hambridge, the *Sunday Times* wrote an infamous editorial about the state of football. Blaming the Bradford fire on 'the disgraceful mismanagement of professional football as a whole', the second paragraph gave the soundbite of the age, 'British football is in crisis: a slum sport played in slum stadiums and increasingly watched by slum people, who deter decent folk from turning up. Death on the Bradford scale has brought home, brutally, just what an appalling state football is in. The game needs cleaning up and revitalising every bit as much as the rest of Victorian industrial Britain.'

There is no doubt of the hyperbole attached to that opening sentence and in truth it grates today to read such a sweeping generalisation about football fans. It was difficult to disagree at the moment it was written, however, that there had to be momentous change. Any argument against was destroyed by May's final horrific act. At the European Cup Final at the Heysel Stadium in Brussels, Liverpool and Juventus fans clashed in a ground barely appropriate for such a big event. Before kick-off, as the stadium began to fill, rocks and bricks literally kicked out of the crumbling stadium walls and floor were thrown between the two sets of fans. Tickets available on the day had turned a 'neutral' section into anything but and the police had been slow to react to the mounting trouble. Tensions continued, bottles joining bricks, and then fists were being thrown by supporters who could reach each other. Eventually a surge by Liverpool fans and a retreat from Juve's collapsed a retaining wall, killing 39 people. In total over 600 people were injured.

The game, somewhat unbelievably, was still played. Juve won 1-0 but nobody cared. David Lacey wrote in *The Guardian*, 'The result seems irrelevant, the details meaningless.' Margaret Thatcher asked the FA to withdraw English teams from European competition for the foreseeable future but was usurped by UEFA and then FIFA who banned them anyway without a defined end. That domestic block would end up lasting for the rest of Bobby Robson's time in charge. There was also a move to expel England from the next World Cup as an immediate punishment by FIFA but they relented after the FA worked tirelessly to present the case for the defence.

So little of 1985 had actually been about football.

* * *

During May, England actually played twice. Although football had been placed in context by the tragedy at Bradford and Birmingham 11 days earlier, they travelled to Finland knowing just two points would guarantee them a place at the 1986 World Cup. Bobby Robson stated that anything less than a win was a failure. You can guess what happened next.

The very worst was avoided and England were grateful yet again to Mark Hateley as his second-half equaliser eventually earned them a point. It had been a frustrating game for all. Finland started well, opting for a physical approach that caught England cold. The visitors may have expected the side who rolled over at Wembley. Instead they got 11 footballers with something to prove. Finland went ahead just five minutes in from a set-piece and should have doubled their lead six minutes later, Terry Butcher and Peter Shilton doing just enough to scramble the ball away from danger. England slowly worked their way into the game but struggled to create genuine opportunities against a team happy to play percentage football and little more. Hateley's goal was just but you could not make much of an argument for more. A point closer to the World Cup but another game in which England had struggled creatively.

A few days later and the Saturday before the horrors of Heysel, England and Scotland would contest the first Rous Cup, a trophy nominally there to celebrate Sir Stanley Rous's 90th birthday but more as an excuse for the two auld enemies to keep playing each other. At the behest of the Prime Minister herself the game had been switched from Wembley to Hampden Park. There were a few excuses thrown about around issues on public transport but the real reason was the very real fear of another riot at the home of football live on television. The switch and enhanced policing combined towards a relatively trouble-free match although there were visible flashpoints in the crowd during the first half. There had also been scuffles reported throughout Glasgow on the day. It seemed to be confined to one area of the ground, *The Observer* wondering if 'the South London chapters of the National Front had decided ill-advisedly to take an away engagement'.

Hampden's eight-foot-high steel fence also helped. Watching the game in 2020 it's jarring to see the silver wall running around the bottom of three stands and then starkly cutting one into two for segregation. So soon after the Bradford fire and with other horrors to come, it remains an unsettling thing to observe behind the tableau on the pitch. There are several doors in it, locked but with a policeman stationed at each, most managing to keep a back to the game. Each stand is a sea of flags, scarves and faces with barely any room. It's a visual and chilling reminder of both sins past and sins to come.

The game itself was a fairly decent one compared to the dourest of Home Championship internationals. High energy and feisty throughout, it lacked genuine quality but didn't want for effort. Several tackles from both teams would have earned red cards and a couple of bans today. As it was, a yellow suffieed in most cases, some just a stiff talking to. On the pitch the tension spilled over into a few coming togethers that defused themselves as soon as a referee appeared. Scotland were a good side and when the two last met in 1984 they had failed to give a good account of themselves. Here with a noisy crowd behind them they were determined to put that right and did, winning 1-0 thanks to a Richard Gough header. England played okay in a game that turned into a dogfight. They were unlucky too. There was disappointment at losing to the Scots but the newspaper inquest into this performance didn't run too deep. There just wasn't the appetite at that moment.

Straight after the Scotland game the squad was headed for sunnier climes as another summer tour had been arranged, this time to play in a three-team test tournament for the 1986 World Cup at the Azteca Stadium in Mexico City and then against the USA in Los Angeles. They arrived in Mexico and the following morning took part in their first warm weather training session. Robson was already thinking ahead and had leapt at the chance to come and investigate likely conditions for the following summer.

That evening the entire team, including their manager, settled down to watch the European Cup Final together. Merseyside was represented in the room by Liverpool's arch-rivals Everton who had risen as a huge force in English football and just won the title, a full 13 points clear of the Reds in second. They were represented by four players – Gary Stevens, Trevor Steven, Peter Reid and Paul Bracewell – all of whom were looking forward to playing in the European Cup next season having also won the Cup Winners' Cup that year.

As events at Heysel unfolded and then the true horror was confirmed over the next 24 hours, a very real diplomatic situation was looming. England's first game in a week's time was against Italy, but it was in the balance – although a cancellation would have been catastrophic to the two countries' footballing relations for a long time to come. Bobby Robson spoke to his Italian counterpart Enzo Bearzot who was thankfully in agreement they should play. The next obstacle was that several in the local authorities felt it best for England to return home. Talks between them and the FA quickly put that idea to bed but Robson's players were told in no uncertain terms to behave themselves on and off the pitch.

A Heysel memorial service was arranged in Mexico City and both sides attended. It was a much-needed show of unity, but the English were cast by all as the villains. There was no way or evidence to argue against that at the time either. Ray Wilkins and Trevor Francis were playing in Italy and were pushed for press duties. Mark Hateley was too but he chose to say nothing. Wilkins and Francis both gave somewhat scripted brief interviews to ITN expressing their own grief but desire to return and play in Italy without hesitation.

On the day of the game the national anthems and then two minutes of silence were observed impeccably by both sides who mixed together in a line before kick-off. The vast Azteca, capable of holding up to 115,000 spectators, was an eerie quiet with just 8,000 there. Robson had stressed the importance of good behaviour yet again so fouls came with an immediate apology from anyone in a white shirt. Even Terry Butcher acted after one bad tackle 'as if he had stepped on a kitten' according to David Lacey.

England lost 2-1 thanks to a terrible decision to award Italy a last-minute penalty. Gary Stevens's well-timed tackle on Pietro Vierchowod was bizarrely judged a foul when no one in an Italy shirt even claimed for it. Nobody dared complain. England's goal came from Hateley, a good header from a brilliant John Barnes cross. Hateley had six goals from his first 11 internationals and with the emergence of Lineker they looked like they would be England's front two for a long time to come. But he would only score three more in his next 21 caps as he was expected to become more of a provider for his strike partner, a role he wasn't suited to.

The rest of the tour passed by with very little drama, which pleased everyone involved. Bobby Robson used training camps to get his players used to the heat and the altitude with an eye to the following summer. One day off saw the squad play cricket between themselves, Lineker proving himself still an excellent batsman. Results may not have particularly mattered but they actually lost 1-0 to Mexico three days after the Italy game. Robson picked an experimental team and told them to be on their best behaviour again. Just as with the penalty against Italy, they suffered an interesting refereeing decision when Viv Anderson's header was disallowed for a foul on the goalkeeper. But despite the defeat, England had actually played quite well.

To that end they got their reward with an excellent 3-0 win over West Germany in the last game of the mini-tournament. The Germans had arrived late and not really got used to the fierce heat or breathlessness of playing at the Azteca. England capitalised, Peter Shilton even saving an Andreas Brehme penalty in a dominant and clinical performance. Typically, Bryan Robson set the standard with a great finish for the opening goal. Hoddle's nonchalant outside-of-the-boot pass and Kerry Dixon's touch allowed an off-balance Robson to volley home from the edge of the area. Dixon, in only his second cap, got a brace in the second half to stamp home their authority.

Finally the trip moved to the USA and a 5-0 thrashing of their hosts. Very little was learned from the game due to the poor standard of opposition but notably Lineker scored the second and third goals of his international career. His first of the game was a stunning volley, Hoddle again the chief provider. The players returned to their digs to find that several of their rooms had been broken into and anything of value not in their hotel safes had been stolen. It had been a trip completely overshadowed by Birmingham, Bradford and Heysel, with actual results of no importance, and about preparing for a competition they had yet to qualify for. Bobby Robson stayed on to look into potential venues to use as base camp for both the group games and a switch for the knockout stages. On his return, English football had changed.

* * *

With the ban for English clubs from all European competition confirmed, Robson was looking at a future where his players were liable to face either moving abroad or a life without testing themselves against the very best. He understood the decision but knew the consequences. 'We were in the wilderness, detached from mainstream continental action and ideas. I'm sure this hampered the tactical and technical development of our players,' he wrote in *Farewell but not Goodbye* in 2005.

The matter at hand was to get over the line and qualify for the 1986 World Cup. A win in their next game would guarantee it, but after Romania away, Romania at home represented their greatest challenge. Robson went for an attacking line-up, including Hoddle who produced his best appearance in an England shirt, in his first World Cup game since Spain 82. He scored his side's first-half goal, taking a brilliantly worked free kick from Sansom and stroking home an opener.

The problem was that Romania were a very good side with a genius in their ranks. Hagi was a footballing free spirit few could cope with. His ability to drift into space and neither sit in midfield or attack but the half space in between was unlike anything this England side had faced before. He was everywhere and in the seventh minute he hit the bar from fully 30 yards and had Shilton completely beaten. Just before half-time he ghosted through the entire back four and hit the bar again with a delightful chip over the goalkeeper. Both efforts were applauded by the home fans who knew they were watching a special player. It's no exaggeration to say that England looked okay until the very second Hagi was on the ball.

An equaliser was coming, and it arrived shortly before the hour. A stunning one-touch passing move through the midfield ended with striker Rodion Camataru holding off Gary Stevens to score. The goal had a suspicion of handball about it but rarely has an equaliser been as deserved. After that Romania seemed content with the point and offered very little. England, as ever, struggled to break down a side now playing without much adventure. A 1-1 draw was absolutely fine in the grand scheme of things but still the rubber-stamping proved elusive.

Their final two qualifiers were at home to Turkey and Northern Ireland. On the day of the Turkey game, Romania, proving to be the wild card of the group, would play Northern Ireland at home expecting to win and force England to need something to seal things. Surprisingly they managed to lose 1-0 and hand England qualification without them kicking a ball. Lineker's hat-trick, a lovely run and finish for Chris Waddle's first England goal, and a typically Bryan Robson-ish Bryan Robson goal saw them past Turkey and into a frankly ridiculous goal difference swing to not finish top.

England played their final qualifier against Northern Ireland in November with the pressure off. The goalless draw didn't matter but it only came about because Pat Jennings had a spectacularly good game at the age of 40. England created plenty but Jennings was incredible on the night. The Irish only needed a draw to qualify themselves and there were conspiratorial headlines in Romania who still had a chance. Anyone who bothered to watch the game could have seen that here were two teams who wanted to win. Qualification over, England and Northern Ireland were both safely through to Mexico 86.

It had been a truly terrible year. On top of the hooliganism and tragedies, a deal had not been struck with the TV companies after months of negotiation, meaning that only England's games had been shown on live television in the season to date. Eventually the Football League would do a deal in December that saw league games return to TV in 1985 in limited numbers but it had been another brick in the wall of the fans' disengagement with the game. Violence, death, decaying stadiums and falling numbers of supporters both at grounds and at home. English football was in free fall.

1986

WORLD CUP years are different. They're full of sticker albums, coins with players' faces on and a mascot everywhere you look. They're previews, endlessly studied newspaper pull-outs and an anxious wait for to see the opening credits for the first time. It's planning your life around three games a day and then watching highlights of a match you saw live. You just know you'll never forget that player for the rest of your life because of that one thing he did in an otherwise forgettable game. They are a joyous overdose to happy addicts and a few weeks of devotion for the passing fan. In short, a World Cup year feels special because a World Cup year *is* special.

English football's *annus horribilis* had been 1985 but this new year provided a potential way to put the sport back at the centre of the conversation. Mexico 86, a festival of football to which England had earned an invite, would start on the last day of May. Bobby Robson's England had reason to be confident as there were early signs that a good team was coming together. Winning a second World Cup might have been out of reach but a semi-final and a notable scalp or two along the way felt possible.

Domestically, the much-mooted ID card system the Prime Minister was a known fan of was still in its early stages by the turn of 1986. Some clubs were already making plans or having trials to introduce a form of the card of their own design but there was widespread resistance. Most chairmen felt the scheme would lower attendances even further and be of little use anyway. The shock of the previous year's outrageous loss of life had already meant several inquiries and investigations had taken place and some suggestions had already been implemented. English football felt different. Not yet safer, but at least slightly more aware of itself.

Sentencing was getting tougher by mandate too. On the year's very first day of court, a 22-year-old Peterborough United hooligan named Barry Fox was given three years in jail after an incident at a game from October. While Fox was trying to scramble up a wall to escape, a special constable pulled him back. The police officer was attacked and knocked out by Fox for his trouble. Once arrested Fox, and others, were now to be given the toughest possible sentences and charged with grievous bodily harm.

The effects were minimal in that there were still incidents around nearly every game, but the lawlessness of the outright rioting across pitches had subsided. Policing was also being upped in the hope that a sheer weight of numbers would deter all but the most determined at the actual matches. It had become impossible to discuss English football without mentioning hooliganism. The balance needed to be redressed in favour of the actual sport.

When the Prime Minister had involved herself, things started to change but it was proving a slow process. One of the biggest issues so far had been just how out of step politicians were with those involved in football and its fans. After Heysel, some of the suggestions had been ridiculously misjudged, such as 'Goalies against Hoolies' which aimed to get 'the more articulate goalkeepers' to do interviews with media networks denouncing football violence. In papers released in 2014 it was even considered whether Margaret Thatcher herself should give an interview to *Shoot!*. Eventually it was decided that the magazine would be 'an inappropriate platform'.

Reading through the papers, most freely available on the National Archive website, there is a sense of real frustration from the government. The main issue throughout is a push-back from clubs on anything that required a decent level of investment or infringed on their control of the game. Some of the measures they had been able to introduce, such as Leon Brittan's argument that 'alcohol is a major contributory factor in violent and disorderly behaviour in football grounds', resulted in the banning of alcohol within sight of the pitch and that still holds today. Others, like using Watford chairman Elton John as the face of a campaign against football violence because of his profile, just seem vaguely silly.

Goalies against Hoolies did get an interview on Piccadilly Radio in Manchester, and it involved England keeper Gary Bailey, but it was actually Bailey as host with the Prime Minister as his guest in August 1985. It's a fascinating time capsule that does sum up the government's inability to understand the causes of football violence and only deal with the consequences. Through various lines about the finance of CCTV being fitted at grounds and the ID card system's finite detail, there is nothing that actually speaks to the football fan. By 1986 things had calmed a little but conduct by England supporters at the summer's World Cup would be scrutinised at every turn.

Those who did want to follow England now knew where they would be staying. Bobby Robson, for the second time, was grateful for an okay draw as England had been placed into Group F. The downside would be they would be based around Monterrey. This meant lower altitude than some venues and fierce heat. They would avoid the very worst of it as all games were due to start at 4pm local time but it would still be uncomfortable for English bodies used to domestic temperatures. Acclimatisation training would be essential. The upside to the location was that they would play, in order, Portugal, Morocco and then Poland. They would be expected to beat all three.

Early preparations were proving difficult as proposed matches were organised and then cancelled by authorities worried about violence. Eventually three away games, one each in January, February and then March, were organised before the annual Rous Cup fixture against Scotland. England travelled to Egypt first and won 4-0 with an experimental side. The most notable move was to give a debut from the bench to Peter Beardsley, another attacking player people were excited about.

In February they played Israel in Tel Aviv after an absolutely sweltering day and laboured against a well-organised side. England's eventual 2-1 win in the close evening heat was hard-fought but unconvincing. Beardsley started this time and for as long as his lungs allowed was their brightest attacking option. England were grateful to their captain and talisman again, Bryan Robson scoring both goals, one an incredible volleyed finish that would win the BBC's Goal of the Season award.

At a time when Bobby Robson's focus was going into preparation he was coming under attack in the press with a renewed vigour. The tabloids still believed he should go – one had even run it as a Saturday headline in 1985 months before the tournament in Mexico was due to start. Now in early 1986 he was coming under fire for circumstances out of his control. Emlyn Hughes, a man who repeatedly used his *Daily Mirror* column to settle scores without fear of a right of reply being given, laid into Robson for the two rearranged friendlies and how little actual preparation he felt they afforded him. 'What do the Football Association and Bobby Robson think they are playing at?' he wrote of the Egypt fixture, adding that the Israel game to come was a 'joke trip'. Brian Clough joined the chorus in *The Sun* and on TV questioned Robson's team selection, plus they had realised that Robson bashing went over well so *Saint and Greavsie* questioned the merits and performance of the Israel game only in the negative. Jimmy Greaves always believed that Bobby Robson stood the best chance of getting things right. In two years' time his patience would be pushed to the limit.

The FA had been grateful to both Egypt and Israel for agreeing to play. A game against Spain had been cancelled after talks between the two authorities came to the conclusion that it was too much of a risk. Other countries around Europe were considered but travel was too easy to be comfortable in regard to England's away support. A final friendly was arranged to be played against the USSR in Tbilisi, both a country England's fans would struggle to get to in numbers and once there dare not misbehave. It was also a chance for Robson to redeem some personal pride after the dismal performance against them at Wembley in 1984. His players responded and put in an excellent shift despite a refereeing performance that upon watching now is absolutely mystifying.

Three minutes after Gary Lineker was denied a penalty, despite clearly being taken out by goalkeeper Rinat Dasayev, the USSR were awarded one for a Viv Anderson challenge that looked innocuous on every replay. Aleksandre Chivadze struck the post to keep it goalless at half-time. England were good and eventually won 1-0 thanks to a lovely goal from Chris Waddle after a terrific one-two with Beardsley that spanned a full 40 yards. They could have added to it too but eventually saw the lead out to the final whistle. They had been composed, defended well and attacked intelligently. A performance that not even Emlyn Hughes could be annoyed about.

April's Rous Cup marked the moment that Robson began to finalise his squad for the summer. A few potentials moved into the probables column after a 2-1 win in a frenetic game. As with the previous year's match, tackles were flying in from the off. Any that came from a white shirt were cheered wildly by the home proportion of the 68,000 people at Wembley. Terry Butcher's powerful header gave England the lead, and a second from Glenn Hoddle provided some breathing space. A second-half penalty and rally made for a nervy end but the home side held out. Thankfully the blood and thunder on the pitch was not matched on the terraces bar a couple of comparatively lightweight incidents. This was helped by Wembley's new steel fence that would eventually have steel spikes across the top.

Aston Villa's Steve Hodge had an excellent game after a very solid debut from the bench against the USSR. Trevor Francis had struggled and this would be his last cap. At 32 years old and with Hateley, Beardsley and Lineker all now in the picture and Kerry Dixon next in line behind those three, it was fairly inevitable that he wouldn't get a swansong in Mexico. Waddle was proving to be a question mark – often unplayable, often anonymous – and Hoddle still only seemed to play his best football sporadically at international level. Robson had his core pretty much written in ink, but there were still plenty of places currently in pencil up for grabs. The Rous Cup was England's for the first time, and their next game would be the first of the trip to Mexico.

* * *

Bobby Robson's eventual 22-man squad raised a few questions but was largely as expected. Trevor Francis's omission was obvious and made for some easy copy across a few newspapers as the striker opined that he never had a realistic chance of reaching Mexico despite being selected to play against Scotland. There was no mass opposition but also no doubting that it made England's attacking options look inexperienced with Peter Beardsley's inclusion in what would have been Francis's place.

A broken leg in an FA Cup semi-final had curtailed Mark Wright's chances of playing that summer, a collision with Southampton club-mate Peter Shilton causing him to be stretchered off. This meant three centre-backs and a couple of players who could cover if needed rather than taking four specialists as had once been in Robson's mind. There was a strong core – Shilton's experience, Sansom and Butcher never let their country down, Bryan Robson was everything, and then Gary Lineker had just scored 38 goals in his first season for Everton, been named FWA Footballer of the Year and was being heavily linked with a move to Barcelona. That core was supplemented by a mix of seasoned professionals who everyone knew what to expect from and the unproven but promising. The list in full included goalkeepers Peter Shilton, Chris Woods and Gary Bailey; defenders Viv Anderson, Kenny Sansom, Gary Stevens of Everton, Terry Butcher, Alvin Martin, Terry Fenwick, and Gary Stevens of Tottenham Hotspur; in midfield were John Barnes, Chris Waddle, Trevor Steven, Steve Hodge, Bryan Robson, Ray Wilkins, Glenn Hoddle and Peter Reid; the strikers were Gary Lineker, Mark Hateley, Peter Beardsley and Kerry Dixon.

Robson also placed Martin Hodge, Stewart Robson, Trevor Francis, Dave Watson, Paul Bracewell and Mick Harford on his standby list.

As David Lacey wrote in *The Guardian*, the squad, on paper at least, looked a little 'strong on elbow grease but short on inspiration'. Creativity, the bane of any England manager to date (and going forward too), was the main talking point across those analysing the squad. Hoddle was brilliant on his day but those days did not come frequently enough in an England shirt. He had become a divisive player and a magnet for criticism when selected unless he produced a man-of-the-match display – a benchmark way beyond anyone else on the pitch. Barnes and Waddle were notable talking points too as Barnes had not pushed on from that goal in Brazil significantly as all had hoped, and Waddle was capable of the sublime and the ridiculous. Jeff Powell of the *Daily Mail* felt both should 'count themselves fortunate that the manager is sticking with wingers'.

Bobby Robson had his men regardless and was sticking by them. In his 42 games in charge to date he had used 61 players to refine them down to these 22. He also now had two official warm-up games and a few unofficial ones to lock in his first 11. After flying out to Colorado Springs and the Broadmoor Hotel the acclimatisation training stalled when their first day's schedule was ruined by a blizzard. The weather changed and soon enough Robson could take his squad to train in the higher temperatures and altitude they needed. Their first game was against a local United States Airforce Academy side but they would be without any of the Everton players involved in the FA Cup Final, who were flying out a few days after everyone else. It didn't matter as they eased to an 11-0 win, Hoddle enjoying himself against significantly weaker opposition.

Three days later they played South Korea in another unofficial match and won 4-1. The most notable goal was yet another brilliant Bryan Robson volley. Those in the know within the England squad held their breath every time the captain went in for a challenge as he had been dogged by a shoulder injury and was not fully recovered. So far so good as he was an impossible man to tell to slow down anyway. They would round the week out with an official fixture against Mexico in Los Angeles.

England's 3-0 win over the Mexicans was impressive but alarming in equal measure. They had strolled into a three-goal lead by half-time and been completely dominant barring an early chance. Beardsley played really well and scored his first England goal. A midfield three of Hoddle, Wilkins and Robson controlled the game expertly, allowing Mexico no time on the ball and yet finding plenty for themselves.

The second half should have been an exercise in preserving energy through passing and possession. It became a struggle just moments in, with several players clearly wrestling with the heat on an intensely warm day at the LA Coliseum Stadium. It was sapping energy, strength, breath and ability. The desire was there, but Ray Wilkins in particular had to take every moment he could to sink to the ground and catch some air. Every throw-in took a few seconds longer, every goal kick an age. Worse was to follow as Bryan Robson chased a ball down to put out for a corner and in the course of sliding put his hand on the ground to steady himself. His shoulder dislocated for a third time since his original injury and he was immediately removed from the game. It was popped back in while he was on the pitch but the weakness was such that everyone involved knew that one bad fall could mean the end of his summer.

A 3-0 win looked great in the record books but there had been a toll. The players clearly had a way to go to acclimatise and the captain was hanging by a thread. Back home, somewhat bizarrely, Sir Alf Ramsey had decided to wade in and, first, criticise England's current manager for not asking him for help as he had taken England to Mexico in 1970, but then a few days later the press also published a private letter Ramsey had received from Robson thanking him for offering to help but there was no time left for a meeting.

Ramsey's bitterness towards the FA, who had lost Winterbottom when he still had plenty to give, in part acted out a vendetta against himself, banished Revie, and had only ever seen Greenwood as a stopgap, was understandable. What was incredibly poor form was to act on it by attacking Robson via the newspapers in a needlessly vicious way. It was a lesson learnt though, 'I would never criticise another England manager while he was trying to do his best for himself and his country,' wrote Robson in later life, 'because I knew just how much it could hurt.'

Robson has said in several books that he asked to speak to Ramsey who refused or rearranged every attempt as far back as when he had taken over at Ipswich. There were others he reached out to who refused to help but then used any platform they had to bemoan all the ways the England manager was getting it wrong regardless of any actual evidence. Brian Clough was one who felt he should have had the England job and grew worse on TV and in the papers as the 1980s moved on. Clough's ire was often not just for the boss but his players too, regularly saying individuals weren't good enough or shouldn't be there. He also loved a dig at the FA at any opportunity for anything he saw as either bad form or overstepping their mark. Often he was right on that particular front. Clough could be even-handed; he didn't look for ways to criticise, but you could be sure he would have taken them if they presented themselves.

This media approach was lapped up by the tabloids who knew they could get a day or two easily out of an offhand comment from someone, and then make another story of Robson's response even if that was silence. This was perhaps why Robson created small groups, a close circle with an even closer inner circle to that. For example, there were some in the squad who had no idea quite how serious Bryan Robson's injury was despite training with him daily. In four years' time this ability to create a group and build a wall around them would serve him well. The genesis of that was happening in Mexico.

Bobby Robson was also grateful, even if it had happened in circumstances he would have loved to have changed, to have Don Howe with him virtually full-time for most of the year. Howe had left his job as Arsenal manager in March in acrimony as he resigned after learning a couple of managers, including Terry Venables and George Graham, had been asked about replacing him while he was still in the position. He would not take another role at a club until he joined Wimbledon in 1987 as Bobby Gould's assistant manager.

A final warm-up game against Canada before moving to Monterrey had been arranged and it was an absolute stinker. After heading to Vancouver the whole affair had a distinctly unwanted feeling, even more so when Lineker was lost to a suspected broken wrist in the second half. England won 1-0 thanks to Hateley's tap-in, a goal that somewhat unbelievably at the time would turn out to be his final one in an England shirt. There was a sense that everyone was desperate for the World Cup to start as the calm before the storm had long given way to anxiety and injury. After the brief Canadian trip they finally moved to their base in Mexico, the Camino Real hotel, eight days before their first group fixture.

In those eight days the touring party were busy. A couple of players immediately fell ill and were treated with strong antibiotics, while one of the medical team, Vernon Edwards, had a heart attack and was hospitalised. The intense heat meant a hard schedule was just impossible so training was measured and steady, and everything took a little longer.

Bryan Robson was being treated with kid gloves and nothing was to be said to the press about his condition. Lineker had provided some good news in that there didn't appear to be a break as first reported, just a bad sprain with possibly a hairline fracture meaning he could play in a light cast. The local professional side, CF Monterrey, were beaten 4-1 in a match played at a decent tempo that importantly everyone came through unscathed. On the Friday the World Cup actually started, and on the following Tuesday England made their entrance.

* * *

'World Cup Wallies' screamed the *Daily Mirror*. 'England suffer the shame of the biggest shock so far here in Mexico,' wrote Harry Harris as the back page made their feelings clear on the performance against Portugal. Each tabloid had their own variation on a single theme: losing 1-0 had not been in any way good enough.

It wasn't just the red tops either. *The Guardian* was relatively neutral ('England's Bubble Bursts' was about as tough as it got) but the real knife wounds were inflicted by David Miller in *The Times*. Headlined 'England must own up to having no great players', the article got worse from there. The game had seen 'an average performance by an average team' in Monterrey, 'a city of unmitigated grime that makes Liverpool seem jolly'. The reference to Liverpool is quite extraordinary reading in 2020. Bryan Robson had been clearly hampered by injury and played both through pain and within himself, but his manager 'should have protected him from that misery when he selected the team'. The England captain was 'just another player', a slightly better review than Glenn Hoddle's who was 'a passenger'. Chris Waddle received a paragraph all to himself, his vision extending only to 'the end of his own toe caps' and that it 'would be helpful if Waddle's colleagues had more idea what to expect of him'. An extraordinary write-up of a very ordinary game from a newspaper that prided itself on its reserve. Until it wanted to grandstand a little, that is.

It's tough to know what could have gone much more wrong for England's opening game of Mexico 86. After welcoming much cooler climes than expected including a few days of rain, the Tuesday started gloomily again – perfect for the English temperament. Almost as soon as the coach arrived at the Tecnológico Stadium the clouds gave way to intense, oppressive sunshine. The instant change in conditions now suited Portugal far more. As they had in Los Angeles, several England players wilted as the match went on.

The captain was as unfit as David Miller had suspected but Lineker was also suffering too, not with his arm but with a stomach ache. They were also up against their oldest enemy – a team who wanted to sit back and nullify the little creativity they were up against. Hoddle and Ray Wilkins couldn't find the angles to hurt Portugal enough; Robson lacked his usual midfield energy. The chances they did create fell to Lineker and Hateley who both had bad days in front of goal. Terry Butcher was all bite in defence and no brain, the heat clearly affecting his judgement and he picked up a silly yellow card with a wild tackle.

As the game dragged on a Portugal goal felt inevitable with huge spaces opening up across the pitch as legs failed white shirts everywhere. With 15 minutes left substitute Paulo Futre, just on and the last thing Kenny Sansom wanted to see running at him, skipped past a weak challenge from the left-back. With absolutely nobody willing to sprint to stop the cross he picked out an unmarked Carlos Manuel who tapped in with no defender within six feet of him. The fact that by the final whistle England were grateful Portugal missed a couple of chances to add to their lead tells you all you need to know about what they had left in their legs collectively. After the match, Peter Shilton had lost 6lb and took a little over two hours to produce the urine sample the doping regulators required from him due to dehydration.

The newspaper recriminations carried on until England's next game against Morocco where things went even worse, albeit they escaped with a point from an awful 0-0 draw. After a week's worth of false accusations about rifts in the camp and rows over the captain's fitness, England blew it against far weaker opposition again. Not only were Morocco technically inferior but they played open enough for even a modicum of an average performance to have earned a winning goal.

In 100-degree heat England had the first half from hell. Not only did they spend the first 15 minutes hanging on as Morocco were absolutely fearless, by half an hour in they had created nothing but a Terry Fenwick header that was well off target. Fenwick played the entire World Cup with a hernia that needed immediate surgery. It would be fair to say he never looked at his best during the summer.

Then things got worse as Bryan Robson went down under minimal contact in the penalty area and stayed down. Within seconds the world was aware the shoulder had gone again as a player who liked to appear impervious to pain writhed in agony. As he was walked slowly off the pitch a few minutes later in a sling it was almost a given he had played his last football of this World Cup.

Then Wilkins, frustrated and suffering in the heat, had a moment. Called offside after taking a corner that had come to nothing, he threw the ball at referee Gabriel González two minutes after he had been booked for a foul. A red card followed, England's first at a World Cup finals, for one of the players usually least likely to give in to such petulance. A horrible first 45 minutes followed by a slog in now near 110-degree heat for the ten men left to try and grind out the draw. At the final whistle they had earned it but were met with a series of boos and jeers from those who had travelled.

As expected, the newspapers only ramped up their criticism, most opting again for variations of the first off the press *Daily Mirror*'s *1am Sports Special* headline, 'Disgrace'. Emlyn Hughes, not exactly a master of understatement, said he was 'ashamed to be English' in his ghost-written column. The *Daily Mail* made 'England's Nightmare' its front page. A single point from their easiest games in the group, no goals scored, Ray Wilkins suspended for two games, Bryan Robson likely out of the tournament, and the full glare of the press turned on them. Something had to change.

In an interview given to *The Independent* in 1998, Terry Fenwick claimed that in a team meeting after the Morocco game it was he who questioned Bobby Robson's lopsided 4-3-3 system, 'I was so annoyed about things that I just stood up and spoke my mind.' He recalled that he told Robson, 'Unless we got back to a system we were used to he might as well book a flight home.' This notion of Fenwick leading a mutiny and saving the World Cup, with the blessing of his team-mates it should be added – 'Peter Reid and Alvin Martin were on their feet agreeing with me' – is a romantic one to him I'm sure, but the events play out differently in other versions of the story.

Robson did indeed hold a team meeting that turned into part autopsy, part therapy session. One of the many things he was good at was letting senior professionals have their say, and then making them feel like they had influenced the changes he was going to make anyway. After an hour of talking among themselves and airing frustrations, they left in a better place mentally for the winner-takes-all final group game against Poland. Vitally, they relaxed. The tension of playing at a World Cup, many for the first time, had infected the squad. An afternoon spent playing cricket after the meeting eased the mind and soothed the soul.

For that final game Robson did ring the changes. He switched from a 4-3-3 to what he called a 4-2-4 but in modern parlance we would say was a traditional 4-4-2. Out went the injured Robson, the suspended Wilkins, an ineffectual Hateley, and Waddle who had shown promise but was sacrificed for the system. In came Peter Beardsley to play up front with Lineker and provide some more pace. Trevor Steven, Peter Reid and Steve Hodge came into midfield to do Hoddle's running for him.

The results were instant. England's back four – Sansom, Butcher, Fenwick and Stevens – all looked more comfortable with the higher work rate in front of them and a better line of defence before they were needed. Even in the heat England looked busy rather than laboured as confidence and adrenaline gave them an extra ten per cent. Reid was wasp-like in midfield, playing like a man who knew he was there to be a platform for others, particularly Hoddle where possible. Finally, Lineker and Beardsley just worked together without effort. They had an unspoken mental link from the off. Their understanding of space and movement reduced each other's required work rate and gave England, at last, a cutting edge.

Poland were by far the best team England had faced in the group and yet were 3-0 down by half-time. Lineker's hat-trick had absolutely ripped the heart from them, each goal an excellent striker's finish. That the first came just seven minutes in helped England settle enormously, and the interplay that led to Steven's low cross between Lineker and Beardsley had a ruinous effect on the Polish defence. They were pulled into positions they didn't want to be in a way England usually had to suffer others. The celebrations of the goal from all were a huge release and watching now you can see the tension lift from Lineker in particular. Their World Cup had begun.

Lineker's second was not only the best move of the game but England's best attacking move of the whole year to that point. Beardsley's superb switch to pass the ball down the line first time, Hodge's timed run and curled cross, and then the finish of a man who knows he's going to score before he's touched the ball were a joy to see. The third, a poacher's goal from a corner, was the icing on a first half that was the antithesis of the previous one against Morocco. Any lasting tension walking into the dressing room was evaporated by an exhausted Peter Reid exclaiming, 'We're winning 3-0 and some fucker must be playing well because I haven't touched the fucking ball yet!' Cue laughter everywhere.

England didn't expand on their lead, but they didn't need to as 3-0 was more than good enough for second place in the group. They moved to Mexico City for a round of 16 knockout game against Paraguay. Not even substandard accommodation, so bad a switch was required before the game to share a Holiday Inn with the Italian squad, could knock them out of their rhythm. The general sense of relaxation even led to a visitor to the dressing room pre-game: Sir Stanley Matthews, a hero of Bobby Robson's and he hoped inspiration to others. The England manager even allowed the BBC to film the meeting as he introduced the squad individually to the man he considered to be the greatest-ever English player. Terry Fenwick was suspended after a yellow card against Poland so in came Alvin Martin, but other than that the team was unchanged. On the footage you can see a relaxed group of players now at ease in each other's company. A list of 22 names had become a squad, and a squad had become a temporary family.

The result was the same – a 3-0 win for England – but the game was vastly different. A slower start did still bring a first-half goal, another Lineker finish from a Hodge cross, but Paraguay were better than Poland had been. England's defence was tight and controlled in the main but Shilton was called upon twice to make good saves.

But the second half turned nasty. Lineker had been a thorn in the side of Paraguay's defenders and off the ball their captain Rogelio Delgado elbowed him so hard in the throat that he was struggling to breathe. As Lineker was stretchered off to recover, co-commentator Jimmy Hill was horrified and said, 'Lineker abused, brutally, deliberately, and cynically by the South Americans, Scotland said they wanted no part of World Cup football if it was like this … and I wonder if we are going to be left feeling the same.'

In Lineker's absence, Beardsley scored a second, following Butcher's shot in and gleefully pouncing on a fumble by the goalkeeper. Lineker would add another after his return, his fifth of the World Cup, but the mood had darkened again. Butcher was spat at, Martin elbowed, and every England tackle was met with either a raised boot or a dive. The referee had lost control and his refusal to award a penalty after a clear and frankly pathetic dive by striker Roberto Cabañas saw him physically pushed by no less than five Paraguayan players. He didn't book any of them.

The match ended and England celebrated making the last eight knowing their fate ahead. Bobby Robson was delighted during his on-pitch interview and looking forward to the 'marvellous' game in front of them. England would play

Argentina in the 1986 World Cup quarter-final, a country with whom they had immediate political history. More pressingly, they would have to find a way to stop one of the greatest-ever players in world football.

* * *

England's fans, their 'uglies abroad' as the *Daily Mail*'s Ian Woolridge had taken to calling them, had behaved better than expected so far. There had been incidents, fighting at the Paraguay game in isolated areas for example, but the full-scale invasion had not materialised. This was in no small part down to the Mexican police's approach in preparation. When England arrived in Monterrey a local newspaper had run photos of fans arriving in the city under the words 'Los Hooligans'. The police had made their messaging clear via various local channels – they were going to assume every England fan was a hooligan and if they acted like one they would meet force with force.

The FA too had been working tirelessly to help in any way possible, well aware of the extensive case they had to make for England to be allowed to come to this World Cup. The bulk of the travelling contingent were behaving fine and even mixing with locals at neutral games. Part of the FA's strategy had been to vet as many people buying tickets as they could and work to stop them falling into known troublemakers' hands. Secretary Ted Croker had also been working tirelessly to deal with incidents and condemn where required. Everyone involved knew they were on a tightrope – Croker was desperate that England be allowed to stay in this World Cup, and the fans had to accept that they were up against a police force who wouldn't ask a question twice.

This had been backed up by a riot involving Mexican fans after their 2-1 victory over Belgium. Celebrations turned to a mass gathering at a monument in Mexico City, and the drink flowed into the night. Eventually that led to an impromptu protest against the government via song and then bottles were thrown at police vans. Rather than make any attempt to calm the situation, reinforcements were called and attacked the football fans indiscriminately. News of the fighting spread across Mexico and various supporters' groups – 187 people were injured by baton attacks, and 45 were taken to hospital.

The lack of easy access to games, the distance to travel and the 'welcome' waiting for them had reduced England's nastier following but there had been, of course, an element who had made their way to Mexico. Croker had been forced to publicly apologise for National Front logos appearing on flags at England's first game against Portugal. The NF group who had arrived in Mexico had also given Nazi salutes during the national anthem and then in the first half unfurled a banner protesting the innocence of a recently jailed member of theirs for hooliganism-related crimes.

They had become a highly publicised minority as photographers in particular took any chance they could to record their idiocy on film knowing it would always sell to newspapers hungry for sensationalist angles. Even the *Daily Mail* was lamenting the attention paid to a small group, there only to promote their repugnant ideology, with its reporter commenting, 'Foolishly, I fear, TV cameras and press photographers focused their attention on them. The moment this happened the apes redoubled their performing tricks. They were still at it 15 minutes after the end of the game.'

Here though was a game of genuine concern ahead. The NF contingent would cause trouble regardless as it was all they were there to do, but Argentina were perhaps the worst possible opponents in such a massive game at that moment in time. Both sets of fans would start from a position of hostility towards each other due to the recent history of the Falklands War and work up from there. Not everyone would want to create incidents, of course, but there was no doubting the capacity existed for hundreds or more to be drawn into a mass collision.

Bobby Robson, for his part, insisted on keeping all talk focused on football. While both FAs and the British and Argentine ambassadors worked with the Mexican police on special measures aimed at limiting the opportunities for violence, the England manager kept his language measured. Ahead of his first game in charge of England against Denmark in 1982, Robson had been drawn in a press conference that had ended up with him taking questions about playing for your country in comparison to fighting for it in light of the recent end of the Falklands War. This time he would not be fooled into saying anything that could be twisted by the press from either side.

England's players were warned repeatedly not to refer to the war, even at the last minute in the dressing room pre-game by FA chairman Sir Bert Millichip. Argentina's squad were not given the same instructions, goalkeeper Nery Pumpido proudly stating to journalists that winning would represent 'double satisfaction after everything that happened in the Malvinas'.

Besides the fans, England had something else to worry about. Well, someone else: Diego Armando Maradona, comfortably the best player in the world. Maradona was a contradiction in human form; the physical manifestation of hypocrisy. He was made of both cannonballs and candy floss. He was the subtle knife you never felt slit your throat, and the train you could see coming for miles as you laid tied to the tracks. He would drift on the pitch into the isolation of space while looking for a crowd to cause trouble with. Maradona was football's first peace-loving warmonger. You might keep him silent for 89 minutes, but he only needed one to sing a full aria. In reply England had Peter Reid.

Reid was given the job of getting as close as he could to Maradona at a point in the Argentine's career when that was near impossible. Gary Stevens had been considered as Reid was carrying an ankle injury, but the midfielder's all-action performances against Poland and Paraguay meant if he was fit he would play. Fenwick was restored after serving his suspension but apart from that the 11, and the formation, remained the same: Shilton, Stevens, Sansom, Fenwick, Butcher, Steven, Hodge, Hoddle, Reid, Lineker, Beardsley. Bobby Robson gave what Terry Butcher described as a pre-match speech that still gives him 'a tingle' when he recalls the words today.

Just shy of 115,000 fans packed into the Azteca Stadium on another breathlessly hot day. There was an edge to the air, emphasised rather than expunged by the heavy police presence. There had been clashes before the game but they had been small and relatively easy to deal with. The national anthems were booed by small sections of the crowd, England's far louder than Argentina's but barely audible over the stadium tannoy system. The day felt like a powder keg ready to go at any time, the authorities' role being to keep extinguishing the fuse.

The first half passed by relatively quietly, tackles rather than quality providing the notable moments. Fenwick was booked in the eighth minute for a foul on Maradona that came at the end of his first run at a cluster of white shirts. He was feeling his way into the game and it had already been noted that Reid was supposed to be his jailor. Reid himself had already felt the full force of a crunching tackle from José Luis Brown and after treatment his ankle had held up. Beardsley had the game's best chance but found the side netting from an impossible angle with the keeper stranded.

There had been incidents between the two groups of fans but the police were largely on top of things. A Union Jack had been snatched and burnt but a large number of the reported 20,000 police officers at the ground, some in plain clothes, immediately moved in to separate a group who had run at each other. At half-time there was the first major flare-up as two England fans made their way behind a goal into what was largely Argentinean territory with a Union Jack. This caused a surge towards them and a signal to others around the ground to take things up a notch. The atmosphere soured in the heat and the isolated incidents began to cluster together like a cancer. The players emerged back out on to the pitch but the chants around them had changed. The Argentinean Barras Bravas sang that the English were all 'sons of whores!', pointing at a group of fans specifically. 'What's it like to lose a war?' sang the English in retort.

On the pitch, Maradona scored the two goals of the decade in the 51st and 55th minutes, sending his fans into the raptures. You have seen each a thousand times. One was a moment of high devilment, the other a run where you could *actually* detect the hand of God. Bobby Robson's reaction to both was the same: disbelief. The handball for the opening goal was no less a miracle than the run past Beardsley, Reid, Butcher, Fenwick and Shilton for the second. The referee, Ali Bin Nasser, came to a decision to give that first goal despite all evidence to the contrary. One of the World Cup's, and indeed football's, definitive moments.

England rallied and got back into the tie via Lineker's sixth goal of the tournament. John Barnes's introduction from the bench changed the game and his cross was headed in by the eventual Golden Boot winner – England's first player to earn the honour. Unfortunately Maradona had ascended to another level, repeatedly leaving anyone who stood in his way in a tired, tangled heap on the floor. It had been a sensational performance to go along with each goal.

In the final ten minutes the game went ragged. Argentina hit a post and then shortly afterwards, Fenwick's lunge at Jorge Valdano should have seen him sent off. There was still time for Lineker to come within a centimetre of the equaliser from another Barnes cross. Barnes had come on for Trevor Steven for his only 16 minutes of football at this World Cup and nearly rescued England's hopes. At the final whistle, Maradona ran for the bench arms aloft. His team-mates celebrated like they had won it all. In a way they had.

The clashes had continued in the stands but the policing meant the very worst was avoided, meaning a collective sigh of relief for each FA. A televised riot was feared, but in the end a small group of English fans ended up shaking hands with the Barras after full time. There were clashes around Mexico City long into the night but very few arrests were made as a more immediate form of deterrent was employed where necessary by police. The *Daily Mail*'s front page just about summed things up for England, 'Beaten By The Magic Man!'

After the game the dressing room was filled with a mix of anger, exhaustion and resignation. England had risen through the tournament and left on both their highest note since 1966 and yet still one of their darkest clouds of disappointment. They had come up short when faced with a genius. No shame, but also a sense of deep injustice over that first goal.

That handball occupied most of the newspapers for the next couple of days. The tabloids had a new footballing villain to take up the real estate they had once reserved for the England team and manager. The fact that Argentina went on to win the World Cup only upped the injustice across the tabloids. Any question of Bobby Robson not taking England onwards was immediately dismissed as ridiculous, the FA chairman stating he had given the idea of replacing the manager 'not a moment's thought'. Robson too had been energised by his team's performance. 'We were close to a marvellous success,' he told the press. 'We should do well in the European Championship.'

* * *

The autopsy into England's summer was mercifully short, all evil conveniently blamed on Argentina's number ten. The fans had, on the whole, not let the country down by the simple virtue of the absolute worst not happening. A low bar, but such was their reputation at the time. England's first game of the new season would be in Sweden in September for a friendly in which the whole side played like they had a hangover.

As usual with the September international, England looked half-cooked and were lucky to only lose 1-0 on the night. The side had a different feel to the summer 11 cast as heroes from the moment Gary Lineker scored his first against Poland. Viv Anderson was brought back in for Gary Stevens, Alvin Martin partnered Butcher and the pair suddenly looked so incompatible it would be the last of Martin's 17 caps. Barnes earned his starting place again and struggled to link up with Kerry Dixon, while Ray Wilkins returned but had started to look like he was being left behind.

The element that followed England into Europe with only one thing on their mind returned but in smaller numbers. The FA's screening process was weeding out those with convictions and gradually thinning the herd, even if the brainlessness remained. The Argentinean embassy in

Stockholm the afternoon before the game was attacked by a small group of fans, with bricks and planks of wood thrown at the windows. In total there were only five English arrests for serious offences and reports shifted in tone to suggest they had been attacked by a Swedish group looking to take the crown of Europe's most unwanted.

English football was also in a period of serious reflection. Gary Lineker and Mark Hughes had moved to Barcelona already, and Ian Rush had agreed to join Juventus for the start of the 1987/88 season after a year back with Liverpool on loan. This was due to complications around the foreign players allocation in Serie A. Glenn Hoddle and Bryan Robson were both being linked with potential moves abroad along with a handful of others at the higher end of the English game. Terry Butcher had finally moved from Ipswich after a decade in their first team but headed north to join Glasgow Rangers. Joining him was Peter Shilton's backup in the England squad, Chris Woods. Mark Hateley and Ray Wilkins were both staying in Italy with AC Milan, alongside Trevor Francis who moved to Atalanta. The English First Division was bleeding its top talent and not attracting them to come back.

There was also the usual move from the press to point fingers at not just the European ban, the falling crowds and the violence, but also the style of play. English football felt old-fashioned. Maradona looked like he had come from another galaxy over the summer. Bobby Robson was reminded of his role as national director of coaching and the need to shift focus to something more skilful, more modern. Change though he knew, as always, would be glacial. Four years in the role had taught the England manager to lower expectations so they were easier to surpass. 'We would be all at sea if we tried to develop that kind of national game from within our First Division,' he responded when asked about shifting to a continental passing game. Away from the press conferences though, he knew that was where England needed to be heading.

1987

IN FEBRUARY 1986, the draw had been made for the Euro 88 qualification groups. Having once held hopes of hosting the tournament, England had now been reduced to accepting a staged draw. Despite a frankly terrible record in the competition they were placed in with the top seeds. This had very little to do with their performances to date; indeed since that third-place finish in 1968 under Ramsey they had only qualified for the final tournament once – the ill-fated 1980 finals where they didn't make it out of their group. What it did mean was that they couldn't draw Denmark, Spain, Portugal, the Netherlands, Belgium or France. Those countries were all close enough for large numbers of England fans to travel to, or where they had recent history of excessive violence.

There was still danger in the draw. Everyone was desperate to miss two games against Italy in particular with the police investigation into Heysel still ongoing. The act of bumping them up the rankings was felt vital to avoiding some of the obvious flashpoints as it meant that a more controllable scenario would play out. England likely would have one, two or even three teams from Great Britain in with them, making policing the fans their own responsibility for a couple of games minimum. Alongside that they would probably face longer trips to countries where supporters might struggle to either misbehave or get there in the first place.

They were drawn into Group 4, one of three to come with the jeopardy of only the top-placed finishers qualifying as it was made up of only four teams: England, Northern Ireland, Yugoslavia and Turkey. Again, Bobby Robson couldn't have asked for much more from a qualification group. Turkey had proved poor opposition in very recent history, Northern Ireland held no secrets, and Yugoslavia were good but inconsistent – in the previous 12 months they had held an excellent France side to a draw but also lost to East Germany. If England won their three home games and picked up even a point away they could and should have been fine by virtue of the other three cannibalising themselves results-wise.

Robson had long accepted the fact England would be journeying to places where their support might be limited, and he had embraced it. 'I'm absolutely delighted we're able to concentrate on the football; it's nice to rid ourselves of potentially difficult fixtures,' he told a reporter after breaking off from a family skiing holiday to talk about the draw. 'What people don't realise is how much it affects the team when we have trouble.' At that time he had yet to see what Mexico 86 would bring on and off the pitch.

The campaign to reach the Euros in West Germany would begin in October 1986 with a good display overall at home to Northern Ireland. The fixture's regularity meant Wembley was a bit nonplussed about it all and was less than half-full on the night despite the summer heroics. One man who had been front and centre of that cast in Mexico, Gary Lineker, had another memorable night. Already enjoying life with his new club Barcelona, he returned to England in the sort of form where the ball seemed to find him in the penalty box rather than the other way around.

His second on the night, England's third, was a special goal. Glenn Hoddle won the ball in midfield and flicked it towards Peter Beardsley. He then did what he always did and looked for Lineker's run. England's number ten took a touch that ran him wide but no matter, as from just inside the box he turned and flighted the ball over the goalkeeper and in off the inside of the post. It was the finish of a man playing at the outer limits of his confidence, backed by the surety of form. At full time there was only one person the press wanted to ask the manager about. Bobby Robson replied, 'Gary has become just about the greatest striker in the world at the moment, Maradona is a wonderfully gifted footballer, but will he score as many goals?' Every conversation still required a mention of Diego, English football's current pantomime villain.

The final game of 1986 was another home qualifier and another good result. This time it felt like a definite stride on the path to West Germany as Yugoslavia, England's main rivals in the group, were beaten. The game ebbed and flowed but the home side were far more clinical. Chris Woods started in goal as Peter Shilton was injured, and Mark Wright was recalled having recovered from his broken leg but on the night was understandably off the pace. Bryan Robson was injured again, fast becoming a recurring theme, and this time England turned to Gary Mabbutt for a recall a shade over three years since his last cap against Hungary in 1983. Mabbutt played well and scored his first international goal with a terrific header.

A second came just before the hour from the unlikely source of Viv Anderson popping up in a striker's position for a tap-in. Yugoslavia had by far shown the greater invention, but England had taken their chances. At 2-0 down the away side pushed forward and missed two golden opportunities –

the first an open goal horribly skewed high and wide by their captain Zlatko Vujovic. England held on even when reduced to ten men for the final seven minutes after a clash of heads saw Glenn Hoddle and Steve Hodge both having to leave the pitch injured. With one sub already used, Ray Wilkins was brought on to replace both men. They were barely clinging on as first an almighty goalmouth scramble saw the post come to England's rescue, then a few minutes later Woods was grateful for Predrag Juric hitting a shot straight at him under minimal pressure. Vujovic then hit the post again after a well-worked free kick.

The game finished 2-0 and England had done well to ride the storm and get a vital three points. With Yugoslavia having previously beaten Turkey it was good to now have the breathing space, and a draw the same night between the other two teams in the group left England going into 1987 with a healthy lead at the top of the table already. Win their remaining home game against Turkey and pick up a win from the three away, and it was looking like job done.

The Yugoslavia game marked the end of Wilkins's international career after 84 caps. He had captained the country ten times, scored three goals and been England's Mr Reliable for a chunk of that period. Unfairly he had earned a negative reputation and a couple of particularly silly nicknames for passing sideways. In truth his job was often to take the ball from a defender and look for a Hoddle or a Robson in front of him. It wasn't always fireworks and rollercoasters admittedly, but often it was the platform better thought of players needed. He had become a facilitator when he was capable of more. Before the decade was out Wilkins would join the English legion at Glasgow Rangers and win two titles and a League Cup there. His red card against Morocco in the 1986 World Cup had marked the beginning of the end. The emergence of Steve Hodge, Mabbutt who was now being chased by Manchester United for a transfer, and Paul Bracewell, plus Peter Reid who was still in the manager's thinking, had sealed it.

So 1987 lay ahead and by the end of it England could be, and from this position should have been, preparing for a European Championship. The only question was whether they could find a way to make it difficult for themselves.

* * *

With care taken in the draw to limit opportunities for England's following to cause trouble, the domestic game had continued to make steps. There was still a disconnect between the clubs, the Football League, the FA and the government but strides were at last being made. Ludicrously, Luton Town had been thrown out of the 1986/87 League Cup for refusing to have away fans at the ground for their tie against Cardiff. Prime Minister Margaret Thatcher had demanded action after the infamous Millwall game at Kenilworth Road, but the fact that Luton had taken their own and were thrown out seemed to represent a complete lack of common sense. League secretary Graham Kelly explained, 'The rules state that 25 per cent of tickets must be allocated to the visiting club and the committee have decided that Luton must conform to the competition rules.' Safety was second to the Football League's authority, it appeared.

Major incidents were less frequent but still occurring. In September 1986, a month before England played Northern Ireland, Leeds United fans attacked a fish and chip van that then burst into flames, eventually completely burning out at the top of a terrace at an away game against Bradford City. The match was being played at Odsal Stadium as Bradford's Valley Parade was still being renovated after the hellish fire there the previous year. It would reopen in December with a friendly against an England XI managed by Bobby Robson.

Trouble had started with fans fighting in the terraces and then a grass fire being lit. A surge of fans surrounded the van before rocking it back and forth. Eventually the first flames appeared and as they quickly took hold, Leeds fans threw stones at the police and arriving fire brigade, then ran on to the pitch to both escape the smoke and try to get to the Bradford supporters who had not left immediately. The players had been taken off the pitch and the match was abandoned with Leeds 2-0 down.

That incident had been policed heavily and where once the fans would have got away with minimal arrest numbers in the chaos, 75 people were actually taken into custody at the game, then more in the aftermath after widespread television and local newspaper appeals. CCTV footage of the incident is available on YouTube and is utterly shocking to view now. The romanticised view of hooligans that emerged in the late 1990s and early 2000s is nowhere in evidence as the fear on people's faces as they scramble away from the fighting and the flames stays with you. That film came thanks to cameras fitted as part of the government and police initiative to combat hooliganism. A new weapon at the time in the longer-term fight against violence in the game.

As arguing continued about paying for innovations in grounds and new laws for football clubs regarding crowd control, the police policy to arrest first and ask questions later, coupled with far heavier sentencing, was starting to make a path to try and reclaim the game. There was a long way to go still, as the riot at Odsal proved, but hooliganism was no longer a life with very little legal recrimination.

This approach had been coupled with a slightly different tack across the media. By the turn of 1987 there had been stories in nearly every newspaper of just how widespread the issue was across the continent. Hooliganism had miraculously spread. In reality it had always been there, but high-profile incidents in the Netherlands in particular had helped create a new sense of perspective. Distance from European competition thanks to the ban had created a platform from which to observe for the English press. The Dutch league's discussions about whether to play games behind closed doors after a match between Excelsior and Den Haag was abandoned when an explosive device was thrown on to the pitch had caused a wave of think pieces.

In an article for *The Times*, Simon O'Hagan had laid bare the issues around Europe. The Italian league was struggling to police games and arrest figures were rising, with violence at nearly every major fixture now reported. In West Germany fans rioted at a match in Munich and tear gas was fired at the police, who responded with their own in kind, at a major incident among many smaller ones now happening every weekend. Dutch side Feyenoord's fans had gone on the rampage at a UEFA Cup tie against Germany's Borussia Monchengladbach, and 71 arrests were made, but vandalism across the city had caused damage worth thousands of pounds and many fans had been hospitalised. At a game in Greece a fan was killed by a flare fired indiscriminately into a crowd. O'Hagan wrote, 'The so-called English disease of hooliganism is contagious, even if it has taken a little while for the germs to spread.'

England's issues with football violence were complex, societal, and still there. However, early in 1987 there was further evidence of the resources now going into ending it as the police carried out dawn raids well away from actual matches. Twenty-seven Millwall and West Ham fans were arrested for hooliganism-related offences. Thirteen of them were immediately sent to trial while the others were questioned, and more arrests were made. There was a long way to go but if 1985 had been a darkest hour, there had at last been a necessary reaction from the police force.

England opened their on-pitch year in February with a friendly against Spain. The match was played in Madrid at the Bernabéu Stadium and the two FAs had long talked about putting the game on after deciding against it the previous year. After working hard on a draw that put hooligans into a difficult position, it always seemed like a foolish fixture to put on. The inevitable is classed as such for a reason.

Where once England hooligans had virtually free rein to run riot and fight the police they now were being targeted themselves. On the day of the game, the newspapers all talked about the 'Ultrasur', a group of fans who 'followed Real Madrid' and 'modelled themselves on the Britain's soccer hooligans' according to the *Daily Mail*. The fixture, it had been hoped, would provide evidence English football's exile from European club competition should be reviewed by UEFA. It didn't. Four England fans were arrested in Paris on their way to Spain for fighting with locals two days before the match.

Their element were met by Spanish fans in force, and neither side emerged with anything other than condemnation. Three England fans were stabbed the afternoon before the fixture and some supporters' coaches were targeted by bottles and stones as they made their way to the ground. The England fans travelling by rail caused havoc on a train coming to Madrid from the north. Spanish police made 12 arrests when it eventually arrived. The outright worst was avoided, the lowest of low bars again, but that was largely due to the vast number of resources and riot gear around the stadium before, during and after the match.

Bobby Robson and Don Howe take training in 1983

Allan Simonsen's penalty gives Denmark the win at Wembley and England miss Euro '84

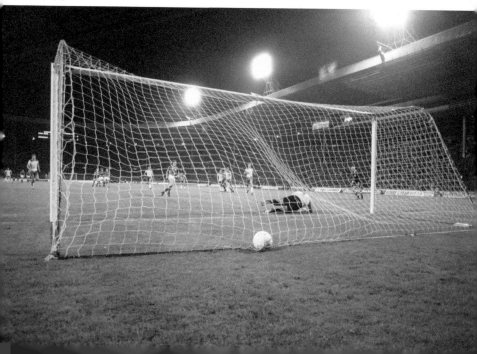

*Barnes against
Brazil, 1984*

*Police strategise on
the pitch during
1985's infamous
Luton v Millwall
game*

The two Robsons, Bryan and Bobby, chat watching a warm-up game in 1986 against Monterrey

Gary Lineker, England's striker supreme, celebrates scoring his second and England's third against Paraguay at Mexico '86

Terry Butcher and Peter Shilton get a front row seat to Diego Maradona's finish for the goal of the century

England's fans make themselves heard in typical fashion during Euro '88

*Marco van Basten scores his first goal against
England and Euro '88 becomes a disaster*

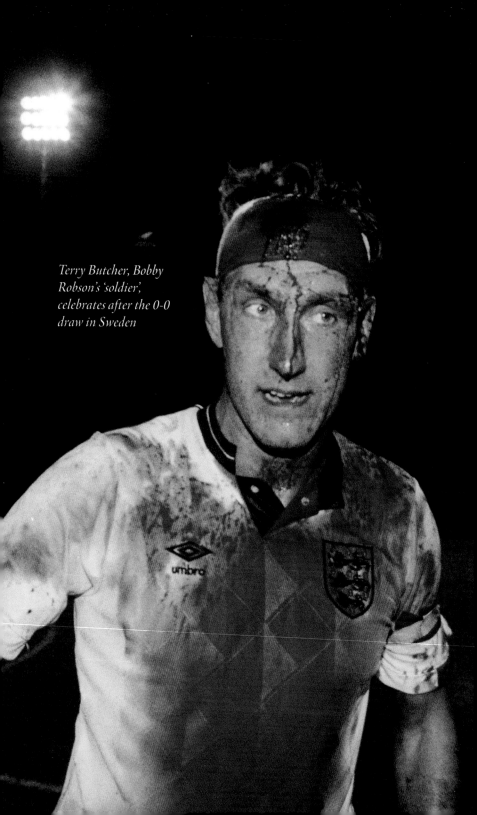

Terry Butcher, Bobby Robson's 'soldier', celebrates after the 0-0 draw in Sweden

Bobby Robson fumes at a press conference called in response to the leaked news of his departure in 1990

Paul Gascoigne begins to enjoy himself at Italia '90 with a man of the match display against the Netherlands

Gary Lineker's face says it all as David Platt scores in the last minute against Belgium

Gazza waves goodbye to the England fans after the semi-final penalty shoot-out

The game itself produced one of England's best
performances since taking Brazil apart in their own back yard
in 1984. Off the back of the injustice of the World Cup exit
they were in good form and again it was Gary Lineker who
took the plaudits. He scored all four in a 4-2 win for the away
side who had been dominant barring a brief burst from Spain
in the first half. The match took place on Bobby Robson's
54th birthday and he could not have wished for more from
his side in lieu of a present. Peter Beardsley had again played
a huge role, being involved in three of the goals and providing
a constant waspish presence that no defender could get a
handle on. Young Arsenal centre-back Tony Adams made
his debut and partnered Terry Butcher well. On the pitch at
least, England were starting to feel exciting.

That form was taken into their first away qualifier in
Northern Ireland in a very professional, no-thrills 2-0 win in
Belfast. England had weathered early pressure then taken the
first real chance they were presented with when Mabbutt's
long throw was nodded on by Butcher for Bryan Robson to
steer home. Chris Waddle added a lovely second, curling in
from 20 yards just before half-time. From that moment on
England knew their work was done and they kept the ball for
periods of the second half. Some teams might have pushed
on for more but on the night everyone in a white shirt or
in the away dugout was content with a third win and no
major injuries. Such was their confidence, Chris Woods was
brought off the bench for Peter Shilton in goal to give him a
few more minutes in England colours.

Northern Ireland had provided little resistance, but
England were in a good vein of form. They were finding the
net with ease and only Mark Wright was a current question
mark when picking the squad as his form was wobbling still.
He had not yet returned to the same level after the injury

that kept him out of the World Cup. Longer term, it was felt that he was still the main option to partner Butcher but at that point it was felt that it might be prescient to look at Adams again.

They took a commanding four-point lead at the top of the group to Turkey for their last qualifier before the summer's Rous Cup fixtures. Having put 13 past them in qualifying for the World Cup, hopes were high of a similarly easy ride. There would be no such comfort this time. Turkey had been stung by a chastening qualification campaign and returned for this one redesigned as an ultra-compact unit whose only desire was to not give an inch away cheaply. England toiled against two lines of five. This was not the old problems with creation returning, but a mark of how far their opponents had come in a short space of time.

A late injury to Butcher saw Mabbutt switched into defence alongside a second cap for Adams. Neither were troubled by a team whose attacking brief only stretched as far as shots from distance. Bobby Robson had gone for goals, Lineker naturally keeping his place, but after England had lost Beardsley to injury he was alongside Clive Allen, a striker just about to finish an incredible 49-goal season. The partnership didn't work as both wanted to be in the same spaces. Beardsley's true position was as a ten to Lineker's nine, drifting behind him and taking defenders with him. Here the two true centre-forwards just got in each other's way. Allen had a goal ruled out for a marginal offside decision and was subbed off for Hateley while still remonstrating with a linesman about it.

Allen had been on the tour in 1984 and was wasteful in the games against Uruguay and Chile. Another blank here meant it was clear the transition to international football was not comfortable for him and his path was blocked by the un-droppable Lineker anyway. He would play once more for England in a fateful 0-0 draw against Israel in 1988. After five caps and zero goals his time at the top level was over.

The goalless draw and point still left England in a commanding position going into the summer and a break from qualifiers. It did sow a tiny seed of doubt about the return game against Turkey at Wembley to come in October but the time to worry about that was nearer the match itself. Bobby Robson was sanguine about the result opting for a cliché in his press conference – 'a point gained rather than a point lost' – but it had been a speed bump when England had been approaching something like their top gear. The Rous Cup was next and prestige opposition as, in a format, change Brazil had been invited to Wembley. Optimism was still high.

* * *

The summer of 1987 was another one of change in the First Division. Despite repeated pleas from the Football Association to UEFA to review the European ban, there had to now be an acceptance that nothing was going to change in the shorter term. Bobby Robson was disappointed and felt it hindered his players' progress but was also completely understanding of the position in regard to the element he called 'animals' following the English game.

Liverpool's once dominant position in the league had recently been threatened by their local rivals Everton taking two titles in three years. The Reds' response that summer was to take two of England's best to the club, John Barnes arriving from Watford for £900,000 and Peter Beardsley from Newcastle United for a then-record of £1.9m. Another England player on the move was Peter Shilton, whose time with Southampton was done after nearly 250 games but a turbulent couple of years personally. A gambling habit was taking hold and he had been forced to give an interview with his wife to deny the headline 'Shilton Is A Wife Beater' in *The Sun*. A move to Derby County had been brokered and taken, and Mark Wright joined him there.

Ian Rush left for Juventus and joining him in waving goodbye to the First Division was Glenn Hoddle. Hoddle had been linked with moves abroad since before the European ban but finally Monaco and their new manager Arsène Wenger bought him for £750,000. It had been a big year for him as in April he and Chris Waddle had reached number 12 in the music charts with the single 'Diamond Lights'. Their follow-up release, the lamentable but ironically titled 'It's Goodbye', was scuttled by the move.

In and among the various transfers taking place involving players in the squad, England played two Rous Cup fixtures. Traditionally the FA invited the World Cup winners to Wembley for an international the year after their triumph. While the offer was not always taken, this time the decision was made that Argentina and their hand of God would not even be extended the courtesy. Brazil were instead the chosen recipients and their acceptance gave a chance to open up the Rous Cup to a third team so Scotland could have their own showpiece game.

Just three days after one of the great FA Cup finals, between Coventry City and Tottenham Hotspur, Wembley was full with 92,000 fans again. Brazil were not quite their 1982 vintage but were still one of football's biggest draws. The game was also being shown live on ITV who at half-time had a special guest. Once David Pleat had finished his brief analysis, Diego Maradona joined them with Ossie Ardiles as translator. After a brief exchange, host Nick Owen immediately turned to the first goal in the quarter-final the previous summer. 'Does he admit it was handball now?' he asked Ardiles. 'No, no, he's not going to admit it, never,' came the translated reply.

After the hiccup in Turkey, Bobby Robson picked another attacking side with two wingers, Barnes and Waddle, either side of Peter Reid and Bryan Robson. Up front Lineker had his favourite partner again with Beardsley back from injury and on the night was absolutely brilliant. At times he was nearly unplayable in the first half. The crowd were treated to a very entertaining 1-1 draw, a great Lineker diving header after lovely work and acceleration from Beardsley cancelled out by Newcastle-bound Mirandinha's tap-in. Wembley was a happy place to be for the night, free of British rivalries or a need for aggression at a perceived foe. Lineker had to borrow a pair of boots from the manager after his own fell apart in training. There was nothing that could make him miss a beat at this point, however.

Making his debut on the night was Stuart Pearce, Nottingham Forest's left-back who had a tough time against Muller but did enough to show he had a future. It was a meteoric rise for a player only four seasons into his professional career. As recently as the end of 1986 he was still placing adverts in the Nottingham Forest matchday programme for his company's electrician services. That debut against Brazil taught him a lesson. 'That if I played well it would be worth two caps – one for the game I played in and the next because I would keep my place,' he wrote in his autobiography. He was right too as he lined up four days later to play Scotland at Hampden Park.

England's second game of the year's Rous Cup was the moment an arduous season caught up with everyone on the pitch. Both teams were booed off at half-time after a frankly awful first half. The second 45 minutes could not have got much worse, but still only raised the pulse briefly.

The 0-0 draw and reports of arrests and violence around Glasgow ended the season on a sour note. Brazil would win the tournament by beating Scotland 2-0 a few days later. England's form over the year avoided too harsh a judgement but the game was genuinely one of the dullest of Bobby Robson's entire time in charge.

During a break before the first friendly of the new season in September, Robson travelled to France to watch England's under-21s compete in the Toulon Tournament under manager Dave Sexton. Overall, they disappointed, which was no real surprise after a series of injuries and drop-outs caused a wholesale change of squad pre-tournament. However, one player impressed and Robson would keep an eye on him going forward – Newcastle United's mercurial Paul Gascoigne. Gascoigne scored a goal with Robson watching where he caught a Moroccan goalkeeper out at a free kick and picked the space at the near post. Just the sort of improvisation England often lacked.

The September friendly international away in West Germany was as bad as it was felt all England September internationals were. Under Robson, over the years England had played five games in the month and won only once, 1-0 over a very poor East Germany side. England lost 3-1 in a game they never got to grips with. The only points of note were Lineker scoring his 20th goal in 21 internationals, a phenomenal record, and the debut as a sub just after the hour of Neil Webb, a cultured midfielder from Nottingham Forest – a club who did a nice line in them. West Germany had been beaten finalists at the 1986 World Cup and played close to their strongest side on the night. Gary Mabbutt lined up next to Tony Adams and had such a bad game that Robson would never pick him again. The Germans just had too much for an England side a few yards off the pace in every position.

With that friendly out the way, England could move on to their final games of the year and their last Euro 88 qualifying fixtures – Turkey at home followed by their trickiest-looking fixture, Yugoslavia in Belgrade. Both would prove extraordinary in their own way.

After the dogged defensive performance in Izmir there was a fear about Turkey coming to Wembley that if England didn't score early it could turn into one of those nights. The manager picked and announced his team early to mild controversy as Glenn Hoddle would not start on a night when he might have expected to. If you know you're going to come up against a locked door, why wouldn't you take a skeleton key? Robson had a different plan and the gentle probing of Hoddle was not required from the start.

Against West Germany, England had faced shock and awe from the very first whistle. The home side had come at them at a high tempo from kick-off and taken the game away from them in 35 first-half minutes. England had conceded twice and been fortunate that was the extent of the damage as it could conceivably have been double or worse. That start, no easing your way into the game, impressed Robson and that's what he wanted from this team.

'All six attackers are proven goalscorers,' he said when asked about picking Steven, Robson, Webb, Barnes, Beardsley and Lineker to start. The intent was to be clear from the off. Hoddle came up in the press conference and Robson admitted to having had to have a conversation with the Monaco midfielder who felt he should start. Hoddle's best work came in games where he had time on the ball with willing runners ahead of him so he could hit spaces rather than feet. His best form with England put him ahead of anyone else on the pitch, but his normal level could appear to be almost languid. He was the player everyone pointed to when England were on song and the one most sought out to criticise when not. His cause for this specific night had not been helped by 'his supine performance in Dusseldorf' according to *The Guardian*'s David Lacey. Having watched that game myself, it would be fair to say he had struggled to get any sort of control in a midfield that never wanted to stop running.

The need for goals had been emphasised by Yugoslavia pulling to within a point of England at the top of the group before kick-off with a 3-0 demolition job on Northern Ireland, who were having a miserable campaign. A win and England need only avoid defeat on their trip to Belgrade to qualify. Their destiny needed to remain in their own hands.

England's higher-paced start not only rattled Turkey but it worked and got an instant reward. Hoddle's replacement, Neil Webb, involved himself immediately in a move that started after good work by Tony Adams having the courage to play a high line. The ball worked its way to Webb in space who curled in a lovely cross that was just beyond Lineker. Thankfully, as they had been working on in training, the winger was to make the two a three in the box where possible. John Barnes timed his run perfectly to touch the ball in for 1-0 with just over a minute on the clock.

One became two shortly after, Sansom intercepting a loose pass and drifting a ball towards a waiting Lineker. A striker in the form of his life, he used the pace on the pass to guide the ball into the bottom corner for a lovely finish. Eight minutes gone, 2-0 up, England could relax and play football. It was four by half-time, Barnes getting a second after a wonderful run from his new Liverpool team-mate Peter Beardsley, and Lineker's ability to be in the right place at the right time serving him well yet again.

With the job all but done and thinking back to that performance against Northern Ireland there might have been a temptation to switch off and preserve their energy second half but they were enjoying themselves too much. On the hour Bryan Robson turned Webb's shot in for a fifth, and then Beardsley's clever header made it six a few minutes later. The cross had come from Hoddle, on at half-time for Steven, to enjoy the fun. One of the only questions left was whether Lineker could get his fourth England hat-trick. He answered with a lovely touch from a Robson pass and then a chipped finish for the seventh. Webb had been brilliant on the night, with two assists and a shot that hit the post on his stats sheet, but beyond that he was a constant presence in midfield who looked forward with the pass every time. His goal with just a minute to go, the home side's eighth on the night, was no less than he deserved.

There had been criticism, rightfully, of England's approach after the dreadful game against Scotland and the collective rabbit-caught-in-the-headlights feel of the West Germany friendly. Here they had answered and not only left their destiny in their own hands but also effectively taken goal difference out of any difficulties. Cyrille Regis had earned a recall after a fine season and a half with Coventry City and his 19 minutes off the bench would be his last at international level. Adams had played well yet again and his partnership with Butcher was looking good. Webb had been excellent on the night and provided everything Peter Reid would have done but with more invention besides. With the ability to now have players of the quality of a Hoddle or Waddle on the bench, genuine game-changers, plus the most in-form striker in world football, there was nothing to fear from the final game ahead.

Bobby Robson decided to keep his team secret and wanted to announce it an hour before kick-off in Belgrade, 'I don't see why their manager should be able to pick his side after seeing mine.' This plan would have worked if the day before the game the press hadn't been invited in to watch England train at the Red Star Stadium. They all clearly heard Robson name his team, and then watched them train in formation in a game to finish the session. Now that the secret was out everyone knew he was going with the same 11 that had started against Turkey.

He also went for the same approach – go at them from the off. Robson was aware of the danger of playing for the draw they needed, something his predecessors would have been consumed by. His reward for the bravery was an opening half an hour of the best football any of his England sides had ever played. And the whole game would go down as comfortably one of the country's best-ever away performances.

By the 25th minute England had four goals against one of the most up-and-coming sides in Europe, in a stadium that everyone had warned would become a cauldron. They had been sensational too, with the game live on TV at a time when most children had just arrived home from school. That evening there would be a plethora of heroes to pretend to be in back gardens across the country.

Three minutes in, Beardsley's clever slide to almost tackle the ball past Mauro Ravnic had deserved the opening goal it brought. It was a great piece of quick thinking to get to a ball both defender and goalkeeper thought they had covered. Clever play from a very clever player. Then came a gift. Ravnic inexplicably picked the ball up for a second time in the penalty area to give away an indirect free kick from an angle just past the penalty spot. Bryan Robson touched the ball to his side for Barnes to lash home. Two goals to the good in their hardest fixture with only 17 minutes gone.

Then it got even better. After a corner was half-cleared and then pushed back towards white shirts in the middle, Robson's smart swivel and finish put them three to the good and they were almost qualified with barely a quarter of the game played. Yugoslavia were stunned. England's passing was crisp and their finishing was clinical. In the 25th minute things began to feel surreal as Adams headed in a fourth, making it 12 goals in their last two qualifying games. Unbelievably, England had also managed to avoid finding a way to make life difficult for themselves.

A consolation goal with ten minutes left to play was the best that Yugoslavia could muster as England were controlled, precise and confident. Those who played in that game nearly all remember every minute. Butcher, a player who the writer Brian Glanville had criticised heavily and questioned whether he should still be in the side at that point, was brilliant throughout and described it as one of 'the most defining games of my entire career'. Bobby Robson said on the night it was 'the greatest result of my career' and in later life admitted that it was 'one of the best displays and results of my eight years'. England had been excellent without the need for caveats.

The press too, for once, had been impressed. 'Bobby's Finest Hour!' ran the *Daily Mirror*'s back page, a newspaper for whom criticism had become currency at several points. Nigel Clarke would often approach writing about England as that of a surgeon with a scalpel in hand, but he had not a word of negativity to offer. The *Daily Mail* went with 'Best of the lot!' to describe what had been a pleasingly efficient qualifying campaign. David Lacey's usual *Guardian* flourish was evident in his opening line, 'England qualified for the 1988 European Championship yesterday with the air of men who had taught the natives how to make fire.' Even *The*

Times, a surprisingly brutal paper when it came to Robson's England, had to admit the performance 'had sent a shudder down the spines of all the contenders for the European title' with a 'dazzling victory of extravagant ease and conviction'.

These were heady days to be a fan of England, and with qualification done it was time to not only look forward to next summer's European Championship but to do so with hope. Robson had evolved 'Dad's Army' into a young, attacking side with Lineker as a fulcrum but others helping too. After his blinding run of form, ironically England's most reliable striker had not scored in perhaps the best performance of the campaign. No one cared, least of all Lineker. West Germany was calling, and perhaps destiny was falling Bobby Robson's way.

1988

SPORTING SUCCESS or failure is often a movable feast. One person's miserable collapse is another's glorious victory. These boundaries move with the times too. In modern football we are getting used to ethereal concepts like 'winning' a transfer window. Actual results are the only quantifiable measure but even they can't always be trusted to tell the full story. In 1988 England lost every game of their European Championship. Definable failure. Also, barely half of what happened. Context, as ever, is everything.

For a start they found themselves in a group with two teams who would play out the final and a side on the cusp of becoming the greatest in their country's history. England's first game was a cup tie and they realised too late. The second was against a generational 11 with a player in era-defining form. They then drifted through their third as ghosts, unable to qualify and consumed only with thoughts of the plane home.

On top of the draw's twists of fate they had to do it all without the player who had come to define their defence, lost to injury. Their easiest way to balance that scale was taken from them as the striker best placed to do it had no idea he was ill. Others were off form, carrying injuries or finally no longer to be relied upon. Expectations had been too high from the off, but the summer of 1988 was a confluence of catastrophes for which the blame would not be equally shared. The fans had rioted, the players were miserable, the press was in full attack mode and the manager at a loss. England's 1988 could barely be described as a rollercoaster because they have ups to go with the downs.

* * *

Perhaps the warning signs that all might not go as well as hoped were there in England's first fixture of the year, an away friendly against Israel in Tel Aviv. With only 20 places available for the summer squad – a slim-looking total of 17 outfield players in that – Bobby Robson wanted to look at some options over a few upcoming friendlies. Steve McMahon was called into the squad but told he would make his debut from the bench as England looked for natural longer-term cover for Bryan Robson. Luton Town's Mick Harford, a striker on the long list for Mexico 86, was also told to expect to make his debut at some point in Gary Lineker's absence. Clive Allen was given a last chance to start but knew he would be substituted unless he played his way into being unremovable.

Terry Butcher was missing. He had broken his leg in a challenge for Rangers against Aberdeen just a week after that magnificent victory over Yugoslavia. Alex McLeish had stood firm, with Butcher in the rare position of taking a shot. His follow-through swing on to McLeish's planted leg broke his tibia. Terry Fenwick was recalled, his last game having been the quarter-final against Argentina 18 months previously. Everton's central defender Dave Watson had also been called upon having made appearances on both the South American tour of 1984 and the North American tour of 1985. They would both be competing to play alongside Mark Wright, now approaching something like his best club form again.

By the time of kick-off, England looked radically different to the side that had won 4-1 in Belgrade. Chris Woods had recovered from a bruising Old Firm game earlier in the year that had left him with a fractured rib. He was in goal, ahead of him Gary Stevens, and a recalled Stuart Pearce played either side of Wright and Watson. McMahon had been promoted to a start as Bryan Robson travelled home, a slight thigh strain meant1 he was ordered to return to Manchester United to prepare for an FA Cup tie against Arsenal. Partnering McMahon centrally was Neil Webb, while John Barnes and Chris Waddle would play on each wing. Up front Peter Beardsley would start and be captain on the day with Allen alongside him. Only four players had survived from the game in Belgrade due to injury, form and Bobby Robson's desire to look at his hand beyond the trump cards.

Tel Aviv suffered a huge downpour the day before and the day of the game. The conditions left the ground a mixture of pond and ploughed field in places, and perfectly fine in others. The result was a surface that nobody dared trust. What transpired from the disrupted team and fractured pitch was a disorderly England performance. Webb, Waddle and Barnes all hit the woodwork in the first half and yet the away side had not been dominant at all. In reality they were lucky to be goalless at half-time as a very tight offside had seen a stunning volley from Israeli striker Shalom Tikva ruled out.

The second half ended up as muddy as the pitch which got worse as the game went on. Fenwick was given 16 minutes of international football from the bench as a replacement for Wright, who had again struggled at international level. Harford came on for Allen who had missed presentable chances in both halves and was also now finished in an England shirt. A squad reduced by injury to only 15 players had very little else on the bench to change things. They ended up with a goalless draw against a side who had not won a home game since beating New Zealand 3-0 in 1985.

Fenwick's England career was at an end as his sub appearance would be his last. A year later he wrote, with the journalist Brian Woolnough, a diary of a full season with Tottenham Hotspur under Terry Venables. In it he joined the swathes of people criticising Bobby Robson and the England set-up. At the time of writing it, Fenwick was 30, at a high-profile club and with experience on his side. Where he might still have been a viable option, he decided to not so much burn his bridges as to blow them into pieces. In various places he posed that the England manager screamed 'blue murder' for more time with his players and then 'they waste the time' anyway. Robson was 'too nice', 'the coaching was poor' and Fenwick decided he should 'expect a better standard from the England manager'. Even Don Howe wasn't safe as 'his ideas on football are boring'.

Nobody from the England side emerged with any credit from the draw, other than McMahon who had at least done nothing wrong on his debut. Defensively the Wright/Watson partnership had not gelled and both full-backs had been hampered by the worst of the weather making a mess of the wings; see also Barnes and Waddle. Webb had a strangely unenergetic performance after two all-action games against Yugoslavia and Turkey, seeming to stroll into position rather than burst into space. It had all led a toothless display that only emphasised the importance of Bryan Robson's dynamism and Lineker, scorer of two goals in the Spanish Cup semi-final on the same night, up top.

Bobby Robson was also not immune to criticism for changing his team. He had been forced to defend the fixture in the first place, as he had in 1986, with England still in a beggars-can't-be-choosers situation when trying to arrange away friendlies. It had all ended up feeling completely unnecessary.

The same couldn't be said for the first home friendly of the year, a scintillating 2-2 draw with the Netherlands. This game had become a sighter for both countries as the draw had been made for the Euro 88 group stage. Group 2 would contain the two teams plus the USSR and the Republic of Ireland. It looked tough as the USSR were a rising force and Ireland had just won their sixth game in a row. The Dutch were at Wembley for a real-time preview for Robson and his staff. They looked formidable opposition.

Ruud Gullit, booed by a section of idiotic England fans throughout, was mesmeric on the night. He was involved in everything and felt unlike any player they had faced before. His speed of thought was equally as good as Beardsley's, and his touch even better. His athleticism was past that of even a fully fit Bryan Robson and he remained untouchable in the air throughout. He gave Adams, Watson and Sansom nightmares for an hour before pulling up with cramp and exiting to avoid injury. If England were to beat the Dutch in the summer they would have to come up with a plan to defend against him properly.

As good as Holland were on the night, England did just about deserve the draw. Lineker's well-taken opener led to a frenetic ten minutes in which they ended up 2-1 down. Adams scored an own goal as he tried to stop a cross reaching Gullit, and then John Bosman's header put them ahead after Gullit had bullied Sansom off the ball. England were losing in a game at Wembley for the first time since being booed off against the USSR in 1984. Adams redeemed himself in the second half with the equaliser and became the first England player to score at both ends in the same game.

Both teams left with a mutual respect for each other but quietly confident. The Netherlands were happy enough that on several occasions they had pulled the opposition defence and midfield around enough to work the space for their strikers to operate in, and Gullit was clearly better than anyone in direct opposition to him. England knew that they had held their own, Butcher was on the way back, and five players had played in a very rough and tumble Merseyside derby just three days before the game. They expected to be stronger come Dusseldorf in the summer.

A drab 0-0 away to Hungary came and went in April with Bobby Robson again using a game to look at some of his options. Gary Pallister made a solid debut as another defender to consider, and Stuart Pearce came off with an injury that he recovered from but then unfortunately aggravated, badly this time, later in the season. Ultimately it cost him his place at the Euros. McMahon and Bryan Robson partnered each other for a formidable midfield that didn't create enough. Robson, however, was sensational in a game that never deserved a performance like that.

With the Euros to come the press were relatively content with the odd barbed comment, the constant aside that England had been left behind by the European ban far more than they had in reality, and a collective 'let's see what the summer brings'. It was, as the *Daily Mail* among others pointed out, time for the 'wholesale experimentation' to stop and settle on a squad that would take them through the upcoming Rous Cup, and then on to West Germany.

At this point the news had come through that Butcher's leg had not healed correctly so he would not be available until September at the earliest. It was a huge blow both on the pitch and mentally to the England camp. Butcher was one of Robson's most trusted lieutenants, certainly the most reliable defender at his disposal. The squad had lost a leader. Butcher was irreplaceable, and the best anyone coming into that position in the team could hope for was to keep his place warm until the broken leg had healed.

The programme was determined that the Rous Cup's two fixtures and then a friendly against Switzerland would be their warm-up into Euro 88. Bobby Robson picked a 24-man squad to cover those fixtures, and to provide an England XI for Alan Hansen's testimonial to be played just after the season ended. There were no real surprises other than a call up for Chelsea's Tony Dorigo, an enterprising left-back called into the space Pearce's injury had left.

Two days after Wimbledon won one of the most extraordinary FA Cup finals in history, England played at Anfield for the testimonial at just above walking pace. This sense of preservation lasted into the first Rous Cup fixture at Wembley, the annual encounter with Scotland. England were grateful to find the Scots in the midst of a transition from the 1986 World Cup squad into the side who would take them forward without the likes of Graeme Souness and Kenny Dalglish. The fixture lacked the blood and thunder of a few recent encounters, and England were allowed to dominate. Beardsley's wonderful dummy and combination with Barnes opened the scoring just 11 minutes in. England gratefully settled into the game and saw the 1-0 win out.

The slim margin of victory didn't really reflect the home side's dominance. They had played to push on and go ahead early as they did against Turkey and Yugoslavia. When they realised the challenge was not as great as it had been previous years there had been a considerable effort to conserve energy. This continued the following Tuesday night against the year's invited guests, Colombia. England were good enough for a 1-1 draw but never really reached anything like top gear. For the visitors, Carlos Valderrama, as Gullit had done, glided through the match with a silken touch and an eye for a pass that England's midfield and defence weren't quite sure how to answer. Colombia were on their way to becoming a very good side, but thankfully for England they weren't quite there yet and the Rous Cup was won for a second time.

The final friendly, a 1-0 win over Switzerland in Lausanne, was an exercise in not getting injured. Lineker's goal on the hour settled a game that didn't matter. After the final whistle a 24-man squad became 20. Robson cut young QPR goalkeeper David Seaman, central defender Pallister, plus two strikers – West Ham youngster Tony Cottee, who had featured three times from the bench but was yet to make an impact, and Mick Harford, unlucky for a second tournament running.

One moment of significance from their last friendly before the Euros was Peter Reid's appearance from the bench with 11 minutes to go. He would go to West Germany but not feature, that cameo in Switzerland proving to be his final outing in an England shirt. He had been a huge part of the 1986 World Cup squad and was an immensely popular player. Reid came to international football late, just shy of his 29th birthday on his debut, but never once looked out of place. He played 13 times for England but it's a marker of his impact that it felt like much, much more. The central midfield options of Robson, Hoddle, and now Webb and McMahon, made him fifth choice. He left a decent legacy but his race was run.

All eyes now turned to Sunday, 12 June and England's date with destiny. A tough test lay ahead, but most felt this was a better squad than the 1986 one, including the manager.

* * *

Bobby Robson's men came into the game against the Republic of Ireland as favourites to win – always the worst possible scenario for an England fan regardless of the opposition. As one myself I can tell you our default position is to wish for too much in public through bravado alone, but actually expect very little in private. It's not the despair, I can take that, it's the hope I can't stand, as an out-of-breath John Cleese once said on film.

The bookies had been swayed by some emotional betting and the lingering injustice of the exit from Mexico 86. The press had agreed and several newspapers had tipped England to not only make it through the group but to win it all. Pundits were slightly more measured, but most felt England should beat the Republic comfortably and concentrate on not losing to the Netherlands next up. A possible win/win or win/draw would put them in a good position with two to qualify from the group for the semi-finals.

This sense of confidence had even spread to the England coach on the way to the ground. Relaxed was good, Mexico 86 had taught them that, but Jim Rosenthal was invited along and filmed a team who to a man could have been on their way to a training session. Kenny Sansom even had the chance to do his impressions live on ITV. His Frank Spencer was quite good; his Ronald Reagan less so. There was a sense that in playing Ireland, a team stacked with players from the First Division, there was no fear of the unknown. They had completely underestimated the situation.

For a start they had no idea just how fired up Jack Charlton had his team to play the English. He knew how important this was to the fans who rabidly cheered the squad arriving at the stadium, every single man from coach to player getting their own ovation. He primed his players to feed from the energy provided in the stands. They did not disappoint.

He also fed into their egos, as Ireland were the lowest-ranked team to qualify and written off by most as whipping boys. Even after the game the *Daily Mirror* would describe them as 'the tournament's no-hopers'.

Tactically, the Irish found a simple way to close England's midfield down by letting Frank Stapleton drop deep to provide an extra man in there. They also had their full-backs, Chris Hughton and Chris Morris, protected by the industry of Ray Houghton and Tony Galvin who worked tirelessly to close down Barnes and Waddle. Two layers of defence out wide and an extra body centrally to stop Robson or Webb creating meant that England were in trouble.

With the plan in place to restrict their opponents to as little space as possible, an early goal would be vital in giving Ireland something to defend. They pushed Aldridge up to make a nuisance of himself and their midfielders joined him at the slightest hint of a presentable opportunity to do so. In the sixth minute England suffered their first quantifiable disaster of the summer.

It's the rarest thing to see a back four give away a goal in which every single one of them made an individual error. Firstly, Wright and Stevens got themselves in a horrible mess trying to deal with a simple ball that Frank Stapleton wasn't even looking to win. Wright jumped into Stevens who had not heard his call or looked a foot to his side to see the defender claiming it. Wright mistimed his jump anyway and the ball dropped on to his head rather than him getting to it with any purpose. Both were now out of position as Galvin hooked it hopefully across. Sansom then completely misjudged the bounce of a ball he should have cleared easily and kicked it high and behind himself into danger. Adams braced himself to head clear but was unaware of Aldridge's desire to win the ball. He made no challenge as the Irish striker headed back towards a green shirt. Houghton had jogged into the space vacated by Sansom's rush to clear the ball initially and nodded in a goal that seemed to suddenly turn the stadium green.

From that moment on and with a huge upset in sight so early, Ireland dug in and stuck to their plan. No England player could get a foothold in the game. Glenn Hoddle was brought on for the ineffective Webb on the hour and things improved slightly but still the Irish kept their discipline. Despite it all England lay siege to the Irish half. Lineker missed several chances, a couple he should have buried in truth. Beardsley also missed two good opportunities, and Hoddle clipped the crossbar.

The defeat was celebrated on the whistle in scenes similar to those England players had trudged by after losing to Argentina in 1986. The 1-0 loss was a huge upset, and a poll in 2015 by RTÉ 2's *Soccer Republic* named it the country's greatest-ever result. England had come into the game too relaxed, had been unable to overcome the Irish tactically and even then missed enough chances to have won the game.

In reality, there were holes in the squad before they even took the pitch to play Ireland. Beardsley's listlessness in front of goal had been caused by the same thing that was hampering Barnes from reaching his best – both had just completed an epic first year with Liverpool. Between them they had played 96 games over the course of the season, both subbed off in only three of them, and all but one of those had come after the 70th minute. Liverpool had been quite brilliant in only losing twice in the course of winning the title, while Barnes and Beardsley had contributed between them over a third of the 87 league goals score. Both missed a single game over the league, FA Cup and League Cup campaigns. As a result, both were playing despite desperately needing a break.

Chris Waddle was coming into the Euros on the back of a tough year. He had received some harsh criticism for not bringing his club form to an international shirt and found himself in and out of squads at the end of the qualifying. He had been thankful to have been picked for the Israel friendly but underperformed again, this time with a reason. Knowing something was not quite right, both the England doctor and then his club medical team suspected a hernia.

He had the operation but by his wife Lorna's admission was 'quite impossible when not fit' and did not look after himself while initially recovering. Not long after the injury had been operated on, he sneaked out of hospital to visit Madame Tussauds with another patient, as one example. Later, having been sent home long ago, his then club manager Terry Venables surprised him in a pub to get a progress update. Waddle then returned in April and while technically fit he was nowhere near his best and struggling to find his once-electric pace again.

Waddle had also suffered a small injury in one of two unofficial games organised by Bobby Robson in the run-up to the tournament. Before leaving the country they played non-league Aylesbury United and somebody forgot to tell their opponents it was a friendly. Mark Hateley, Trevor Steven, Lineker and Waddle himself all received treatment over the next couple of days for knocks and injuries caused by hard tackles on a less-than-ideal pitch.

On arriving in Germany another friendly was organised and again the local non-league side had not received any memo to go easy. Steven was again injured, this time to the point of him having to miss the Ireland match, meaning Waddle's natural replacement from the start or bench was unavailable. In the same game, Wright and Stevens both picked up knocks just a few days away from that group-opening clash, and Lineker had received a kick to the ankle and was subbed immediately.

With Butcher missing, several carrying injuries big or small, Barnes and Beardsley out on their feet and Waddle struggling, the last thing England needed was Lineker to be in anything less than top gear. He was coming to West Germany on the back of another 20-goal season, his second in Spain, but his lack of sharpness against the Republic of Ireland would be repeated and actually worsen across the next two games.

Lineker had struggled so badly that he had asked not to play in the final match against the USSR. The management team felt he had to, more than anything to set an example to others they felt were trying to hide from more criticism. He came off after 70 minutes having 'never played in a game where I was so certain I shouldn't be on the pitch', as he told *FourFourTwo* in 2015. After wrestling with severe fatigue and illness he then started losing weight – an issue when he was not carrying any excess in the first place. He returned home and was hospitalised, before eventually being diagnosed with hepatitis shortly after the tournament had finished. Bobby Robson visited him to apologise for refusing his request to rest.

On top of the actuals were several unquantifiables. Sansom, so long England's Mr Reliable on the left, was approaching 30 and suddenly looked vulnerable and destined to lose one-on-ones against anyone with pace. Hoddle, supremely talented but only in games built for him to thrive, looked markedly slower and was now the wrong side of 30. Then there was the spine; nobody who played in his position looked like they were the same class of defender as Butcher. The decision to play 24-year-old Wright and 21-year-old Adams against Ireland was a mistake against players as streetwise as Aldridge and Stapleton.

From the excitement of the Turkey and Yugoslavia games, England had regressed, struggled with injury, and Bobby Robson had trusted in some he might have been better questioning. It suddenly looked like it would take a miracle to get something from Holland. On the day God must have been busy with other things.

Watching this match in full now it is worth saying that there are a series of sliding doors moments that could have seen it go in another direction. England were not actively bad at any point, and Bryan Robson's goal was worthy of a match against the eventual winners of the tournament. What they couldn't reckon with was a side of the quality that came to Wembley earlier in the year adding a player the calibre of Marco van Basten.

He was clinical at a level no one in a white shirt could get near. Where he took Gullit's wonderful outside-of-the-foot pass and turned past Adams to score his first, Lineker hit the outside of the post when gifted a chance and an open goal by Koeman's header. When Van Basten took Gullit's pass in his stride and scored his second, Hoddle had only hit the inside of the post with his free kick. For the hat-trick Van Basten reacted first at a corner and slammed the ball home. Lineker had snapped at England's best chance after the Robson equaliser and put the ball wide.

The 3-1 loss was compounded by Ireland and the USSR drawing that evening, rendering the unlikelihood of England getting through now a mathematical certainty. Bobby Robson mixed the side up for the final game, now a dead rubber against the Soviets, and almost inconceivably having told them to play for pride things got worse as they gave in to another chastening 3-1 defeat.

Hoddle's error gifted a goal with just three minutes gone and seemed to set a fairly dismal tempo. At the group's end, England had played three, lost three, scored two and conceded seven.

Before facing the USSR, Bobby Robson said he was 'devastated' by the defeats to Ireland and the Netherlands. Afterwards he admitted to being ashamed. While 1987 had ended with so many reasons to be positive, 1988 had proved them all to be smoke and mirrors. There was still time before journeying home for Bryan Robson to punch Peter Shilton after an argument in the hotel bar. The pair quickly reconciled over breakfast the following morning. The wheels had not so much come off as flown away never to be seen again.

The England party headed home having wanted to go since the moment the full-time whistle blew against the Netherlands. They were not returning to any sort of peace. The players were under fire, the manager now *persona non grata*, the fans had done the inevitable and the newspapers were in their element.

* * *

Having built England up pre-tournament in a rare show of positivity, the tabloids took losing to the Republic of Ireland exactly as you may have suspected. By the tournament's end the anger had become a frenzy and even the broadsheets were joining in.

The *Daily Mirror*'s Nigel Clarke took it all personally. 'He promised us so much,' he wrote in his back-page reaction piece that the sub-editors had headlined 'RUBBISH!' Clarke had ghost-written Sir Alf Ramsey's columns criticising the England manager over the years. With the circulation war with *The Sun* now in play, he positioned himself as Bobby Robson's biggest critic going forward from Euro 88. His colleague Harry Harris was on match report duties and tore into the England players and manager for committing 'suicide' with their 'complete and utter shambles' of a defence.

The Sun, *Today* and the *Daily Star* all lined up to join in kicking 'England's bottlers'. By the time of the game against the Dutch all had basically written off England and their manager regardless of result. The 3-1 defeat, and then Ireland's later draw with the USSR, confirmed the exit and the vitriol could really start. 'English football is draped in a black cloak,' said *The Times* in a relatively mild report compared to the *Daily Mail* which claimed it was 'on the road to oblivion'.

The inquest was already at full speed and the verdict had all but been decided by the time England met the USSR. The result gave a confirmatory nod for the coverage to not only continue, but to get personal. The *Daily Mirror* decided to just outright ask who would now take the England job such was the damage done by Robson's tenure, 'Clough? No! Venables? No! Kendall? No! Howe? No! Sexton? No! Taylor? No! Wilkinson? No!' The paper's answer was actually to give the job to Bryan Robson somewhat bizarrely, but only after letting the current manager limp to the end of his contract to give the captain time to prepare.

The Observer preferred to take the view that no single person was to blame, rather that everything was wrong and lumping it all on the manager was misjudged. The great Hugh McIlvanney wrote, 'It is hard to have a decent wake when so many people are confused about the identity of the corpse.' Bobby Robson was seen as an issue but one of a myriad facing English football. It would be wrong to remove him, McIlvanney wrote, when all the problems would remain. There was no real cheerleader anymore for the England manager. Or the team. It looked like things might well get worse before getting anything like better.

All who were busy demanding Bobby Robson's blood were to be disappointed. He was asked by the FA chairman if he wanted to remain in the job and despite elements of doubt and an offer to resign if requested, he said yes immediately. Unfinished business more than anything. Millichip spoke to the press himself to make clear there was 'no likelihood of Bobby Robson being dismissed'. Privately both men knew there was a rebuilding job ahead. The tabloids had their upturn in sales from Robson's team's miserable Euros, and a template had been set. It was going to take character to get through the next few months if England did not win their next couple of fixtures handsomely.

It would be fair to say that one of the reasons Robson survived the catastrophic summer was that the FA could only fight fires on so many fronts. As badly as the team had performed, the fans had been even worse. From the moment of their arrival in Germany things had soured. There had been reports of almost immediate incidents in isolated parts of Stuttgart. Most of it had been vandalism, driven by alcohol, with whispers of fighting with local fans. In relative terms the Saturday night had been quiet although an undercurrent had infected the city. Very few arrests were made but the atmosphere was undeniable.

In the wake of the loss to Ireland, a local hooligan mob came looking for England fans. They found and attacked a large group of them at the railway station in Stuttgart. CS gas was used and, heavily outnumbered, the English fans took several beatings. Eventually armed police mobilised to stop the riot but the genie was out of the bottle. That night violence broke out wherever England fans gathered, locals beaten in retribution despite having nothing to do with the gang that attacked initially, and bars smashed to pieces for the trouble of having served the English for an hour or two. Disparate groups of fans raged into the night in what the *Daily Mail*'s front-page headline called the 'Battle of Stuttgart'. Police had been forced into several baton charges as the English appropriated anything that could be used as a weapon.

In the morning and with things slightly calmer, German authorities were at pains to point out they were under no illusions about their own country's hooligan issues. The wider blame for a continued night of violence lay at England's feet and certainly the newspapers were in no mood to offer any caveats. Most knew the value of these stories beyond just moral outrage at this point. The more lurid the details the better. Photographers had become vital to the process and they were dispatched to find trouble. Nearly every newspaper from red top to broadsheet carried photos all along the same three themes: smiling yob being taken away; hooligan attacking police officer; massed gang in England shirts and flags in aggressive pose.

To make matters worse, the Sports Minister Colin Moynihan had flown out for the game. His high-profile appearance and then the night of violence that followed brought another call for action in parliament. The problem was there was little that could be done as the fans migrated slowly to Dusseldorf for the game against Holland. Over 100 arrests had been made in Stuttgart but ahead lay an even bigger challenge. The Dutch element were notorious themselves at this point and there was a real chance that the whole city was about to explode.

Violence, vandalism and arrests followed England across the country. The newspapers, the authorities and even the Prime Minister condemned the behaviour in the strictest possible terms, as always, without offering solutions. Alongside each report of an incident was yet another public figure calling for England to be banned from taking fans to away fixtures or for offenders' passports to be seized, but nothing could control what was happening on a nightly basis in Germany. The rhetoric was that something would have to be done in the future. Meanwhile the riot was happening at that moment.

The night before the game against Holland saw the worst of the violence as English and Dutch fans clashed with each other and with locals in Dusseldorf. Over 300 England supporters ambushed Germans returning to the city via train after their match with Denmark. That set the tone for another 40 arrests, plus further baton charges, smashed windows, overturned cars and innocents attacked. By the time the England team was returning home after losing to the USSR there had been arrests well into the hundreds, and injuries to hooligans, normal fans, police officers, innocents and rivals. Calls to ban fans from travelling were now coming from the Sports Minister himself in sheer exasperation at the hopelessness of it all. Bert Millichip was having to field questions about whether England should be allowed to even compete for the chance to go to the next World Cup.

The English had left a stain on the tournament in more ways than one. At every level there seemed to be another huge problem to sort. Two days after the squad's return journey from Germany, Don Howe was hospitalised with a suspected heart attack. It really could not have gone any worse. The future looked horrendously messy at best; a deep black hole at worst.

* * *

The end of Euro 88 also spelled the end of three international careers. Firstly, Dave Watson would never be selected again after 12 caps, all under Bobby Robson. He had looked a prospect when taken to South America in 1984 but four years later had come up a little short. Terry Butcher's imminent return limited his opportunities, Tony Adams was also well ahead of him, and young Nottingham Forest defender Des Walker had impressed in the under-21s and was now worth a look longer term.

It was also the end of the road for Kenny Sansom. After 86 caps it had been a gradual decline and while still a supremely gifted player he just was not quite where he used to be. A few months after Euro 88 he left Arsenal after eight seasons when replaced by Nigel Winterburn for the same reasons. Sansom had rarely let his country down, and to date he remains the 12th most-capped England player of all time. Stuart Pearce had emerged as first choice and provided a very different option to Sansom, who would be briefly recalled to a squad in light of an injury to Pearce in 1989 but was not chosen to play. As a player who contributed to England's time under Robson enormously, it's perhaps a shame he didn't get to join the exclusive 100-cap club as Shilton had just done in the summer.

The final player discarded after the Euros was more controversial. The great Glenn Hoddle debate was 56 caps in. There was no doubting Hoddle's obscene level of talent, but harnessing it to the rest of the England team had proved elusive. At his best he glided through international games and looked unplayable. At his worst he had been almost anonymous. Perhaps the issue with Hoddle was not that he couldn't find his best, but that he couldn't find a way to be a consistent seven out of ten for England. Often nine, more often five, his refusal to compromise to something more prosaic was, and is, in some ways admirable.

It is always said if Hoddle was Spanish or Dutch he may well have won double those caps and more. They would have built their side around him. The trouble was he knew it.

He did not leave quietly and gave a series of interviews, not rounding on the manager as others might but condemning the whole system. One of the harshest of these was, somewhat surprisingly, given to *Shoot!* magazine in a piece headlined 'I weep for English football'. He attacked a lack of focus on creation over the obsession with combat, 'The truth is that we are lacking technical ability and until our outlook on the game changes, that situation will remain … at home youngsters are ashamed if they haven't got what everyone calls "fighting spirit" yet overseas their pride is hurt when they can't control the ball with their first touch – that's the difference.'

With Hoddle gone, England did face a lack of creativity but there were options. Neil Webb had sunk to everyone else's level over the summer but his promising start still held some hope. There was also a clamour to pick the player everyone was talking about, Paul Gascoigne. He had just moved to Tottenham Hotspur for a record fee and had played excellently for the under-21s. The issue was he was still raw and incredibly impetuous. England under-21 manager Dave Sexton had already had to warn him earlier in the year that if he was booked again he would be subbed off immediately. 'We've been doing this for some time and I don't remember having too many players cautioned,' he said in defence of the policy. Whether Gascoigne was to be trusted or not was one thing, but you certainly couldn't ignore him.

First up for England after the summer was the annual September fixture. This time it would be Denmark who came to Wembley for a friendly before the World Cup qualifiers began, providing tough opposition for a game Bobby Robson really needed to win. As soon as the focus from league football switched back to the international matches the attacks on Robson started again.

The tabloids decided, upon seeing Robson's refusal to stack the team with debutants, that his selection was 'spineless' and 'senseless'. *The Sun* called him 'the clown of English football'. In the face of growing pressure, Robson wanted to keep his spine together so Butcher was straight back in, Shilton started despite being just a few days from his 39th birthday, Bryan Robson partnered Webb in midfield, and Steve Hodge was played in an injured John Barnes's place for his first cap in over a year. Lineker was still not fit enough to play so Mick Harford started as England's number nine.

On the right wing, Robson did bring in Arsenal's supremely talented youngster David Rocastle. He was another who had been impressive at youth levels for England and did fine on his debut, as did Des Walker, a 65th-minute substitute for Adams. Walker immediately settled in and looked for all the world like he could do everything Adams could but quicker. Harford missed a good chance in the first half and was taken off for Tony Cottee with 20 minutes to go. Neither man produced anything noteworthy and this was to be Harford's last game for England. Woods had the second half in goal as Robson pondered Shilton's future.

Then, with five minutes to go, the player the press were really clamouring for made his debut. Paul Gascoigne was 21 years old with lightning in his boots. He had way too short a time to make an impact but he would get his chance further down the line.

England's 1-0 win was important after the toil of the summer. For a start it broke the losing habit. Denmark were good and Michael Laudrup had been a seriously impressive youngster at Wembley in 1983, but now he was genuinely world class. He wriggled free but couldn't find his range several times as England clung on to a vital, morale-boosting clean sheet. Their goal came from a nice volley from Webb who was better on the night. Wembley had welcomed just shy of 26,000 fans but the small crowd was a natural response after recent results on and off the pitch. It had been a six out of ten night but for their manager that had been enough.

As expected, there were several in the press who disagreed but collectively there was little to really criticise about the friendly. Robson's demeanour in media conferences before the game had changed in the light of the abuse he was now receiving. He was spiky and shorter with his answers. After the match he was asked about the summer and the negative public feeling more than the actual game they had just won. He'd had enough. 'You know as well as I do that West Germany was all about the last defeat,' he replied to the question that tipped him over the edge. 'Russia was the only bad England performance in two years and you slaughter people because of that, you would not let it go!' With that he cut the press conference short and left with a parting shot, 'You write what you want, the team has won, the team has said it all.'

After the slight respite of beating the Danes, England moved on to a game that mattered, their first in trying to qualify for the 1990 World Cup in Italy. The draw had been made back in December and had not been as kind as the one for 1986. England were again in a four-team group, one of three in UEFA qualifying, but this time there was a safety net in the form of the two best runners-up from those also reaching Italia 90. There was work to be done though. Sweden were first up and had beaten a Robson side in their last meeting, a horrible September friendly shortly after the World Cup in 1986. They had also been drawn with group outsiders Albania, who represented the unknown, and Poland. England had never faced Albania but knew all about the Poles. Having beaten them 3-0 in Mexico, confidence might have been up were it not for a couple of high-profile failures against them in the 1970s.

Sweden came to Wembley in October and at a time when Bobby Robson was desperate for a win. As opposition they were the last thing England needed right at that moment in time – solid, compact, excellent on the break, and on the verge of becoming a really good side. They were also coming into this qualification run on the back of some great results and had given England a warning in April by tearing Wales apart in a friendly to win 4-1.

The first half was cagey. Waddle, recalled to the starting 11 much to his relief, had a goal ruled out for offside but England struggled to create anything meaningful. In return Sweden offered patience, waiting for a mistake to come. They very nearly got their reward when captain Bryan Robson tried awkwardly to pull out of a tackle with Robert Prytz but clattered into him in the box. Prytz's exaggerated fall convinced the referee of Robson's innocence but on another night it might well have been given.

England tried to be more proactive second half. Gary Lineker, recovered but not at his sharpest, flashed a header over after good work from Waddle and Barnes. Waddle was having a good game and his superb through ball sent Lineker through but he ran wide and missed the target. Chances came and went, and Waddle was unlucky not to get a penalty when hacked down, but with seconds left England thought they had got their win when Lineker found his finish from Beardsley's lovely deft touch only for another offside flag to deny them. While the BBC were still showing a replay, the final whistle was blown. Somewhat unfairly after an okay performance in a very tight game, England were booed off.

Bobby Robson, quite rightly, defended the performance but relationships with some in the press were close to breaking point. When asked about the booing he preferred to ignore it and pretend it hadn't happened. 'That's gossip,' he replied. Yet again he had a go back at his assembled detractors – 'you generate the hate and I have to suffer it' – but he already knew what would await him over the next couple of days in the tabloids. 'I am having to work in a hostile environment and that is not easy … the attitude of the press has changed, they are much more volatile than they were and there are sections generating hate,' he continued, knowing the words wouldn't help his cause at all. 'They can brainwash the public.'

The Sun, having called the England manager 'Plonker!' on its back-page headline the day after the game, set up the 'Robson Hotline' offering readers the chance to ring up and 'let the men who run our national game know just what the country really feels about Robson'. On the Friday the paper ran its *Sun Sport Special* on 'the man making England a laughing stock in world football'. Robson ('six years a loser' according to Brian Woolnough) had already refused to quit and now there was word from Dick Wragg, the chairman of the FA's international committee, that they would 'never sack Bobby Robson, never'.

In its special, *The Sun* found room to run Stan Boardman and Bernard Manning's 12 favourite Bobby Robson jokes, a series of photos of Robson from the press conference after the game under the headline 'The Face of a Flop', and the odds for the next England manager – Graham Taylor and Terry Venables were the two favourites. John Sadler, the writer who 'gives it to you straight' according to his by-line, called for Brian Clough yet again, and added, 'The FA should crawl up the M1 to land him.' Analysis out the window, this was a feeding frenzy.

The *Daily Mirror*, and its chief hatchet man Nigel Clarke, was just as bad. 'GO! In the Name of God GO!' ran a soon-to-be infamous headline. The *Mirror* had been linking managers to the job on a weekly basis, Howard Kendall even having to go so far as give an interview in early October to rule himself out of the running for a job that wasn't available. Clarke's piece after the draw against Sweden was hyperbolic to the point of tedium. When you open with the lines 'Bobby Robson was booed out of Wembley last night. And now he should be kicked out of his job' there really isn't anywhere else to go.

A few ran pieces not quite supportive of the England manager but far more representative of the actual game that had just happened. Jeff Powell in the *Daily Mail* wondered why 'Robson wants to go on putting himself through this torture – only a psychiatric specialist in masochistic pride might tell us'. The truth was that Robson was wondering too but decided to answer by throwing himself into his work.

The final fixture of the year was an unwanted friendly against Saudi Arabia in Riyadh. The FA were paid well for an England side to fulfil the fixture and Concorde was commandeered for the flying visit. Bobby Robson wanted to play an experimental team supplemented by a few older heads, but his chosen squad was decimated by injuries and withdrawals before they had left. At one point it was down to just 14 players, Brian Clough of Nottingham Forest the latest to pointedly withdraw two of his men – Des Walker and Steve Hodge – without explanation.

A fixture that had been called into question before it had begun went badly. England laboured to a 1-1 draw with five debutants featuring at various stages – Brian Marwood, Alan Smith, Mel Sterland, Michael Thomas and goalkeeper David Seaman. While they had the likes of Bryan Robson, Waddle, Beardsley and Lineker around them there was no rhythm, very little continuity, and in the end they had gone in at half-time 1-0 down. Tony Adams's header in the second half brought England level. They had three goals ruled out for offside (at least one was extremely marginal) but the failure to beat weak opposition was an awful way to round off a terrible year.

Nearly everything about the trip annoyed the England management team – the standard of opposition, the distance to travel, the drop-outs, the performance and the sense of knowing what waited for them back home. Bobby Robson gave the BBC a terse interview after the final whistle as Barry Davies asked him why he hadn't brought on Marwood earlier. Robson took exception, showing the strain, and snapped an answer. Davies had been fairly cutting in his commentary summation of England's performance, offering, 'They came to a desert, and they got lost.' Jimmy Hill in the studio was also heavily critical and felt England needed to bring in a new man to work with the manager and take over in two years. Robson then agreed to a rearranged midnight conference for the written press as the England party were flying home through the night. He shouldn't have bothered as he knew what was coming.

The reaction to this draw was as bad if not worse than the last. The *Daily Star* went for sarcasm and ran a back page that read 'Didn't we do well! England heroes hit new heights (To hold mighty Saudis to 1-1)'. Its reporter, 'Desert Rat', asked the FA to give Bobby Robson a 'ten-year contract and free company camel' and 'declare a national holiday to salute our England heroes'. In its slightly more serious match report, Bob Driscoll stated that the only music suitable for the England manager to dance to was a 'funeral dirge provided by the Arab band'.

The *Daily Express* went with 'Arabian Nightmare' and decided 'there is no end to the futility of Bobby Robson's England'. Star columnist Johnny Giles then gave 'Five reasons why he [Robson] has been a sad failure for England'. The Irish international quite fancied Bobby Charlton to take over. *The Observer*'s Peter Corrigan stated a few days later, 'There is nothing left to admire about English international football anymore other than the obstinacy of Bobby Robson.' In the face of another onslaught there was a truth to that idea. Even Britain's newest paper, the extremely short-lived *The Post* (the tabloid dedicated to being sensationalism-free as ran the blurb), joined in, 'BLIND – He thought they played well against Saudi Arabia. DEAF – He won't listen to the barrage of calls for him to get out now. DUMB – He won't say the words we want to hear: I QUIT!'

As for the two heavyweight tabloids, *The Sun* went with the typically culturally sensitive 'England Mustafa New Boss' and then 'Give Bobby the chop'. However, it lost this round to the *Daily Mirror* and knew it. In one of the most memorable back pages of the era, the *Mirror* retooled its headline from the Sweden game to read 'GO! In the Name of Allah GO!' Nigel Clarke's article was typically biting over what he called 'the final humiliation' for Robson's side. Inside the paper he wrote 'Twenty Facts That Say Robbo Must Go – What an England Wally!' claiming he had 101 and had run out of space.

Robson himself needed police protection on returning from the trip. A press pack pursued him the minute he came into sight in the airport. He and several members of staff were taken off to a private room while the way was cleared for them. The situation was bordering on the ridiculous but 1989 needed to be a better year.

1989

THE TABLOIDS were at war with each other and everyone was now fair game, not just the England manager. Kelvin MacKenzie's reign as editor of *The Sun* had ushered in a new approach to the red top battleground. By 1989 it was in its pomp. Everyone involved had now realised actual news did not sell anything like the number of newspapers a front page like 'Freddie Starr Ate My Hamster' did. The truth had become secondary; the first age of living post-consequence had begun. Starr was followed by that headline for the rest of his life. The incident, of course, never happened and he always denied it, but as James Felton wrote in the excellent *Sunburn* about that very headline, 'When you see something on the front page of a newspaper, people tend to think there must be *some* truth to it.'

There had been the occasional high-profile fightback. Elton John had been pursued by *The Sun* and successfully taken it to court to receive a £1m pay-out and a full-page apology. The stories had been salacious in the extreme as the newspaper printed false testimony involving Elton, orgies, rent boys, sex toys and cocaine. Having to hand over that amount of money must have hurt those involved but, in reality, the notoriety earned was the real currency of tabloid reporting.

In later life, MacKenzie has been asked about this period of time in charge of the biggest-selling tabloid in the country. It would be fair to say he has no regrets. In a 2006 interview he claimed Sir Elton should have to hand back the settlement as, 'It hasn't damaged him at all, has it?' He also denied ever printing lies, 'They were great stories that later turned out to be untrue – and that is different.' All it was ever about was selling newspapers for him; the victims of these stories were utterly secondary.

Bobby Robson had felt the full glare of *The Sun*. And the *Daily Mirror*. And every other newspaper for that matter. The hostile environment he had described after the Sweden game was every bit as bad as it looked. Partly this was down to the FA having the temerity to not bow to the pressure. These were newspapers that boasted they won elections and could make or break a celebrity's career when they spoke. The arrogance of popularity. Robson's treatment was not just about selling newspapers. It was about the FA daring to not listen.

Robson survived this period through the loyalty and love of his closest circle. His dear wife Elsie and family stood by his side throughout. Another he relied upon was his right-hand man. Don Howe questioned whether Robson should continue as England manager under this immense pressure but once the boss told him he was staying, Howe was too. Their relationship helped Robson survive the onslaught if only for giving him someone to vent to on the inside. He reflected on the friendship in a TV interview in 2001 while Newcastle United manager, 'Quite ridiculous, and outrageous, and obscene what happened to me but there it is, that's what happened. Couldn't stop it, nothing I could do about it … he [Howe] was very sensible about it, very intelligent, and he was very supportive of me, so he stood with me, that's why he's been a great close associate of mine and I've loved the fella, and I mean loved him.'

Their friendship and working relationship meant the very best way to combat the press for both of them was just to get on with the job. They enjoyed the work; they were not going to let the back pages spoil it for them. The pressure was real and present throughout, however. A friendly early in the year against Greece was the next chance for a potential open season. 'I'm here to fry Bobby Robson,' the *Daily Mirror*'s Nigel Clarke told ITV's cameras upon arriving in Athens. Rather inconveniently for him, England won.

Robson used the game to look at Des Walker, David Rocastle and Alan Smith again, all three starting alongside some more experienced heads. It nearly turned into a disaster, England gathering themselves together after going 1-0 down to a first-minute penalty. Terry Butcher's challenge was rash, but also just outside the area. The small audience of 6,000 fans cheered or jeered depending on their allegiance in an Olympic Stadium that held over ten times that amount when full. Penalty given, pencils were being sharpened in the press box.

Unfortunately for them England responded, and John Barnes equalised within six minutes. His free kick struck the bar and went in off the goalkeeper's hand. From that moment on, Greece retreated and England attacked until half-time. Better finishing might have seen them 3-1 ahead but it was not to be. The second half turned to attrition as Greece dug in. England rallied and got the winner with 11 minutes to go, Bryan Robson's 25-yard volley the least they deserved in truth.

Notably the crowd of local fans that had bothered to come spent a considerable amount of time goading the small England following. For a change there was very little response even as seats were thrown at them in the wake of the second goal. There had been a couple of idiots who gave a Nazi salute during the national anthem but there was no sign of a National Front flag. In reality it was no step forward, more that hardly any of England's following had come and certainly not enough to misbehave on command. There were so few in the ground that after the final whistle the English could be heard distinctly. Bobby Robson's interview was moved to the tunnel so some agricultural language could not be heard.

'After you've been hit over the head like we have been in the last six months it was a relief to get a win,' he told reporters. It hadn't been pretty, but it had been important. With a couple of ghosts put to bed England then travelled into the unknown and came away from Albania with exactly what they had gone for: a 2-0 win. The result proved to be a brief salvation from the usual press onslaught as England had impressed with their professionalism if not their creativity. Rocastle was neat and tidy, Peter Shilton terrific and Bryan Robson the driving force as ever.

England's inconsistent wing men suffered differing fortunes in the game. Chris Waddle was tasked with playing up front with Lineker and struggled to form a partnership. Lineker was not at his ruthless best yet, still finding his way back into fitness and form, plus he was struggling with new Barcelona manager Johan Cruyff. Waddle did nothing wrong but they drifted through the game rather than gelled.

Barnes, however, was good. Not exceptional, but a level of good he had struggled to find at times in international football. His free kick and performance against Greece had set a tone, and this was another step forward towards consistency. His nicely taken goal in the 17th minute calmed the nerves. His delivery allowed Bryan Robson to head a second just past the hour to settle it.

England, for once, could be completely happy with their work in taking three points from a tight game. Importantly they were already top of the group and next up Albania were coming to Wembley. By the time that game was due to be played English football had irrevocably changed forever.

* * *

Some dates stay with you forever, and rarely for good reasons. They are the moments when everyone remembers where they were whether they were involved or not. Often they are era-defining, and nearly always a dividing line for a before and after. For English football that date is 15 April 1989. Specifically, Hillsborough. An obscene death toll and all from fans who just went to watch the football. A lack of protection from those you should automatically be able to trust with a duty of care. Lies, smears and cover-ups. Ninety-six dead, 766 injured. In a litany of dark days for English football, this truly was its darkest.

There are several books that go into far more detail than I ever could about the disaster, the inquests, and the incredible and inspirational fight by several groups to try to bring some justice and consequence to those who deserved it. I recommend every football fan read at least one. The scenes described on the day – the helpless crush, the heroism, the abject failure of authority – will never leave you. Ninety-six dead, 766 injured. Those numbers should never be forgotten.

Boosted sales figures from negativity around football meant Hillsborough's coverage was always going to lead on blaming fans as hooligans. The extent to which all truth or evidence was ignored to do so by press and authorities remains utterly shocking. Such was the negative feeling towards the sport that as Roger Domeneghetti wrote in *From the Back Page to the Front Room*, 'Liverpool and Nottingham Forest arrived at Hillsborough on 15 April 1989 to be confronted by a police force and ultimately a media which viewed them all as hooligans.' Desmond Morris's folk devils in full effect.

Four days after the disaster *The Sun* published the headline that rightly still shames it to this day: 'THE TRUTH'. That two-word header had been specifically chosen by Kelvin MacKenzie over his other option, 'YOU SCUM'. That word, 'truth', is unequivocal. It is used so there can be no further debate. Before any investigation had been completed, they decided they had their verdict based on word from a police force beginning to understand they were in serious danger of being at fault and second-hand information from a Sheffield MP not in attendance at the game.

Their allegations were appalling. The three subheadings for the article were:

'Some fans picked pockets of victims'

'Some fans urinated on the brave cops'

'Some fans beat up PC giving kiss of life'

Yet somehow it got worse from there. Football fans were described as having 'viciously attacked rescue workers as they tried to revive victims'. An unnamed 'high ranking police officer' said his men faced a 'double hell – the disaster and the fury of the fans who attacked us'. There was even a story about Liverpool supporters shouting at a policeman trying to revive a partially clothed female victim to 'throw her up here' so they could '**** her'. The truth? Lies. Every one of them.

Other newspapers, including the *Daily Mirror*, ran with the same information. The difference was their articles were clear to point out that these were allegations by police officers. There was a growing feeling in most newsrooms, and quietly in government too, that all was not well with the emerging 'official' story. So much so in fact that some papers printed almost immediate stories taking the edge off those reports, or outright retractions. The *Daily Mail* took the allegations and preferred instead to focus on the Home Secretary Douglas Hurd ordering an end to what was becoming a very public war of words between the Liverpool and South Yorkshire Police Federations.

The day after *The Sun* delivered its verdict, it chose to dig deeper into its position in a front-page piece under the headline 'The truth hurts'. While utterly horrific, this approach was one built on experience. Football fans were always hooligans, hooligans were always to blame, blame sold newspapers. But this wasn't rioting at Euro 88. This was a tragedy caused by negligence.

The trap *The Sun* had willingly fallen into was that when you got the reaction you wanted for demonising an entire group for the actions of a vocal and public minority, it was very difficult to stop doing it. Others were not immune to this either. Two days after the tragedy, UEFA president Jacques George, with limited information, said in talking about Liverpool fans that 'this region seems to have a particularly aggressive mentality' and that he had the impression they were 'beasts who wanted to charge'.

English football was in mourning. Immediate perspective is never a comfortable thing. As recently as a week before the game there had been a row about Arsenal's season-ending trip to Liverpool being played three days before the vital qualifier coming up against Albania. It had set the FA at odds with ITV as it had been moved for television. It all seemed so insignificant suddenly.

What Hillsborough did was create a sea change on many levels. Lord Justice Peter Taylor was appointed to produce *The Hillsborough Stadium Disaster Inquiry Report*. The investigation found a consistent failure in the policing of the game and condemned the South Yorkshire Police, adding that their refusal to accept any blame and desire to instead point at the fans as the sole determining factor 'gives cause for anxiety as to whether lessons had been learned'. He also noted that it would be 'more seemly and encouraging for the future if responsibility [by the South Yorkshire Police] had been faced'.

The Taylor Report also identified the abject condition of some stadiums. The steps taken to stop fans entering the pitch at many – high fences and pens for away fans in particular – were actually a huge safety concern. They had become a literal death trap at Hillsborough. One wonders what the Lord Justice would have made of Ken Bates's electric fence if he had been allowed to keep it. Safety standards that had led to the Bradford fire had yet again proved to be so low that innocent people had lost their lives. There had been a failure from football authorities to enact universal guidelines that had to be adhered to, and furthermore failure of government to demand them.

From that awful day came change at a price nobody should be expected to pay. Stadiums were upgraded by mandate across the country to all-seaters over the next few years or moves to new ones taken where refurbishment was not a realistic option. The move away from standing at grounds was, perhaps, one of the fundamental measures to eradicate violence in stadiums due to the easier identification process by seat, the ability to refuse entry to known season ticket holders, and by making it harder to physically move around a football ground. A side effect from an incident not caused by hooliganism.

Policing and safety standards also changed, all for more stringent measures with proper accountability. The disaster and the Taylor Report's 43 immediate 'minimum' recommendations are fundamental moments in time for English football that still resonate today. That figure would rise to 76 in the final report completed in early 1990. As I said previously, I would urge you all to read about the fight for actual justice yourselves.

What Lord Justice Taylor also identified were 'false reports', namely and directly the actions described by *The Sun* as the truth. The Lord Justice pointed out that not one called witness had corroborated any part of the allegations, and those who passed on the accusations couldn't produce anyone to make them stand up to scrutiny when asked to. 'Those who made them, and those who disseminated them, would have done better to hold their peace,' reads point number 257 of the interim report.

This information was another step along the way of football fans trying to reclaim the sport as their own from the clutches of the media narrative. Fanzines, and publications like *When Saturday Comes* and others, had all started with the intention of not only giving a voice to the supporter, but to prove such a thing existed despite what the tabloids wanted you to believe. Now that became their mission.

The first *When Saturday Comes* published after Hillsborough ran with a cover that not only spoke to the incident but summed up the media attitude to football. It simply printed four photos. One each of Graham Kelly, Margaret Thatcher and Chief Constable Peter Wright (the man in charge of the South Yorkshire Police), all with a speech bubble with the words 'it wasn't our fault' in it. The final photo was of a massed group of football fans, again with a speech bubble but this time saying, 'Oh well, it must be our fault again.'

The government had introduced the Football Supporters Act to push through their ID card system. The arguments about this had gone back and forth but those in charge were insistent that anyone going to a game would have to give their passport number ideally (although other methods were being discussed) to be checked and then get a membership card issued before they could buy a ticket at any ground. Football had been resistant and the fall-out from Hillsborough and the now obvious conclusion, if not actual admission of any sort, that the sport's problems went beyond just the fans saw it eventually collapse.

England's game against Albania at Wembley took place on a mild Wednesday evening 11 days after the disaster. Around three quarters of the 60,602 in attendance were seated, with the remaining 25 per cent standing but behind fences that had now been radically reengineered to be instantly removable in the event of a crush. A minute's silence was observed before kick-off and the atmosphere felt different. Liverpool had not even trained since the semi-final, but Steve McMahon and Peter Beardsley took the decision to join up with the squad – Beardsley starting on the night. Barnes had been otherwise committed to attend one of the many funerals Liverpool's players and staff took it upon themselves to be present for, and emotionally withdrew himself from selection. Despite the way they had been treated by some, the whole of Merseyside had reacted with an incredible level of grace and sensitivity.

As the players ran through the pre-kick-off formalities, all with black armbands on, the crowd broke into a chorus of 'You'll Never Walk Alone'. Beardsley was visibly moved. Before the game, Robson had been almost apologetic with the press that it had to be played at all. He had done the only thing he could and pointed to the potential 'boost for our football' if the country won. It was up to the players now.

On a night where, to quote a cliché, football needed to be the winner, English football to be specific, it turned out as well as anyone dared to hope. Lineker broke his lull with the first goal, a simple header for his first international strike in 11 months. Beardsley was the man of the match by some way and added a second to put England in total control less than 15 minutes in. He added a third just past the hour, his brace assisted by Lineker in a role reversal. That goal was the signal to make a couple of changes, including Paul Gascoigne on for David Rocastle and debutant Paul Parker into the fray for Gary Stevens. Gascoigne's first meaningful contribution was to set up Waddle for a fourth goal with a lovely header back across the six-yard box. Waddle had also had a fine game and deserved something tangible from it.

Gascoigne was drifting into space and enjoying himself against beaten opposition. He linked with Beardsley to jink past three players in the box in a brilliant dribble that saw him cross when he should have taken the shot on. With two minutes to go his moment came. Parker spotted his run into space still some 40 yards from goal. Gascoigne collected the ball, shrugged off one challenge and burst between two more. Now inside the box he picked his spot and passed the ball into the net for a brilliant goal, his first and England's fifth. Vindication for the building clamour to get him into the team. An unforgettable cameo.

The night ended 5-0 and with another chorus of Liverpool's anthem as everyone left the pitch. There was only one player anyone wanted to talk to Bobby Robson about post-match. The BBC's Tony Gubba waited a single question before asking about Gascoigne. Robson gave one of the all-time great responses. 'I'm going to spend two hours with him tomorrow to try and restore a bit of confidence, he's lacking in confidence isn't he the boy,' he said, smiling, 'and we need two balls – one for him, and one for the team.'

* * *

Robson and Gascoigne had met long before he was given six minutes from the bench for his international debut against Denmark. In 1981 Gascoigne had taken part in a TV series for transmission the following year called *Robson's Choice*. A bunch of hand-picked young footballers trained at Ipswich Town under the future England manager for a week all captured for television. In Gascoigne's own words, the first thing he did on film was flash the camera a grin and then 'slipped and went straight on my arse'.

Gascoigne rarely did things quietly. As a schoolboy he was a precocious talent, and he knew it. He was close to signing for Middlesbrough, Southampton really wanted him, but he only had eyes for one club, Newcastle United. Having impressed for Redheugh Boys Club and Gateshead Boys he knew the Middlesbrough contract wasn't going anywhere. He had told everybody at school he was going to be a footballer and for most the anxiety and risk involved would have meant taking the first offer he had. He waited though. He knew. He had told people he was going to play for Newcastle, and that's exactly what he did when they finally offered him schoolboy forms not long after his 13th birthday.

At Newcastle he was destined for greatness from an early age. He was moved up when his schooling allowed to play with the full apprentices, all 16 or older. His teachers had little faith in him academically but invited him to join in their five-a-side games after school. Some loved him, and some used it as an excuse to try to put him in his place. Either way, no one could get near him.

Schoolboy forms progressed with age to an apprentice contract and he was made Kevin Keegan's boot boy when he signed for the club full-time in 1982. He spent his apprenticeship near-constantly receiving special or extra training. They got his weight down and his stamina up, and by the middle of 1985 he had made his first team debut and captained the youth team to win their version of the FA Cup. England flew out to Mexico 86 with Paul Gascoigne a Newcastle first-team regular. A year later he made his debut for the under-21s in the Toulon Tournament and was the cover star for that year's edition of the *Rothmans Football Yearbook*. The talk of a promotion to the full international side had already begun.

By the end of Euro 88 the noise had become a chorus, Gascoigne was a Tottenham Hotspur player and that full England debut from the bench was earned. There was a reason he was still making cameos rather than leading the orchestra, however. That innate ability to always be the loudest in the room came with several drawbacks.

In April 1986 Gascoigne received his first red card for punching a Birmingham player off the ball in a tight match they were only winning 1-0 at the time. He then burst into tears as he left the pitch and had to be calmed down as he kicked anything in sight once in the tunnel. Early in his England under-21 career, manager Dave Sexton had been moved to put that restriction on him receiving another booking as he felt he had been lucky to not get sent off. For all his talent his frustration could get the better of him. Some games passed him by and he would often end up lashing out, becoming a regular in the referee's notebook from a young age. Others he illuminated but attracted chaos, managers learning early that the concept of a position didn't often appear in the world of Paul Gascoigne.

Even for all his brilliance in his 25 minutes against Albania he had also shown why Robson was not quite sold on Gascoigne becoming England's future. He had entered the action with explicit instructions to play on the right of midfield. Naturally the first thing he did was head over to the left to try and get a touch of the ball. From there he drifted to the right of the attack, almost making a three as he played so high with Lineker central and Beardsley left. From there he assisted Waddle's goal. After a lonely minute or two actually playing where he was told he decided to try the left again, and then went central behind the strikers for the next five minutes. After that he dropped a bit deeper where he basically played centrally for the rest of the game, giving Parker a whole flank to defend alone.

A tired and beaten Albania had not been able to use his indiscipline to attack in any meaningful sense but Robson was annoyed. In that same interview he explained through slightly gritted teeth, 'At one time I thought he was going to play in the front row of F-Stand as he played all over the pitch except in the position I told him to play!' The talent was obvious but at international level indiscipline cost you. There was a little way to go for Paul Gascoigne to become Gazza.

Robson had been impressed, excited, annoyed and then worried about how to harness this young footballer's enthusiasm. He felt Gascoigne needed to try harder in training and have a better diet for one. He did instinctively know he was special though. 'He's a rare talent which we need to nurture … we need to give him his head sometimes and he needs to be disciplined as well,' he told the BBC. As much as Robson knew the press would beg for Gascoigne's inclusion, he wanted to see some substance to go along with the mountains of style.

After Hillsborough and with what looked like it had the potential to be the most dramatic conclusion to a domestic season ever with Arsenal's trip to Anfield coming three days later, the lack of appetite for the summer's first Rous Cup fixture was understandable. Chile were the year's guests and hardly a draw, so much so that a record low of just 15,628 came to Wembley on a Tuesday night in May.

Robson gave Gascoigne a start and also handed debuts to Nottingham Forest's Nigel Clough and Wimbledon's John Fashanu. Chile had no intention of actually playing football and repeatedly fouled, kicked, pushed and dived their way to a 0-0 draw. Both debutants failed to offer anything more than willing running. Gascoigne stayed in position but couldn't break free of a midfield designed by their opponents to become a swamp.

On the Friday night Arsenal sensationally won the title with a last-minute goal. Culturally the significance of this cannot be understated. Where the Hillsborough disaster brought about the physical changes English football required to resurrect itself, that night at Anfield where it was up for grabs now convinced the right people of the value of domestic football as a spectacle again. Television rights suddenly had a commercial appeal after a decade of cutting to terraces alive with violence and a commentator's condemnation and apology.

There was a long way to go but, faintly in the distance, the very first light at the end of the tunnel could just be seen. This was matched by an increase in actual attendances at games across the season of over half a million people despite the constant reports of violence. Importantly on that night at Anfield, after Arsenal's 2-0 win there was no reaction and no riot. Liverpool fans had seen enough, been through enough, and had been demonised wrongly so they knew something else was needed. Arsenal's grandstand victory was actually met with applause 'without reservation', as David Miller wrote in *The Times*.

The following day England played the annual fixture with Scotland and it only produced a couple of things of note. Firstly, they won 2-0 to take the Rous Cup for a third, and final, time. The tournament would not return and the oldest fixture in international football would not actually be played again until 1996. The Rous Cup had lost its value and yet again incidents occurred across Glasgow as fans fought in isolated pockets. Over 250 England and Scotland fans were arrested, although very few were actually charged. A visible section of England fans in the ground clashed where they could but were pushed back by an eager police force. There was just no need to put a flashpoint into the annual calendar like this.

Secondly, the game saw a new striker enter the England fray. Fashanu had looked out of his depth and struggled against Chile. He was forced off by injury after only half an hour but that was his brief England career finished. Tony Cottee made his first international start and after an ineffective 75 minutes in his seventh cap he was also subbed, and his England career was over. Fashanu's replacement was from the lower leagues, Wolverhampton Wanderers' goal machine Steve Bull. Wolves had been promoted from the Fourth Division in the 1987/88 season and Bull had scored an incredible 52 goals in all competitions. They had then been promoted from the Third Division in the season just gone and he had scored an equally mindblowing 50 more. Robson had been forced to look further down the divisions due to the availability of others, and Bull did not let him down.

In the 82nd minute he jumped for a long Stuart Pearce cross that actually hit his back and then broke his way. Bull lashed in the loose ball with the finish of a man high on over 100 goals scored in two seasons, to add to Waddle's first-half header. England had their first-choice striker in Lineker but had been looking for a better quality of backup for years. Many had tried and failed but maybe Robson finally had his man.

* * *

Exactly a week after England's trip to Glasgow their World Cup qualification aims took a huge leap with an excellent performance against Poland at Wembley on the first Saturday in June. With a full-strength team to pick from and two away games to finish the group it was vital they won this one, and they did in some style.

Gascoigne was not trusted but nobody could really complain after a comprehensive 3-0 victory. Shilton equalled Bobby Moore's record of 108 England caps and was rarely troubled as Bobby Robson asked his men to get on the front foot early again. Lineker's excellently taken goal from the tightest of angles was scant reward for their first-half dominance. Poland were poor, far from the challenge some had built up. The Des Walker/Terry Butcher defensive partnership was flourishing and snuffed out what little danger there was.

Barnes added a second with 20 minutes to go, volleying in Stevens's cross. Neil Webb added a third after a defensive calamity and the job really was done. Since the start of the year England had beaten Greece, Albania twice, Scotland, Poland, and drawn with Chile. It might not have been breathtaking throughout but the slow rebuild after the last six months of 1988 was on course. They finished off the season four days later with a very tired 1-1 draw in Denmark. The game had been organised to celebrate the DBU's centenary and ended up being heavy in substitutes and light on quality.

England would not play again until a vital qualifier in September away to Sweden, although that was not to say that Robson would be out of the news. In mid June allegations were run in the tabloids that the England manager had not one, but two mistresses. The first was Pauline Ridal and Robson was forced to admit a brief indiscretion in a story riddled with 'errors, inaccuracies, distortions of the truth and lots of discrepancies'. The tabloids had taken the most basic of facts and put them through their own hyperbolic filter yet again

'What I did was daft, I was pretty stupid,' he told Lynda Lee-Potter in 2002. Elsie stood by him, for which he was eternally grateful, as did the FA who moved to announce immediately they would be taking no action despite the tabloids suggesting yet again he should quit. The *Sunday Mirror* was not satisfied, however. It found a second alleged mistress who had 'kept a diary'. This was going to be turned into a salacious tell-all book that would shame the nation. Janet Rush's tome never made it to publication, if it ever existed in the first place, and indeed if any of the alleged affair took place. Personally, I have my doubts. The *Mirror*'s Monday edition decided that 'the latest revelation must put his England future in doubt'. It didn't, Robson choosing as ever to throw himself into his work again. A fortnight of tabloid stories, heavily enhanced or outright fabricated, and still they couldn't get their man.

By the time of the trip to Sweden, Robson's mood towards the press was particularly low. The day before the game, with England allowed to train on the pitch at the Rasunda Stadium in Solna, there were two questions to be answered. Would Gascoigne be trusted to start in such a tight game with Bryan Robson unavailable due to injury, and would the more defensively suited David Rocastle start or Waddle and Barnes to go for it? Robson trained his team in formation in what he thought was secrecy, unaware many in the press corps were watching while eating at the stadium restaurant.

Gascoigne was not in the starting line-up, while Waddle and Barnes both were. At the press conference held later it became apparent the word was out in both the English and Swedish media about his planned surprise to play Waddle. Robson, paranoid after a summer of headlines from the red tops, was extremely angry.

He refused to confirm that he would be going with that team in spite of all the evidence to the contrary and called anyone who had made an effort to view the training 'cheats and spies'. Most who had seen were only at the ground to grab something to eat before the press conference. He was absolutely insistent that 'there is value in secrecy' as he was asked again about his team. 'We tried to keep D-Day secret,' he said now with any lingering sense of perspective long gone, 'and Adolf Hitler didn't tell us when the Germans sent over their doodlebugs!'

The training ground team was still *the* team on the day with Terry Butcher picked as captain. England needed two draws from these two away games to qualify. What followed was a tense and cagey match, with neither side willing to risk the loss. In the 27th minute, Swedish striker Johnny Ekstrom rose and clashed heads with the England skipper. Butcher was a bleeder; he had suffered a very dangerous injury as a result of a broken nose that wouldn't stop gushing blood for days in 1982. The situation had become life-threatening at one point and he had needed almost continuous transfusions.

Here the gash to his head opened immediately. The best the England medical team could do was to wrap his head in bandage until half-time when they could stitch it properly. Butcher bled through the wrap almost instantly and went off at the interval for treatment. They cleaned it up, doctors working double time to get him ready before the bell for the second half, but only seven of the ten stitches needed were completed. Butcher went out for the second half and started to bleed almost immediately again. Not long after his first header he was covered.

Both teams continued to gently probe rather than go for it, and both had chances to score. England's best fell to Waddle who went for the near post when far was the option and missed. Butcher continued on until the final whistle, and at the end even his socks were covered in blood. Yet another one of English football's iconic images was born as he celebrated a 0-0 draw and vital point. He walked off smiling despite losing blood from his forehead and now a secondary cut by his eyebrow caused by another clash of heads. Butcher had become the walking embodiment of something a section of English society cherishes – the bloodied hero, the gallant warrior.

He made the front and back pages the following morning with each photo used a slight variant on the same theme. His manager was still in hyperbolic mood but rightly claimed it was the bravest performance he had ever seen. Butcher's heroics had set the tone for the team on the night with a point earned through hard work and discipline. Even Gascoigne, on with 20 minutes to go as the result of a bad injury to Webb, dared not misbehave in front of the captain. Steve McMahon was dropped deeper to sit in front of the defence, covering for Gascoigne's tendency to wander. Both worked hard and helped see the game out to the delight of the manager.

Webb's injury would unfortunately go on to define his career. While he played on once recovered from the ruptured Achilles tendon he was never quite the same player. He still had more to give in an England shirt yet but he was never again an automatic first choice as it looked like he might be at one point. A good player who looked for a time like he might be a great one, he wouldn't feature for England again for nearly ten months.

Off the pitch it had been another sorry night according to the newspapers. All ran headlines about violence across Stockholm. 'They Shame Us All Again' screamed the *Daily Mail* in a report on clashes with police, vandalism, burglary, and made it appear the night had become something out of a war film. Some 102 England fans were arrested before the game and violence had started on a ferry on the way over – 'Soccer's Ship of Shame'. In total over 100 England fans left the country under deportation orders.

However, many fans returned surprised at the level of press the violence had earned. With the Hillsborough coverage no doubt a factor, quite a few had learned that all wasn't as it was always told. In his seminal book *All Played Out*, Pete Davies devotes a chapter to the 'headlines on acid' and 'strange news from Stockholm' where it became clear to him that there had been violence and hooliganism, but not on the scale described by the newspapers. For example: 'One store that the papers said was smashed to smithereens,' he wrote of a Channel Four investigation that backed up his theory, 'hadn't been touched.' In the days before social media and live coverage there was also no need for tabloid accountability it seemed.

The result left England with the job of going to Poland needing a point to be sure of qualification. Again they were tight, controlled and disciplined, and relied on a hero to save them. This time it was Peter Shilton who had a memorable game. Now 40 years old, he produced a string of first-half saves to keep England in it as Poland fought for their World Cup lives. The second half settled down a little but all in white were grateful that a last-minute shot from Ryszard Tarasiewicz hit the bar with the goalkeeper finally beaten. Another 0-0 draw, another precious point and England qualified as one of the best second-place finishers.

They ended the year with two home friendlies as preparations began. A very strong Italy side were held 0-0 at Wembley in an impressive performance that saw debuts from the bench for Dave Beasant, Mike Phelan, Nigel Winterburn and a certain David Platt. Then in December, Yugoslavia were beaten 2-1 with Bryan Robson scoring twice, his first after 38 seconds. It rounded out a year in which England had not been beaten and been impressive in games to varying degrees. All eyes were now on next summer. Bobby Robson's second World Cup could surely not provide the drama of his first.

1990

January

On 9 December 1989, Bobby Robson nervously awaited his team's fate in the 1990 World Cup draw. His luck had deserted him after they made hard work of Mexico 86's group stage despite being given all they could ask for. Euro 88 qualification had been negotiated but they had to beat an extremely promising Yugoslavia side twice. As reward they had been handed the toughest group possible. What would fate bring Robson now?

In one of football's starriest-ever draws, footage was shown of Pope John Paul receiving a model of the World Cup from FIFA president Joao Havelange in a private Vatican audience for officials and organisers. Then at an indoor arena in Rome a cast of football's living legends was assembled including a reunion for Pelé and Bobby Moore. They watched Luciano Pavarotti sing, Sophia Loren defy ageing, and the names drawn one-by-one almost as an afterthought.

Two days previously, England had been announced as sixth seeds, to grumbling across Europe. The Netherlands felt their Euro 88 win should have given them preferential treatment; Spain had a better record in recent World Cups having matched England's and also qualified for 1978. Their argument was not just with England but also fifth seeds Belgium. FIFA had worked out a formula to determine it all, but the details didn't really add up. Havelange had also previously stated that Spain would be seeded come the draw. FIFA defended their position. Everyone knew what was really going on.

What the seeding meant was that England could and would be placed into Group F. The significance of this was that all games in that group were to be played on the islands of Sardinia and Sicily. After Heysel there was a serious concern about England's fans coming to the Italian mainland. Confining them to an island was seen as an easy but key part of the strategy to combat hooliganism. Once the draw was made, the British government went further and requested all England's games were played in Sardinia to avoid any travel at all.

Group F, on paper, looked hellish for England. First, on 11 June they would play Jack Charlton's Republic of Ireland. After Euro 88 and with this Irish side now established as resolutely difficult to beat off the back of only conceding two goals in eight qualifying matches, it looked an incredibly difficult first game. A few days later they would play the Netherlands, whose Ruud Gullit and Marco van Basten were now mainstays in the Milan side that had just won back-to-back European Cups. The Dutch were installed as favourites to win the group immediately. England would finish on 21 June against Egypt who represented everything the English struggled against – a team happy to sit deep and get bodies behind the ball.

Fortunately, hope came in the form of the structure of the draw. First and second would qualify for the knockout rounds, and four of the best third-placed finishers from the six groups would also go through to make a round of 16. If England could get a win and a draw, they could likely afford to lose one and still qualify. It was a decent margin for error but Euro 88 loomed large in the rear-view mirror still.

Domestically, the year started with John Barnes struggling with a persistent hamstring problem. He had missed the Yugoslavia friendly in December with the injury and there were rumours he might be out for a longer spell if it went again. Bobby Robson was sold on two wingers at this point and to lose or not have a fully fit Barnes for the summer would be a huge blow. Bryan Robson was dealing with an injury, a groin strain, but was expected back within a few weeks.

Paul Gascoigne was in the news as ever. On New Year's Day he got frustrated during a goalless draw with Coventry City and cracked a bone in his arm after lashing out at midfielder Lloyd McGrath. A few days earlier his Spurs side had been playing Nottingham Forest. Gascoigne's performance had been so erratic that Forest manager Brian Clough had been moved to leave his dugout and tell him to get back and help his Spurs team-mates in midfield.

Gascoigne, in a plaster cast, met up with a provisional 30-man England squad for a two-day get-together that Robson had organised in lieu of an arranged game. All those invited except the Arsenal contingent turned up, as Nigel Winterburn, Michael Thomas, Tony Adams and David Rocastle all withdrew through injury. The players met at Lilleshall where they underwent some basic fitness and health tests. Webb, now recovered from the Achilles injury but not having played yet, was invited. All were given a couple of talks about what needed to be done for the summer including diet and acclimatisation advice. Robson was leaving nothing to chance.

The surprise inclusion was Manchester City midfielder Paul Lake, who was promising but already struggling with injuries. Aston Villa winger Tony Daley was also included and had been brilliant during the season. If Barnes was injured Robson would have to consider his options and Daley was versatile enough to play on either flank if required. All were informed that the England manager would be naming a squad of 40 in April that he would then be refining down to the 22 he would take to Italy. The likes of Shilton, Butcher, Robson and Lineker could start learning enough Italian to convince a waiter, but there were plenty of other places up for grabs.

England also had their first friendly of the year confirmed as Brazil would visit in late March. Then Czechoslovakia would come to Wembley, and then Denmark and Uruguay in quick succession, before leaving for Sardinia. Bobby Charlton had been asked about England's prospects after being drawn in the same group as his brother Jack's Republic of Ireland. He immediately tipped England to win the whole tournament and Ireland to not get out the group.

February

The Taylor Report had been published in full by late January. Subsequently football was back on the agenda for parliament throughout for the next few weeks. The recommendations to be implemented meant huge change for the English game. Stadiums across all professional leagues were to be made all-seater with government input and approval required via the Advisory Design Council. Where terraces were to be used during building works, far stricter protocols on capacity numbers, safety certificates and crush barriers were to be implemented immediately.

Football clubs were also tasked with a far higher set of minimum standards on matchdays across the board. The police force the same. Responsibility was to be taken for every aspect of a crowd watching football and a duty of care maintained. Greater punishments and bans were to be handed out to any fans found to be breaching any aspect of the new system. Safety was now paramount, zero tolerance the way forward.

The conclusions of the Taylor Report caused debate about all aspects of football, so much so that Bobby Robson even ordered his players not to overreact when and if they scored at the World Cup. The idea was to keep the reaction on the pitch at a level that they hoped would be reflected in the stands. 'They [goal celebrations] are bad for the game, for fans, and they're dangerous too,' he told the assembled crowd at the gala dinner to launch the brand-new Sir Stanley Matthews Award for sportsmanship. English football was finally doing something about English football, even if they appeared to be starting at a comparatively micro level for macro problems.

Robson then joined FA chairman Bert Millichip in Stockholm for the draw for Euro 92 qualifying. Both were disappointed to not only face the Republic of Ireland again with all that entailed, but also Poland who could be difficult as their last away game had proved. The final team were the much-improved Turkey, who were no longer an easy ride. Millichip used the trip to restate his case that the government needed to implement a second part of the Football Supporters Act to give the courts power to stop known troublemakers from travelling to watch England.

On the pitch Gascoigne was back for Spurs in better form, the bit now between his teeth in regard to getting into that World Cup squad. Barnes was okay, still being nursed through, but the main worry was Bryan Robson who returned to training only to break down the very first time he kicked a ball.

The England captain's appalling luck with injury was a deep concern at this point. Since starting his professional career in 1976 he had broken his right leg twice, torn his ankle ligaments, broken his nose twice, infamously dislocated his shoulder three times, suffered several concussions including one in an incident where he swallowed his tongue, bruised his ribs, fractured his left leg and played on it, pulled each hamstring more than once, and now was suffering with a groin injury that wouldn't go away. It was eventually diagnosed as a tear bad enough to have surgery. He would be out all of March and well into April as a minimum.

March

The newspapers shifted their agenda slightly, but the overarching message remained the same: Bobby Robson could not remain in the job. The World Cup and the draw for the Euros both afforded a chance to look forward. That and a lack of actual international football year to date presented a window to speculate.

The tabloids continued to snipe at any and every given opportunity. At this point everyone knew both their aim and their reasons. The *Daily Mail*'s Jeff Powell was also reporting that the FA had told Robson to 'Win it or else!' in a story that when you drilled into the detail consisted of a couple of Bert Millichip quotes and an interpretation of the bookies' odds on the next England manager. He was also still adamant that the new man should already be working within the current set-up and learning his future job as they would be 'no better prepared than a Page Three girl suddenly asked to play opposite Sir Alec Guinness at the Old Vic' if coming in from the outside.

The two names that kept coming up were Graham Taylor and Howard Kendall, with Terry Venables most often mentioned as the outsider's choice. Powell would get his wish if Taylor was to get the job as he was brought into the fold to help scout England's upcoming opponents along with, among others, John Lyall, Howard Wilkinson and Dave Sexton. Robson was building a cabal of knowledge to help him over the summer. Mexico 86 had been a good experience overall but the spectre of Euro 88 demanded that he look beyond what had been done before.

One of the favourite current ploys from tabloid to broadsheet was to keep guessing as to the make-up of Robson's upcoming squad. Had Steve Bull done enough? Would Neil Webb make it? Who was covering Bryan Robson? Why was Paul Gascoigne not trusted? Among the wildcards were new names like Matthew Le Tissier, Southampton's unorthodox genius in waiting who had just outscored his career goals tally to date in a single season. Ray Wilkins and Gordon Cowans were both linked with surprise recalls to bring some experience with both in excellent form, but at 33 and 32 respectively it felt like a flight of fancy.

Norwich City's central defender Andy Linighan was also a journalist's favourite when asked for the runners and riders with Mark Wright's inclusion no longer a given. Wright had fallen out of favour when Robson felt he had been too eager to miss the final game against the USSR at the European Championship with what he felt was a minor injury. A few months later the England manager would recount this in his autobiography *Against The Odds* and describe Wright as 'giving himself an excuse if he played badly'. Wright did not take it well despite being given a glowing reference when picked for Robson's 'Dream Team' later in the book.

By the end of the month everyone was glad to have some actual football to talk about. Robson had not been happy that circumstances had conspired to give him over three months without so much as a friendly to look at his team, exclaiming, 'What a joke that is in a World Cup year!' On 28 March

Brazil were in town and finally the footballs were back out of the cupboard at Lilleshall. Webb and Bryan Robson were there only to observe but Bobby invited them to meet up with the squad and feel part of things. There were no surprises, and Gascoigne was included but this was not to be his game. In place of the injured Captain Marvel in midfield, Aston Villa's David Platt was selected. Gascoigne was privately quite nervous about his World Cup chances and the manager's press conference the day before the game did little to calm his nerves. 'I made up my mind a couple of weeks ago to pick Platt,' Robson told reporters. 'He was in good form and Gascoigne was a little up and down.'

Brazil proved to be just as big a draw as they had been in 1987. Wembley was full, with its capacity slightly reduced to 80,000 as seats had been installed in place of all terracing on the Taylor Report's recommendation. Robson played his strongest team and was rewarded with an excellent performance. Brazil played in their blue away kit, something which would provide a decent piece of pub trivia by making them harder to recognise when the footage was used in the video to England's World Cup song, 'World in Motion'.

Peter Shilton was substituted just 11 minutes in as a nasty collision with Des Walker's elbow left him with a cut above his left eye. Chris Woods came on and was rarely tested as England were incredibly neat and tidy for a change. Lineker's stooping header after 37 minutes put the home side ahead and they deserved it on balance. Beardsley's near-post corner was flicked on by Barnes, Platt's late run into the box gave the Brazilian line far too much to think about and Lineker was left in space to nod in.

That was the way it finished after a second half in which England defended well but were grateful neither linesman nor referee thought Stuart Pearce had handled Muller's shot on the line. Having got away with one it felt like their night from that moment on. Careca struggled to find a finish when one-on-one with Woods, and Muller lifted his best chance over the bar.

A few things were decided by the 1-0 win. Woods had sealed the number two spot after competition from David Seaman and Dave Beasant. It was now down to those two to fight it out for the number three position going to Italy. Woods had come on early and settled immediately into the game, so he would be trusted to do so again if required. Waddle and Barnes had both played well and covered their respective full-backs enough to convince Robson that he could risk playing two wingers when playing high-quality opposition. A key part of England's attack was now decided. He also realised that Barnes and Beardsley were again coming to the end of a long season with Liverpool and this time would be nursed through training a little before the tournament to avoid burn out. Gary Stevens was the one player to have had a rough night, the right-back run around by Branco and repeatedly looking the weakest of the back four. His position was one to think about.

The last thing the England manager now knew was that Platt was definitely coming with them. His first start had been against an excellent standard of opposition and he had been consistent, careful with the ball, a great foil for the attacking players with his late runs, and was capable of playing wide if required, central, or behind the striker. An excellent option to now have in the squad.

April

If Brazil had been Platt's audition, the friendly at the end of April against Czechoslovakia would be Gascoigne's. Each of his games in the lead-up was forensically studied and dissected by the press. Early in the month, Tottenham Hotspur played away at Nottingham Forest, a team that Gascoigne had struggled against earlier in the year. Aware he was being watched, his first major action in the game was to start a row with Forest manager Brian Clough that saw him pick up his ninth booking of the season in only the 14th minute.

After that, however, he was nigh on untouchable. Spurs won 3-1 and he had been involved in nearly everything of note, spraying passes about like Glenn Hoddle at his very best. Brian Scovell's verdict in the *Daily Mail* was that he had put in one of 'his most masterful performances'. Seven days later he played against Coventry City, the team he had broken his arm against earlier in the year. While it was not the spectacular performance of the previous week his cross led to Spurs' first goal in a 3-2 win. Gascoigne played with far more discipline on the day, as if he wanted to follow being allowed to light the fireworks by proving he had watched the safety video.

Just two days later Spurs had a rearranged trip to Millwall. Gascoigne was booked for a tenth time but only after repeatedly being hacked down by a midfield intent on stopping him building any momentum. He had been frustrated to the point of a single bad tackle. He had gone much further in games like this before so perhaps a measure of progress. All roads now led to a huge match for Tottenham on the Saturday before the friendly, Manchester United at home with their two formerly injured England midfielders declared fit to play – Neil Webb and Bryan Robson.

With all eyes on him and the game pencilled in to be first on *Match of the Day* before kick-off, Gascoigne turned in a virtuoso performance and revelled in the spotlight. The *Daily Mail* said it was the 'day the student played like a prince', while *The Observer* called him Spurs' 'mischief-maker' who had a 'marvellous time' playing against his England competition. With Bobby Robson watching from the stands, Gascoigne scored the opener with a late run and smart finish. Spurs would go on to win 2-1 with Gascoigne irrepressible at times. In the dying moments he came within a wonderful Jim Leighton save of making it three with a free kick from nearly 30 yards out. He still had time to pretend to kick an injured David Howells, to the delight of the home crowd just before the final whistle. Four days later he was going to start for England. It was fair to say he was ready.

Robson's month had been spent trying to watch each of his prospective squad and fielding questions about Gascoigne. He was pleased to see his captain and Webb back in contention but was aware that both were nowhere near match fit. Mark Wright was finding his best form and was now very much in the picture ahead of Tony Adams who Robson felt needed to improve on the ball. He thought the same of Des Walker but his electric pace overcame so many issues he was also definitely in the 22.

Robson's relationship with the press at this stage was near a permanent breaking point. He was brought into conversations there was no need to be discussed in, he was permanently talked about in the negative, and he was now pushing back. He was asked fairly innocuously what he thought the public opinion was of him right at that moment in time. 'It's you the press who make public opinion,' he snapped back. 'Don't let us kid ourselves about that.'

Clough took time out of his schedule preparing for the Littlewoods Cup Final to criticise the FA for not making him England manager, as he always did in the run-up to a major international tournament. He claimed his political views had cost him the job this time, and then turned on Robson as he never felt that 'the national side has mirrored the excellence of our league clubs'. He did, of course, believe it had nothing to do with the clubs or the long season but was actually about Robson's selections, 'He's got carte blanche, he can take them for four days training, have league games cancelled, have get-togethers – you name it. Pick the right side and we'll compete with anybody.'

The side he picked for the Czechoslovakia friendly did turn out to be the right one and Gascoigne was spectacularly good. If this was an audition to be an extra then he ended up stealing the lead role. But it was a huge pity only 21,000 fans were there to see it. Before kick-off there was a certain amount of scepticism which didn't help the attendance as Robson mixed things up with his selection. Shilton would start but David Seaman was told he was definitely getting the full second half. Lee Dixon was given a debut at right-back as Gary Stevens's place was in jeopardy after the Brazil game. Steve Bull would start up front with Lineker as there was no need to play either of his Liverpool men when they were on the plane already. Trevor Steven would start for the first time since the previous year's 2-0 defeat of Scotland. Steve Hodge was also recalled and was in very good form for his club. The plan was to make a couple of changes at half-time to look at Wright in an England shirt again, his last cap coming in the 3-1 defeat to the Netherlands in 1988. Tony Dorigo would also come on, as while Stuart Pearce had made the position his own there was no harm in looking at his backup.

England actually went behind with just ten minutes gone to a very good header from Tomas Skuhravy. They had looked bright but the first sight of goal from either team led to the opener. There was no panic, with Gascoigne still easing through the gears. Seven minutes later they scored one of the great England goals. Gascoigne's glorious outside-of-the-foot pass from just inside the Czechoslovakia half found the run of Bull. He controlled with his chest, took the ball on the bounce and crashed it in. The pass was a thing of beauty, the finish straight out of a demolition derby.

Five minutes later Gascoigne's near-post corner caused panic in the ranks and eventually landed with Pearce who scored his first England goal. Everyone was in the mood now and the home side were playing some excellent football. Gascoigne came out after half-time and ascended again. Shortly before the hour he glided through two challenges and sent a glorious cross over for Bull to head his second. With ten minutes to go Seaman didn't cover himself in glory when facing a free kick and it was 3-2. That scoreline was far closer than the game had been, Bull missing two chances to get his hat-trick and put the result out of sight.

With less than a minute to go England broke out of defence and the ball found its way to Gascoigne 30 yards from goal. A burst of acceleration put him in between two defenders who couldn't get near him. Three touches took him into the area, and a fourth saw him hit a rising shot past the helpless keeper for number four. An immediate cut to the England bench caught Bobby Robson telling all around him, 'That was fantastic.' Robson laughed then bit his lip. His problem child looked like he might just turn out to be a genius.

May

Gascoigne was now not only in the squad but likely to start in the summer. Many in the press were already calling for Robson to quickly rebuild his side around him before the World Cup began. David Lacey in *The Guardian* had been impressed to the degree that he wrote that Gascoigne had 'practically laughed his way into England's World Cup squad'. That wasn't too far from the truth.

While May should have represented a calm month of diligent preparation, it quickly turned to chaos centred around the manager. The basic facts were these. After long discussions about the future, it became clear to Robson that the FA had tired of the constant abuse and media pressure around him. His contract was technically supposed to run until 1991 but with things coming to a head and the fall-out of any tournament – good, bad or indifferent – usually meaning a fresh start to some degree, it was prescient to talk about it now. He asked if there would be an extended deal and was informed that once the World Cup was over they would be looking for a new manager to take them forward. Thanks for all you've done, but we're going another way.

The contract talks had been sparked by an informal approach directly to Robson from representatives of PSV Eindhoven. The Dutch club had asked if he would be interested in taking them forward after the World Cup and he was. Ultimately he had hoped to be given a new contract as despite all the distractions he still considered managing England the pinnacle of the profession. He now knew it was not to be. With everything that had happened and his relationship with the press nearly non-existent, it was sensible to not only secure a new job but leave the country for the foreseeable future regardless of what happened in Italy. He also had the full blessing of the FA from the off who were honest enough to admit they wanted to go in a different direction.

Once the deal was all but agreed, everyone vowed to not say anything about it until the World Cup was over. Robson wanted to inform his staff personally, then the players, and leave on the highest point they could achieve. It should have been a dignified end to an unsavoury moment in tabloid history. In reality it turned into a bare-knuckle boxing match.

There had been rumours for a while that Robson was going, partly because of the relentless campaign by many in the press to make it so. The *Daily Mail*, *The Sun*, and the *Daily Mirror* all claimed to have the exclusive that Robson had been approached to take over at PSV and the FA were allowing talks to take place. At this point it was virtually a done deal in reality, but all involved felt they could deny their way through the stories.

However, specific details then leaked. The sort denials would not cover anymore. With England due to leave for the World Cup, Robson and the FA had a crisis meeting. They had to face the fact that they needed to admit what was going on as the lies now circulating about the nature of his departure could not stand. Some were framing him as greedy, some as a traitor. Indeed, he would successfully sue the *Today* newspaper for that exact line. Several journalists who had been asking him to leave for years were now outraged in print that he had the temerity to do so.

Nearly all articles mentioned the fact he was doubling his salary or more, most guessing at figures to make it seem like both an ego-driven decision and Robson turning his back on his country for cash. Nearly all also framed it in their news pieces as the England manager telling his employers he quit out of the blue despite the PSV links over a week earlier. It became a frenzy that went past even the 1-1 draw with Saudi Arabia in voracity. According to the *Mirror* in a piece that attacked the FA's handling of the departure as well as Robson himself, England were now 'the laughing stock of world football'. Enough was enough and a press conference was called at Lancaster Gate by the FA with Robson there to defend himself on the day he was leaving for Italy.

Within minutes the whole thing descended into anarchy. First Robson was mobbed on his way in and had to fight his way through a mass of photographers who pushed and fought for a photo of a man walking into a building and then making his way to a desk. The scrum was so bad that Robson called them 'hooligans', a loaded word when used about anything to do with English football. Once the photographers were ordered to leave the room and his post-Italy departure was confirmed by an official statement, he took particular offence to a story that he had been seen handing brown envelopes to each of the international committee, telling them he had resigned and wanted to go now. In response he offered a reward of a million pounds to charity if any journalist could find one of these envelopes. 'There is no truth in any of these stories,' he raged. 'I can categorically state that I have not contacted the FA and offered to resign before the World Cup!'

The level of hostility in the room was higher than at any point in his reign and reciprocated in kind. There was another layer to his anger, one that repeatedly saw him accuse tabloid journalists of printing 'appalling lies' and shouting 'garbage' as a statement was read by Graham Kelly denying most of the story the red tops had been spinning. The scandal around his personal life had blown up again, the threatened book now allegedly being readied for publication and Janet Rush's ex-husband deciding now was the perfect time to sell 'a detail packed dossier' to the *Sunday Mirror*. Robson was accused of leaving because of the allegations around his social life and wanted to completely, and angrily, distance himself from that.

Every detail was replayed in the press alongside the accusations of greed and treachery. This caused Robson and his family great personal pain. A line had been crossed. After a little short of 15 minutes, some spent with Robson on his feet fighting his corner rather than passively sitting behind a desk, he left knowing he had said his piece but it didn't matter anyway, they would write what they wanted to. He was now leaving for the World Cup directly after 'the worst 48 hours of my entire life'.

Earlier in the month, although you wouldn't have known it, Robson had found time to name his squad and also manage England through two warm-up games. The first had been an unremarkable affair against perennial opponents Denmark at Wembley. Walker was excellent, Gascoigne neat and tidy rather than boom or bust, and Lineker's goal proved to be the difference. In eight years Robson had faced the Danes five times, losing the one that counted in 1983, drawing two and winning two.

Their second game and send-off was against Uruguay. A half-full Wembley witnessed England's first loss in 17 and first home defeat in six years. It was a good match and the home side were on the wrong side of more than one refereeing decision for a change. The high point of the 2-1 loss was a stunning goal from Barnes. It would be fair to say that although England pushed for an equaliser, one or two players were acutely aware of what a Uruguayan tackle might do to their summer.

That squad was now settled upon and quietly bonding around ways to keep Gascoigne quiet. The day before the Uruguay game, Robson had cut his group 26 down to a final 22. Missing out were goalkeeper Dave Beasant, defender Tony Adams whose chances had been ruined by the emergence of the now un-droppable Des Walker, striker Alan Smith who only ever had an outside chance anyway thanks to Steve Bull's easy adjustment to international football, and most agonisingly midfielder David Rocastle. Robson's final cut included goalkeepers Peter Shilton, Chris Woods and David Seaman; defenders Walker, Terry Butcher,

Mark Wright, Gary Stevens, Stuart Pearce, Paul Parker and Tony Dorigo; midfielders Bryan Robson, Neil Webb, Steve McMahon, David Platt, Steve Hodge, Trevor Steven, John Barnes, Chris Waddle and Paul Gascoigne; and strikers Bull, Peter Beardsley and Gary Lineker.

June

Before the opening game there was still time for England to disappoint. Tunisia were chosen as a surrogate for the upcoming meeting with Egypt and little went right. Firstly, England were left waiting for over half an hour in a hot coach as the driver had taken the wrong road and was refused entry to the stadium. Then things got worse after kick-off as England struggled on a breathless day to get any rhythm. A couple of half-chances went begging and then they were 1-0 down to a brilliant strike from fully 35 yards. A bobble off the pitch caught Gascoigne out and his wayward pass fell to Abdelhamid Hergal who scored the goal of a lifetime.

The incredible strike gave Tunisia belief and deflated England who laboured on. Butcher, under pressure from writers in the broadsheets who felt he should no longer start when Wright and Walker were younger and faster, had a day to forget. Not only did he struggle with a striker way below his level but a rush of blood saw him booked for a headbutt on a marker at an England set-piece. Robson was not impressed and subbed him almost immediately, to which Butcher responded by storming off, threw his shirt off in front of the bench, and then slumped against an advertising hoarding rather than joining the rest of the players. After the game, Robson defended him, putting it down to competitive spirit. Privately, Butcher was left in no uncertain terms about his conduct.

Bull's last-minute header didn't exactly earn a 1-1 draw, but England got one anyway. In nine days they would play the

Republic of Ireland and now desperately needed a good start. They had beaten a Caligiuri XI mostly made up of reserves and youth-team players 6-0 before the trip to Tunisia, and later in the week they strolled to a 10-2 win over a Sardinian XI, but somehow as the World Cup started England had managed to yet again heap huge pressure on themselves.

As in 1986 they started slowly, although the 1-1 draw with Ireland was a good result to some degree. The way the groups were structured, four points was certain qualification barring something extraordinary happening. This meant one win and two draws. Realistically, three points should also have been enough to reach the round of 16. Getting the first of those was fine, but the performance was worrying. England, as in Tunis, suddenly looked out of step with each other. They knew exactly what to expect from their opponents and largely coped with it. With that side of the game taken care of they should have had the platform to build and create, but nothing happened. Barnes and Waddle struggled to get into the game in any meaningful way, ditto Gascoigne who had started alongside Bryan Robson.

England had even been given a leg up when goalkeeper Pat Bonner completely misjudged Lineker's control of a Waddle cross. He had to watch in slow motion as the England striker scrambled in an opener just eight minutes in. Now having to push, the Irish tried to bully the England back four as they had in Stuttgart but found them in far more resilient mood. With just over 20 minutes to go Bobby Robson tried to see the 1-0 win out by taking off Beardsley and bringing on McMahon as an extra midfielder. Unfortunately, he was ring rusty and having only been on the pitch for two minutes lost the ball to Kevin Sheedy on the edge of the box. Sheedy scored the equaliser and then neither side pushed for a winner in the fear of leaving space and losing.

The fall-out was exactly as expected. Robson, already on his last nerve before leaving the country, was suffering personally as his brother Keith had been taken into hospital after having a heart attack. He had also been informed that several journalists had doorstepped his mother who had been unaware of the news at the time. No less than an absolute violation of his family's life. His press conference had an edge again, and he took particular umbrage to David Miller from *The Times'* questioning. His reward for fighting back was an absolute savage Miller opinion piece, 'Having shared an opening match of barely third division international standing, in which England were outwitted even in that for much of the first half, both camps need to adjust, fast … I cannot recall a more inelegant World Cup match and shall be in no hurry to remember this one.'

The Sun was slightly more route one in that it was just demanding the whole England squad come home before they could embarrass the country further. The 1-1 draw was far from ideal, but in no way was it the disaster it was being made out to be. The press had simply declared their anathema on Robson already and were bitterly hurt they had been ignored so he could leave on his own terms.

The players loved Robson. They respected him professionally, enjoyed him personally, and the press coverage hurt them too. Butcher's ongoing war with the *Sunday Times'* Brian Glanville aside, they were often shielded from the bulk of the criticism by the campaign around the manager. Before their next game against the Netherlands the gun had been turned on them, however.

When the England party had flown out to Sardinia they had been allowed to bring wives and girlfriends with them for a few days before the serious business began. They had been grateful to the FA for that decision, and Robson had been a part of it in trying to get them as relaxed as he could before knuckling down. Now the squad were together without partners they had moved to the beautiful Is Molas Resort, slightly more inland. On 13 June Robson was informed by FA representatives that both *The Sun* and the *Daily Mirror* were seeking statements on a story about a hostess at the hotel named Isabella Ciaravolo. She had apparently been asked to leave while the England team were staying there. There was no actual confirmed detail other than that but the 'rotters' from the tabloids sniffed blood and numbers.

The *Mirror* ran the story on its front page, not wishing to lose ground with its main rival and everyone else followed in that wake. The *Mirror* managed to contradict itself in that its subtitle claimed the 'beauty' had been 'sacked from top job with players', and then in only the second sentence of the main copy was it clarified she had actually just been moved to another part of the resort. The article said it all, or should I say suggested it all, without actually saying anything. There was, however, a big issue for both the major tabloids in this latest arms race: no one had any proof.

Ciaravolo, to her eternal credit, refused various offers to sell her side of the story. She was suffering by insinuation and wanted no part of confirming anything anybody thought they knew. It should be said that in writing this book now, 30 years later, there is still no evidence or testimony from anyone to suggest that she had done anything wrong, or indeed that any England player did. The *Mirror*'s hit piece hurt the players as it resulted in a string of phone calls from home, some accusatory, some sceptical and all unnecessary. The story as a whole had not hurt them so much as one single sentence had, 'At one official disco a number of the attractive hostesses had mingled with the England stars.' A masterclass of tabloid suggestion in one single sentence.

The players now refused to talk to the press and long-term this aided Bobby Robson in turning a siege mentality into a reality. There was no comment on the non-story from the FA or Robson. The next press conference featured a more confident, slightly more relaxed England manager. He had been defending himself for so long that it was now easier to do it for others. The only story to emerge that day was that Dave Beasant was flying out to replace David Seaman who had broken his thumb in training. A straight bat can be an enjoyable thing if you know you are going to get applause from the balcony for playing it.

One player who did give an interview, not to the written press but to the BBC, was Paul Gascoigne. When he arrived with slogans handwritten on his t-shirt, all messages to a handful of beloved people watching, they might have expected the usual sunshine and smiles from him. He was in no mood to give them that, arguing, 'It's a disgrace, there's people that don't want us to win the World Cup, and the people at home, the public, get the wrong image of it.' When even your court jester turns to anger, you know something has broken.

On the Saturday evening England played the Netherlands with something to prove. This was no longer just about putting the ghosts of 1988 to bed and there was a change of system too. Wright was deployed as a sweeper, something many had been asking Robson to do for a long time. It was a formation that England had struggled against historically, but the manager had been less than keen to implement as he felt he had to sacrifice something in another area of the pitch to have it. It had always been the plan to deploy it now though, and it had always been Robson's plan.

The idea that the players revolted and demanded to play with a sweeper took hold and suited several with a grudge over the years. Terry Fenwick's Spartacus moment in 1986 was an example of how these things can be perceived. In his book *The Ultimate Patriot*, Bob Harris, a confidant of the manager and the England squad throughout this time, is unequivocal in his verdict that it was Robson's idea.

Another staunch advocate that the manager had the plan all along was Lineker, even going out of his way in a TV interview with Robson for the BBC to mention it to end the rumour altogether. 'You changed tactics in that World Cup to cope with Holland didn't you,' he asked knowing how loaded the sentence was. 'There's always been this rumour that it was forced on you by the players which I've fervently denied for you on occasions, the truth is you did take players' advice but at the same time you ultimately made the decisions yourself?' Robson laughed and then pointed out they had selected the squad specifically to have the players that could change to a sweeper system when they wanted. If not he would likely have had Tony Adams there with them.

England not only played the Dutch at their own game, but they were better at it on the night, and Robson's men were actually incredibly unlucky not to win. After being denied an absolutely clear and obvious penalty in the Ireland game when Waddle had been scythed down in the box, and now after an ultimately goalless but incredibly encouraging 90 minutes here, they could only hope eventually luck would go with them.

Their destroyers in chief in Germany, Van Basten and Gullit, were handled excellently by the English defence. Des Walker's pace and confidence to step out if required with Wright as his backup meant he could follow Van Basten and effectively nullified him. The Dutch were in trouble themselves. They had started poorly with a laboured and lucky draw with Egypt. England defended well and hurt them when they attacked. Lineker was harshly judged to have handled when scoring in the first half, and Pearce's free kick flew in with barely any time left in the game but was disallowed as it had been indirect. Bad luck but an excellent performance to build on.

The game also saw Gascoigne take on one of the world's best midfields and win. He was superb on the day and involved in everything good England did going forward. He snarled over a felled Gullit when a foul was given against him, he ran at defenders with no fear, he kept dropping the ball into space meaning players suddenly had the freedom to run, and he produced a Cruyff turn that was straight from the pages of *Roy of the Rovers*. The secret was officially out.

England now knew they had a cup tie ahead. Results had conspired that after the Irish drew with Egypt each team was on the same points, goals scored and conceded going into the final round of fixtures. If England could win their last game, they would be through. No need for any other calculation or to worry about what was happening elsewhere if they could just get themselves over the line. Thankfully, and deservedly after their last performance, they did.

It was a turgid affair but that had very little to do with the English team. Egypt had come not to lose and hope that would be enough. In the first half they closed ranks, repeatedly passed back to their goalkeeper, and if all else failed they fouled whoever had the ball. It looked like it could be a long night. For once England found a way.

An hour in, Walker was fouled when on a break. This gave Gascoigne the chance to float a ball in for Butcher and Wright to attack. It was Wright who got there first and glanced a header in for a vital goal. It was then England's turn to form a pack and protect the lead. They did so and qualified from a group that would need lots to separate Ireland and the

Netherlands in second and third respectively after another draw. It had been bad, much better, and then clinical, in that order. They had done enough.

They had also had to play that last game without their captain as Bryan Robson's injury curse had struck again. He had come off for Platt during the second half when his left Achilles tendon gave way as he was running. There had been an old injury in the area and eventually it had flared up again at the worst possible time. He had come straight off and like Mexico he knew his World Cup was over instantly. He flew home for surgery, bitterly disappointed but marginally lucky to have lasted that long. He had injured his big toe before their first game in an incident Gascoigne got wildly wrong in an autobiography. He had been fortunate to not break the toe then but still needed injections to get him through training and games as it was. Captain Marvel had gone home but England were through, so the squad had to focus and move on.

There had been no truce with the press. There had been an upturn in performances and actual results so the very worst of the hostilities had abated briefly. England would now face Belgium, the team who had finished fourth at the last World Cup. They were quite a prospect too as Enzo Scifo was one of the most talented players in Europe. Robson went back to his sweeper system after reverting to a back four against Egypt. The game was on a knife edge throughout and England moved into extra time for the first time since losing to West Germany in 1970.

They managed to win in the absolute best way. After a game where both sides had managed to parry and riposte there were just seconds left when Gascoigne won a free kick 50 yards from goal. He swung in a gorgeous delivery towards substitute Platt who turned having let the ball drop over his shoulder. His volley left the goalkeeper completely stranded and there was delirium in the stands, on the pitch and in living rooms across the country. Robson danced along the touchline. Lineker gave the smile of a man who couldn't believe what had just happened as players rushed to join him on top of Platt. Game over. At the final whistle the England players celebrated with the fans, Butcher and Waddle dancing with them, Gazza screaming at them. A sensational victory and an iconic goal. Maybe their luck had changed.

Those fans there on the night were in heaven. There had been a small charge at a pocket of Belgium supporters in the ground during the game and tensions had been raised. This was England's first match on the mainland and all the talk was of how much trouble they were definitely going to cause. A huge police presence moved in and held the bulk of the English followers in place after the final whistle to allow everyone else to leave. For once they wouldn't have gone anywhere anyway. The reaction by the police was typical of their approach so far. It completely ignored the section of Belgians who had not only been taunting the English knowing they would suffer no consequence, but who had started the charge with one of their own a few moments before the response.

To date there had been incidents, arrests and deportations, but nothing like on the scale even our own Sports Minister Colin Moynihan had predicted before the World Cup. The English had been targeted by many and responded in kind, and the usual idiots had acted as expected, but the fear of the widescale riots and mass violence had yet to come to pass. England's following was also significantly lower than expected and far more disparate. When you are spread far and wide and without the inclination anyway, it's tough to start the riot photographers want you to.

The policing had been heavy-handed in the extreme, which had helped keep incidents down even if just through fear. Upon entry for the game against the Irish England fans had all their coins taken from them and were given stark warnings for merely walking by a police line. Some were left with the feeling that the real hooligans were in uniform.

The Football Supporters' Association (FSA) had set up a 'fan embassy' system to help with practical advice, information and ticketing. Things on the whole were improving. However, they were hearing more and more reports of violently imposed curfews and targeted attacks on England fans. There was a balance to be struck as the English were certainly no victims here and many did what they had always done – let the country down. But self-fulfilling prophecies were coming true. If you tell people wild animals are coming, they will do anything they can to protect themselves.

The fear around the game against the Netherlands had proved unfounded as the mass confrontations from Euro 88 weren't repeated. Again the policing decision was to control the English rather than their opposition who also had a fairly horrific arrest record. An England fan march that the FSA had warned supporters not to attend did turn into a larger fight. There was a suggestion it had been organised by those there to cause trouble as a chance to do just that under the banner of a fan event. The target was not away fans, but the police who responded in kind.

England supporters had been portrayed as violent thugs for so long now that those who actually were needed their moment. The march, charge, chase and counter saw arrests but also injuries to innocent parties along with the guilty ones. Even an FSA volunteer who approached a police chief about the way fans not involved in the violence were being hit at random was struck on the head with a baton in reply.

The press were there for the photographs and headlines, therefore they chose to ignore the stories of groups of English fans cleaning up campsites when leaving and organising good-natured games against locals. Instead, incidents involving tens were reported as hundreds. The approach seemed to be to reinforce the negative messaging from everyone, including our own government. The reality was that the fans as a whole were behaving better than expected. Not only that but they were beginning to feel like they had a team to cherish.

July

England played only three more games under Bobby Robson. It sounds so undramatic when you say it like that. With the exit in sight but the chance to leave with a World Cup in the bag, Robson was trying to get his players to relax, take his plans on board and play with freedom. Fortunately, he had Paul Gascoigne to help with the former and latter of those needs.

Gascoigne could not be described as a calming presence. Depending on if you want to dig down for the truth or prefer to believe various legends told in slightly differing ways, at this World Cup alone he kept Chris Waddle up all night talking the night before a game, led more than one secret raid to a local bar, nearly took the England captain out of the tournament before his Achilles went anyway, smashed his own toe up by bombing into the shallow end of the pool, ran a betting scam that cost Peter Shilton hundreds of pounds, tore around a golf course topless in a buggy and was reprimanded by staff, started a food fight, played tennis in the midday sun (or very late at night in at least one account) the day before a semi-final, and drunkenly scaled a two-storey wall to sneak back into the hotel. And that barely scratches the surface.

What he also did was perform brilliantly on the pitch. In England's next game, the quarter-final against Cameroon, he showed up in the big moments yet again. The match was one of a reasonably dour World Cup's best. Cameroon had been brilliant – no football fan will ever forget the name Roger Milla – and England found themselves 2-1 down with just eight minutes left to play. Gascoigne had conceded the penalty that gave Emmanuel Kundé the equaliser and was now playing on the edge trying to force a goal. Both sides had huge chances in a game where the momentum swung back and forth. England were starting to panic and snatch at theirs. Outwardly there were signs of fear; of losing, reprisals in the press and of failure.

The press had been shut out of England's camp and resorted to long-lensing the squad from trees and walls where possible. The pressure was obscene, but Bobby Robson was doing a superb job in shouldering it for his players. What he needed now, staring into the abyss of elimination, was a reward for that noble burden. The sweeper system had been abandoned with time running out and Butcher was now back on the bench.

England won another free kick, such a huge weapon with Gascoigne's delivery. He floated it in, Cameroon failed to clear and Lineker's quick touch won him a penalty. The contact looked minimal but Lineker was in no mood to ask twice. He scored and the tie nervously moved into extra time. Wright was bandaged after a bad cut to the head, and several players were clearly tired on a warm evening in Naples, so could England find a way through?

Gascoigne came up with the answer in the 104th minute. He burst past a challenge and out of defence before threading the eye of a needle with a ball to Lineker. The striker took a touch, rounded the keeper and was upended for a penalty.

Lineker scored again, England held on to win 3-2, and for the first time on foreign soil, they were in a World Cup semi-final.

That night against West Germany became a cultural milestone for English football. The combined television viewing figures the moment England got through their group were huge and kept growing. Some 19.3m people watched Platt's volley beat Belgium, then 23.6m tuned in for the quarter-final. For the semi, a gargantuan 25.2m people settled down to watch it. Some reports put that figure at well over a million more. The 1980s had rightly seen people turn away from the English game in disgust. The fightback to popularity was almost complete in the course of a single summer. The one for respectability would take a lot longer but at least was also now being fought.

England, with sweeper system in place and Butcher wearing the captain's armband, with Gascoigne and the summer's other huge success story Platt in midfield, really did give everything they could. It is easy to romanticise in hindsight but watching the game again you realise just how good that West Germany side was. They were by far the best team that summer and worthy winners. And yet England ran them so close.

The headlines were that England came from behind to draw 1-1 in normal time, Lineker's excellent improvisation answering Andreas Brehme's deflected free kick. They were denied another penalty and yet again it was Waddle who was fouled, but they had also ridden their luck somewhat at the other end, so for the third game in a row they would move into extra time, where Gascoigne's booking in the 100th minute meant that he wouldn't play in the final if England progressed. His tears created one of the decade's most defining images. 'Have a word with him,' Lineker urged Robson. Paul Gascoigne was now Gazza. Our Gazza.

England kept going in a period of extra time that now truly felt epic and both sides could have won it. Waddle hit the post, Platt had a goal disallowed and the Germans' Guido Buchwald hit the post. The final whistle blew and penalties lay ahead. The game really had everything and this was, perhaps, the only fitting end. They scored, we missed, Pearce and Waddle inconsolable. England were out of the 1990 World Cup.

I'm aware that none of those things are spoilers for anyone reading this book but that game gave us England fans so many defining moments that it's difficult to count them all. It was a bitter pill to swallow, arguably even more than 1996 which, while on our home turf, came when our football was in a much better place. England getting to the semi-final in 1990 should not have happened. Indeed it took the slimmest of margins against Egypt to get out of the group, a 120th-minute winner against Belgium, two late goals against a naive Cameroon who if they had held back would likely have seen the result out, and all against a background of intense media pressure and nervous looks to the stands. The game against West Germany had proved a bridge too far but somehow England had just lost on the finest margin available in football. All of that was unfathomable as the players trudged home after Euro 88.

The fans had also continued to exceed the low bars set for them. The obvious tensions around a Germany game in 1990 did cause incidents but again the much-promised widescale violence just didn't occur. The *Daily Mail* did its best with a round-up pointing out England's hooligans were 'by far the worst in the World Cup'. Their figures were 435 detained with 420 of those deported, 98 official arrests, 35 convictions for football-related offences, and three tried and jailed already. As poor as that was, it was also nothing like what had been promised, the supposed pandemic of the

English disease tearing across Italy. It also didn't account for the fact that England's fans were policed heavier and harder than any other. You don't have to look too far to find a litany of stories of mistreatment or unprovoked attack. There was an ocean of work to be done, but it had clearly begun.

The *Mail*, and others, perhaps disappointed with the calmer seas than expected, wrote articles about widespread violence in England after the defeat. It was meant to feel like almost a coordinated effort when really it was just an attempt to link many incidents to a root cause. No doubt some were a direct result, but others felt tenuous. What was not reported was the England fans unfurling a banner in the stands that read 'Pay No Poll Tax' or the various anti-government chants heard during the first half. English football was trying to reclaim itself from what the authorities kept telling people it was.

Bobby Robson's time in charge of England came to an end in a third-place play-off defeat to Italy that no one wanted to play in. England did win the World Cup's Fair Play Award, a just reward that meant absolutely nothing to anyone there. Robson was off to a new home and a new adventure, but he was leaving as what had seemed the unlikeliest of all things, a hero. He had stayed at the World Cup to receive the award and watch the final, but he was made aware of the scenes that greeted his squad when they returned home.

That's what they were eternally now – his squad, his men, his brothers. Every newspaper ran joyous pieces about how proud they had made them, how they always believed, how they knew they could do it. The *Daily Mirror*, which ran so many nasty, vicious and often untrue headlines over the Robson years, now had one it had no right to, but that did represent the country finally. The newspaper's piece on the crowds and the 'greatest soccer comeback ever' went to press topped quite simply with the words 'We Love You'.

After

'IT WAS the greatest part of my life I think,' said Bobby Robson of that summer. He was fiercely proud of being England manager throughout his eight years in charge. Quite remarkable when you consider what he went through. Those precious weeks felt like karmic reward for a man who had been through a hellish few years simply for the crime of doing his job.

Italia 90 was a moment in time not just for him but for all of English football. An island measured by minutes. In the various documentaries on the subject, interviews, articles and autobiographies of anyone involved, no one can talk about it without a glint in their eye. 'Should have won it,' Robson told Gary Lineker in an interview in 2002. 'Every one of their penalties went right in the corner!' Lineker smiles. He can only offer 'Bloody Germans' as a reply.

The fact is that England should not have won it. The Germans were better, but Robson's side doing what they did was enough. This country wasn't ready to win another World Cup. Our island mentality had been so entrenched that it had exploded into violence. Even with the movement to take football back from the hooligans at a tipping point, a tacit confirmation that England was the best at something was, in reality, the last thing anyone needed. Glorious failure allows the much-needed room to build. Victory expands to fill all space.

Robson had made plenty of mistakes along the way and players in every position over the eight years had let him down to one degree or another. What he did do better than anyone else was survive. Through the torment of a tabloid press throwing hand grenades at each other with not a care if anyone was caught in the crossfire, he remained. His family suffered, it took a huge toll on his mental health, it nearly cost him everything, but he passionately believed that being England manager was the greatest job in the world. So much so that a few years later with his replacement Graham Taylor struggling in the role, he offered to come back. A remarkable sense of duty to a post that had given him his single highest high and every one of his lowest lows.

Robson left the shores on a tidal wave of reappraisal. He would go on to great success in Europe by building on an understanding of football at the highest level with his natural gift for being with people. He would win the league twice with PSV in two years there, then two league titles and the Portuguese Cup with Porto shortly afterwards. Eventually Barcelona did have their man and he won a Spanish Cup and a European Cup Winners' Cup with them. Along the way he worked with the likes of Romário, Ronaldo, Jose Mourinho and Pep Guardiola. Both of the latter two have talked about the value of personality as the legacy Robson left them. Ronaldo said, 'He was like a father to me.'

Robson returned to England with Newcastle United, his other dream job, in 1999. After five years there he was dismissed, harshly, and was critical of the club's hierarchy. He would then take a consultancy role with the Republic of Ireland. The work. It was always about the work. More importantly it was about the people the work brought into his life.

Even more remarkably, Robson had continued to work through several battles with the disease that would eventually claim his life. Cancer had first struck in 1992 and an operation had been required to remove a section of his colon. It was a success, but then three years later in 1995 he needed nine hours of surgery to remove a malignant melanoma discovered when he had been for his sinuses checking. That left him needing to wear a plastic fitting to cover a hole in the roof of his mouth for the rest of his life.

In 2006 and now knighted, Sir Bobby Robson was diagnosed with lung cancer and a tumour in his brain. The operation to remove the tumour left him paralysed. Unfortunately, the cancer returned to his lungs after treatment and he passed away peacefully at home, Lady Elsie by his side as ever, in 2009. He had devoted the very last years of his life to helping to fight the disease by creating the Sir Bobby Robson Foundation. Their work continues to this day and millions of pounds have been put towards the fight against cancer in his name. If you are reading this book and leave with a new level of respect for the man himself, I urge you to consider supporting them.

* * *

The press had learned nothing from their treatment of Robson and set about the newly announced England manager Graham Taylor in the same fashion. His story will be told in another book.

If I tell you *The Sun*'s campaign against him left the enduring image of his time as a mocked-up photo of his face on a turnip, you get some sort of idea what the next four years would bring. To this day, being the England manager comes with an acceptance that you will be a hero or villain, and rarely (if ever) in between.

Robson's group of generals, his spine, all went on to contrasting fortunes. The game against Italy called time on Peter Shilton's international career after 125 caps and three months before his 41st birthday. Shilton had been a goalkeeper for the big moments but that had left him by the time of England's penalty shoot-out. He retired at the age of 47 in 1997 having played in 1,005 league matches.

The semi-final proved to be Terry Butcher's last cap. Forever England's warrior in chief, it is easy to ignore the fact Butcher was actually an excellent all-round footballer too. He and Robson shared a close bond from Ipswich into the England side. Butcher's decision to retire from international football was taken as he knew his knees were not up to playing every game available anymore. England's younger defenders – Mark Wright, Tony Adams, Des Walker and more – were pushing him all the way as it was. He retired from playing altogether just three years after Italy and went into management and punditry.

Bryan Robson and Gary Lineker would both play on under Graham Taylor. Robson had missed so much football through injury that you cannot blame him for taking every chance he could. Three caps in 1991 would be his last and in truth they were given on reputation rather than form. He ended with 90 total, and 26 goals – many of them vital. For a spell Robson was without a doubt comfortably one of the best midfielders in the world. It's impossible not to wonder if without the injuries he might have gone past even Shilton's 125 caps.

Lineker was a man in pursuit of a record that never came. He ended his international career after 80 caps and stuck on 48 goals, one shy of Bobby Charlton's then all-time record for England. He famously had never been booked but his England career ended in 1992 with him being subbed off in a game against Sweden in which they desperately needed a goal – a decision that still baffles to this day. He retired from playing in 1994 after suffering an injury to a toe that would not heal. He transitioned seamlessly into a successful media career that he still enjoys today.

And as for Paul Gascoigne? Well, like Graham Taylor, his is a story that can't be told in a single paragraph. He and Bobby Robson shared a bond and a love for each other. Robson thought he would win England the 1994 World Cup, Gazza believed he could do it. Unfortunately, his life slowly unravelled in a spotlight few have to endure. After 1990, Gazzamania was a very real mass psychosis. He would still manage a huge amount on the pitch and a glorious moment at Euro 96 to boot, but a few short months after Italia 90 his innocence had gone. There's a famous moment in an interview eight weeks after the tournament with Terry Wogan in which he is warned by the host that his dream 'might turn into a nightmare'. It would be fair to say he suffered significantly over the next decade and beyond but at the time of writing this book in 2020 Gascoigne seems to finally be in a better place mentally and physically. I can only hope with all my heart that he stays there for the longer term this time.

* * *

After Robson's time with England, the game, the fans and the domestic leagues evolved into something better. Robson was a small hand on a huge machine that engineered the ground-up redevelopment of our football into a product that no one needed to be ashamed of. The repeated tragedies and violence had been full-stopped by a glorious national moment around the game. Some of the appetite for the old way had disappeared for good.

It's easy to pontificate today about how safe our national game is but there are still underlying issues that football is on an eternal quest to address. The sport, more than any other, is often a reflection of the circumstances and society around it. Alf Ramsey's triumph was one of 1960s England built on hard work and endeavour over all else. He struggled to adapt when the 1970s demanded some style to go with all the substance. A Nobby Stiles was all well and good but where was your Frank Worthington? Robson's time in the 1980s was one of huge societal unrest. Some 11,000 arrests during the miners' strikes, the IRA bombing the Brighton conference, widescale privatisation and all bookended by the Poll Tax riots. Football's violence, death and despair was merely a reflection of the England in which it lived. The 1990s would bring change, hope for the future, and Robson's triumphant summer defeat provided a moment from which to build beyond those who had been fighting to do so already with very little help.

Hooliganism still exists, and it often still blights England's away trips. Racism is still a huge issue in our game too, both visible and unconscious. To say those things shouldn't take away from the huge strides that have been made since the very worst of the 1980s. You can now go to a football match in a safe environment with very little fear of violence or widespread racist chanting and the like. It is an eternal journey to improve on the issues within football we still have, but it is also fine to recognise how far we have come.

The press's coverage of football has also changed. Social media provides ways for managers and players to respond to lies and rumours directly. Standards of accountability are also far higher. There is still money to be made from negativity, however. The recent tone of reporting on Raheem Sterling for instance provides a window into an engrained truth the tabloids refuse to change. With barely a hint of contrition, Robson's England team were spoken of only in reverence after that summer. All is forgotten because we can still sell newspapers that way. Some there, as later memoirs have proved, knew it went too far.

What Bobby Robson suffered, from the professional to personal abuse, has yet to be repeated on quite the same scale. The fact that he is now rightly thought of as one of England's greatest-ever gentlemen is scant reward for all he and his family endured. Who knows what would have happened if he had bowed to pressure and left in 1983 after failure to qualify, or 1984 after the USSR defeat, or in 1988 after the summer collapse, or after any one of the horrific incidences of violence and despair? The only thing we know for sure is that as far as some of the press that had followed and hounded him across his time with England were concerned, it was never supposed to end like this.

Acknowledgements

THERE ARE many people to thank for their help in doing this book and I will definitely forget someone. That being the case I better say to them, thank you. And sorry.

Huge thanks to Nick Miller, Duncan Alexander and Michael Gibbons for some practical help and advice at various points, and to all at Gale who lent me access to their digital archive during lockdown. Thanks to Duncan Olner for the lovely cover design, and to Paul and Jane at Pitch for going with option number two when Covid did for option number one.

Thanks to Daniel Storey for the initial idea and excellent foreword; if there's anyone who loves Sir Bobby as much as me, it's him. Also, thanks to Chris Nee, Ryan Keaney and Steven Chicken for the encouragement and occasional editing. Writing a book can be a lonely business so thanks to everyone for the late night WhatsApps and text messages, and weird conversations about mid-1980s England friendlies.

Thanks to the *Socially Distant Sports Bar* podcast for a soundtrack to research this book, and to Elbow, Hans Zimmer and a load of mid-90s essential mixes for one to write to.

To Mum and Dad, thank you for everything. In particular thank you for allowing me to have a bedroom full of *Shoot!*,

Match, and *90 Minutes* magazines, *Roy of the Rovers* comics, football stickers of assorted years, and anything else football related I could get my hands on from about 1986 onwards.

To Beau, you were one when my first book came out and couldn't walk or talk. You'll be ten and shouting at a little French bulldog by the time my second one does. You are the funniest, cheekiest, sassiest girl I know. Now just occasionally let your old man watch the football please.

And to Penny. Then, now, always, forever.

Bibliography and References

Books

Armfield, Jimmy, with Andrew Collomosse, *Right Back to the Beginning* (Headline Publishing Group, 2004)

Barnes, John, with Henry Winter, *John Barnes: The Autobiography* (Headline Publishing Group, 1999)

Barrett, Norman, with Martin Smith, *The Telegraph Football Years* (Sevenoaks Carlton, 2013)

Beardsley, Peter, *My Life Story* (Collins Willow, 1995)

Bowler, Dave, *Three Lions on the Shirt* (Orion, 1999)

Bowler, Dave, *Winning Isn't Everything: A Biography of Sir Alf Ramsey* (Orion Books, 1998)

Burnett, Rob & Mewis, Joe, *England: On This Day* (Pitch Publishing, 2020)

Butcher, Terry, with Bob Harris, *Butcher: My Autobiography* (Highdown, 2005)

Butler, Byron, *The Official History of the Football Association* (Queen Anne Press, 1991)

Charlton, Bobby, with James Lawton, *My England Years* (Headline Publishing Group, 2008)

Crooks, Richard, *What Was Football Like in the 1980s?* (Pitch Publishing, 2020)

Crouch, Terry, with James Corbett, *The World Cup: The Complete History* (Aurum, 2002)

Davies, Pete, *All Played Out* (William Heinemann Ltd, 1990)

Domeneghetti, Roger, *From the Back Page to the Front Room* (Ockley Books, Second Edition 2017)

Downing, David, *The Best of Enemies: England v Germany* (Bloomsbury, 2000)

Felton, James, *Sunburn* (Sphere, 2020)

Fenwick, Terry, with Brian Woolnough, *Earning My Spurs* (Mainstream Publishing Group, 1989)

Finney, Tom, with Paul Agnew, *Tom Finney: My Autobiography* (Headline Publishing Group, 2003)

Galvin, Robert, *The Football Hall of Fame* (Robson Books, 2005)

Gascoigne, Paul, with Hunter Davies, *Gazza: My Story* (Headline Publishing Group, 2004)

Gascoigne, Paul, with David Wilson, *Glorious: My World, Football and Me* (Simon & Schuster, 2011)

Glanville, Brian, *England Managers: The Toughest Job in Football* (Headline Publishing Group, 2007)

Glanville, Brian, *The Story of the World Cup* (Faber & Fabor, 2018 Revised Edition)

Goldblatt, David, *The Ball is Round* (Penguin, 2007)

Gordon Brown, Jack and Ross, Phillip, *England: The Complete Record* (deCoubertin, 2018)

Harris, Bob, *Bobby Robson: The Ultimate Patriot* (deCoubertin, 2020)

Harris, Bob, *Sir Bobby Robson: Living the Game* (Weidenfeld & Nicholson, 2003)

Harris, Harry, *Italia '90 Revisited: The Players' Stories* (Empire Publications, 2020)

Hart, Simon, *World In Motion* (deCoubertin, 2018)

Jordan, Gary, *Out of the Shadows* (Pitch Publishing, 2017)

Keegan, Kevin, with Bob Harris and Caroline North, *My Autobiography* (Little, Brown and Company, 1997)

Keegan, Kevin, with Daniel Taylor, *My Life in Football* (Macmillan, 2018)

King, Jeff, *High Noon: Bobby Robson's Year at Barcelona* (Virgin, 1997)

Malam, Colin, *Gary Lineker: Strikingly Different* (Arrow, 1993)

Maradona, Diego, with Daniel Arcucci and Ernesto Cherquis Bialo, *El Diego* (Yellow Jersey Press, 2004)

Maradona, Diego, with Dabiel Arcucci, *Touched by God* (Constable, 2017)

Matthews, Tony, *England's Who's Who* (Pitch Publishing, 2013)

McColl, Graham, *England: The Alf Ramsey Years* (Chameleon Books, 1998)

McMahon, Steve, with Harry Harris, *Macca Can* (Pelham Books, 1990)

Morris, Desmond, *The Soccer Tribe: 2016 Edition* (Rizzoli New York, 2016)

Morse, Graham, *Sir Walter Winterbottom: The Father of Modern English Football* (John Blake Publishing, 2013)

Newsham, Gavin, *Hype and Glory* (Atlantic Books, 2010)

Parker, Paul, with Pat Symes, *Tackles Like a Ferret* (Know The Score Books, 2006)

Payne, Mike, *England: The Complete Post-War Record* (Breedon Books, 1993)

Pearce, Stuart, *Psycho* (Headline Publishing, 2000)

Platt, David, *Achieving the Goal* (Richard Cohen Books, 1995)

Powell, Jeff, *Bobby Moore: The Life and Times of a Sporting Hero* (Robson Books, 2002)

Robson, Bobby, *Time on the Grass* (Arthur Baker Ltd, 1982)

Robson, Bobby, with Bob Harris, *Against The Odds* (Stanley Paul & Co, 1990)

Robson, Bobby, with Bob Harris, *An Englishman Abroad: My Autobiography* (Macmillan, 1998)

Robson, Bobby, with Bob Harris, *So Near and Yet So Far: Bobby Robson's World Cup Diary* (Willow Books, 1986)

Robson, Bobby, with Paul Hayward, *Farewell but not Goodbye* (Hodder & Stoughton, 2005)

Robson, Bryan, *Robbo: My Autobiography* (Hodder & Stoughton, 2006)

Ronay, Barney, *The Manager: The Absurd Ascent of the Most Important Man in Football* (Sphere, 2009)

Shilton, Peter, *Peter Shilton: The Autobiography* (Orion, 2004)

Simpson, Paul, *Paul Gascoigne: Four Four Two Great Footballers* (Virgin Books, 2004)

Smyth, Rob, and Murray, Scott, *And Gazza Misses The Final* (Constable, 2014)

Smyth, Rob, Eriksen, Lars, Gibbons, Mike, *Danish Dynamite* (Bloomsbury Publishing, 2014)

Spurling, Jon, *Rebels for the Cause: The Alternative History of Arsenal Football Club* (Mainstream Publishing, 2003)

Stein, Mel, *Chris Waddle: The Authorised Biography* (Simon & Schuster, 1997)

Stein, Mel, *Gazza* (Bantam Books, 1996)

Storey, Daniel, *Portrait of an Icon* (Ockley Books, 2017)

Sutcliffe, Richard *Revie: Revered and Reviled* (Great Northern Books, 2010)

Welch, Julie *The World Cup: An Essential Guide to Mexico '86* (Virgin Books, 1986)

Whitehead, Richard (editor), *The Times' 50 Greatest Football Matches* (The History Press, 2019)

Wilson, Jonathan, *Inverting the Pyramid: The History of Football Tactics* (Orion, 2008)

Wilson, Jonathan, *The Anatomy of England* (Orion, 2010)

Winter, Henry, *Fifty Years of Hurt* (Bantam Press, 2016)

Wright, Billy, *The World's My Football Pitch* (Stanley Paul & Co, 1956 Arrow Illustrated Edition)

Newspapers
Over 1,600 articles were read and researched for this book
including work from:
Aberdeen Journal
Birmingham Mail
Coventry Evening Telegraph
Daily Express
Daily Herald
Daily Mail
Daily Mirror
Daily Star
Derby Daily Telegraph
Financial Times
Huddersfield Daily Examiner
Liverpool Echo
London Evening Standard
Mail on Sunday
News of the World
Reading Evening Post
Sheffield Daily Independent
Sports Argus
Sunday Express
Sunday Mirror
Sunday People
Sunday Today
Sunderland Echo
The Daily Telegraph
The Guardian
The Independent
The Observer
The Post
The Sun
The Sunday Telegraph

The Sunday Times
The Times
The Yorkshire Post
The Yorkshire Post and Leeds Mercury
Today
Western Morning News
Westminster Gazette

Magazines and Journals
90 Minutes
Football Monthly
FourFourTwo
Hot Shot!
Late Tackle
Match
Orbis World Cup 90
Roy of the Rovers
Shoot!
The Blizzard
Total Football
When Saturday Comes
World Soccer

Websites
bbc.co.uk
englandfootballonline.com
englandmemories.com
englandstats.com
fifa.com
football365.com
inbedwithmaradona.com
margaretthatcher.org
mightyleeds.co.uk

nationalarchives.gov.uk
newspapers.com
pressgazette.co.uk
rsssf.com
soccernostalgia.blogspot.com
that1980ssportsblog.blogspot.com
thefa.com
ukpressonline.co.uk
youtube.com